A daughter's memoir
of failed rescues

Killing
Penelope

A daughter's memoir
of failed rescues

Killing

Penelope

kimball

converse

pier

A Lucky Bat Book
Killing Penelope
Copyright © 2017 by Kimball Pier

ISBN-10: 1-943588-52-X
ISBN-13: 978-1-943588-52-7

Cover Artist: Nuno Moreira
Published by Lucky Bat Books
10 9 8 7 6 5 4 3 2 1

This book also available in digital formats.

For Penelope and Gardiner, my beloved parents,
and for my husband Jon who is a saint

Contents

ACKNOWLEDGEMENTS

I AM SO GRATEFUL TO LOUIS B. Jones whose belief in this book and his guidance in writing it over the past fifteen years has sustained me through episodes of discouragement and complete blockage. To my friends and colleagues, Robin Barre, Karen Terry, thank you for wading through the manuscript when it was in its toddlerhood; and to my husband Jon who managed to stay awake as I read and re-read parts and pieces, and who was patient and kind as I experienced memories and relived the traumas, you are my hero and my dearest companion. And finally, my gratitude to the Squaw Valley Community of Writers where I learned so much and felt like I'd found my tribe, and to Jude Harlan and Jessica Santina of Lucky Bat Books whose care and professionalism in making this dream real has meant so much to me.

Penelope

PART I

THE SQUAW VALLEY YEARS
1959-1970

1

WAITING FOR THE GREEN CHAIR

I WAITED AT THE BOTTOM OF THE KT-22 ski lift in Squaw Valley for my favorite chair. It stood out, out of place among the ordinary, like Greta Garbo in a *Ziegfeld Follies* chorus line. There were colored chairs in groups of six—pink, yellow, blue, and white—but there was only one dark green chair with varnished wood slats on its seat. I wondered if it knew I was waiting for it to float down the cable just for me. The forest-green metal would be comforting and inviting, the varnished seat shiny and perfect. I loved that it was still there even though I'd been gone for four years.

It was a sunny day on March 23, 1974, almost two weeks after my sixteenth birthday. My mother, Penelope, was dead. I'd left her to die back in Duxbury, but I'd made up a lie about it so nobody would ever know it was my fault. I planned to tell anyone who asked, "We agreed that I should leave so she could have her old life back." I'd never said anything about social services making me leave Penelope to come home to Squaw to live with my father. It had either been that or a foster home. My father hadn't spoken to me much since Penelope and I had moved away from Squaw Valley in the spring of 1970.

I knew when he called that morning that she was dead. He wanted me to come down to his office right away, but I walked slowly. He was sitting in his study in his old leather chair, the one I'd used to twirl around in when I was little. His nurse, Bunny, showed me in. "Your mother is gone," he said and began to sob. I held him close and didn't cry at all. My tears were locked up in a vault somewhere inside my body. I wondered how he could be so sad about Penelope. He'd gotten what he'd wanted: a new life with Sammie and her kids. He'd left the house for the last time in the spring of 1970, wearing blue polyester pants from J.C. Penney's and white, fake-leather shoes that Sammie had gotten him. He'd left behind all the pairs of khaki Brooks Brothers slacks and leather loafers that Penelope had always gotten him.

I comforted him as he cried, but I hoped it wouldn't take too long. Redheaded Heidi Chisholm was waiting for me outside. We'd planned to cut school that day to ski, defiant and wild as we'd always been ever since we were little. Now I had a really good reason for cutting school. Heidi might get in trouble, but I wouldn't.

2

HANGING ON

H E USED TO LOVE PENELOPE AND me, but my memories were the only
proof I had. There were no pictures of me on his desk or in our house,
and he got irritated when I brought up old memories.

"Hey, Daddy, remember when I was four, and you said I was old enough
to ski? It was 1962, and the rope tow at Papoose, Squaw Valley's beginner ski
hill, was the scariest thing, except for the dark place underneath our stairs at
home. You gave me a pair of wooden skis and bamboo poles for Christmas.
Remember?" He looked away and said nothing.

I remembered that whenever he decided it was time for me to learn something, I had no voice in the matter. He meant well, and, in most things, he
was a patient and thoughtful teacher and mentor, as long as it didn't involve
athletics or playing Parcheesi. An approachable and comfortable doctor,
my father was imperturbable in emergencies, using his snowshoes to make
a house call when his VW Beetle was up to its door handles with snow, to
pull a fish bone from a child's throat or to chat with patients about football
while he sewed up holes in their heads. There were occasions when he'd fetch
a pair of pliers from the VW's glove box and douse them with alcohol to
serve as de facto forceps, like the time he yanked a piece of a 7UP bottle out
of my foot. He was never without his black leather medical bag—inscribed

with his name, Gardiner Pier, MD, in gold letters near the clasp. When I opened it up, it smelled of antiseptic, bandages, and the rubber tubing of his stethoscope, one of my favorite toys. Somehow, after his long days at his office and hospital rounds, he found the energy to pull me into his lap and tell me stories, or to play hide and seek with me while Penelope prepared his favorite hors d'oeuvres of Triscuits and smoked oysters and his evening gin and tonic.

I felt the need he had for me to be exceptional, the daughter who could be more like a son. I was an accident, the result of an illicit tryst in Penelope's shower. He was forty-six years old when I was born. One December evening, he didn't take the turnoff for Tiburon, where his wife and three children lived, ending up instead on Penelope's houseboat in Sausalito. And after a few whiskey sours, the zipper on his trousers failed.

I was barely out of diapers and into big-girl panties, but Gardiner wasted no time in shaping me into a skiing prodigy. After I'd been outfitted in my stuffy red snowsuit and a pair of mittens on a string, he propped me up on the bench in front of Papoose's snack bar while he laced up my boots and shackled me to my wooden skis. He was a madman, a titan, bellowing marginally coherent instructions as to how to manage my equipment on snow while I sweated and struggled against the confinement of my snowsuit. I waddled and weaved, flailing like a little sapling in a hurricane as I hurtled down Papoose, unable to control my speed and crashing over and over until my soggy snowsuit weighed more than I did and tears and snot caked my face.

In my first attempts at grabbing the moving rope on the rope tow, I was yanked to the ground, skis and poles refusing to behave, but I hung on to the rope as Gardiner had instructed me to do. My hands burned as my grip tightened when we reached the end of the line, the rope lifting me off the ground as it approached the squeaking wheelie thing at the top where I was then suspended above the snow. The rope tow operator had to stop all rope tow operations in order to run to the top where I dangled. He pulled me off, slinging me over his shoulder, a sobbing sack of toddler, and carried me to the bottom, depositing me at Gardiner's feet. I begged to go home, but he insisted I practice until I had mastery. And so I was pushed into the rope tow line once again, sniffling and snotty-nosed, hoping that this time I could grab onto the moving rope without falling down and be brave enough to let go before the wheelie thing ate my hat again.

Most children *want* to let go of the rope tow. But I'd had to work so hard to learn to grab it and hang on, and I was so paralyzed about letting go that in my early rope tow days, I repeated the act of hanging on until the very end. I hung on to everything and feared letting go of anything. Maybe that's what comes from being an accident, the abortion that didn't happen in time. I had clung to the walls of Penelope's uterus and insisted on being born.

Penelope seemed never to cling or hang on, not even to Gardiner. When she took me skiing, she coaxed the chair on the chairlift until it swung gently to catch her, and she sat with grace as if the chair were lucky to have a few minutes with her. She would cradle the reins of her horse's bridle with such gentle certainty that he wouldn't dare take advantage of her trust. She steered her Porsche without gripping the wheel. It just seemed to want to go where she wanted it to go. Even when she held a gun, it was as though she had some kind of romance going on.

After burning through many pairs of mittens, I finally attained rope tow proficiency, becoming a fanatic rope tow grabber, a master at timing my grabs so that I remained upright even on the fast rope tow. Skiing down again began to feel like flying, and when I was five, I was ready to graduate to Squaw Valley's multicolored chairlifts. If I couldn't have my green chair, a blue one was acceptable.

But I always waited for my green chair no matter what. I knew what I wanted. I watched for my chance, not wanting anyone to interfere with me. I wanted to choose who might ride up on the chairlift with me, but I preferred to ride alone. I worked my way up through the lift line and lied to people who asked me if I wanted to ride up with them.

"No, I'm waiting for someone," I would say, looking away. Sometimes, I would accept the invitation from a pretty lady or a handsome man. But, mostly, I liked having the green chair all to myself.

3

Letting Go

IN BETWEEN ROPE TOW PROFICIENCY AND riding the chairlift, Gardiner had decided to mold me into the great swimmer he imagined himself to be. I was four and had not yet recovered from my Papoose ordeal. I loved the water and was happy to splash around in the shallow end where I could touch bottom. No need to go underwater or try to float just yet; I had plenty of fun just going up to my chin, pretending I was swimming by jumping up and down and flapping my arms. But he had Olympic dreams for me. So off we went to the Squaw Valley Lodge's swimming pool in his light-blue VW Beetle, with a length of thin rope and one of Penelope's best lemon-yellow guest towels. To begin with, that pool was not heated, and it always had bugs in it. And it didn't have nice stairs at the shallow end to sit on and ease into the water. Gardiner eschewed shallow ends or wading in slowly, one toe at a time. "Wading is for sissies," he'd say brusquely. "We'll have none of *that* crap."

He explained that the towel was for my stomach to protect me from rope burn, which immediately aroused my suspicion that he was on one of his manic missions to teach me something I didn't want to learn. The rope was made into a sort of sling, but it looked more like a noose to me. He then instructed me to step into it, and he tightened the rope around my middle. "Now," he said, pleased with his noose idea, "get in the pool."

8

"But there aren't any stairs," I whimpered. "I have to get used to the water first, Daddy."

"Just use the ladder and go down backward," he said a little impatiently.

And so, quivering with fear, I made my way into the pool while maintaining a death grip on the rails of the ladder down into the cold, buggy water. I felt the rope around my belly creep up toward my armpits as I gripped the side of the pool. I met his command to let go of the side of the pool with an even stronger grip, screaming that I didn't want to learn to swim in the lodge pool, that I *needed* the shallow end of a heated pool that had stairs. He assured me he wouldn't let go of the rope and told me to start kicking with my feet and paddling with my hands. "Swim! Goddammit, Kacey! Swim!" he commanded, as if I should summon my inner trout.

And then he did the unthinkable. He let go of the rope, confident that my kicking and flapping would keep me afloat. I wasn't sure if my toes could reach the bottom, but he was. Devoured by fear, sputtering and gulping buggy water, sure that my body wouldn't float and that the bottom of the pool was hundreds of feet below, I floundered over to the edge and refused to let go.

I wanted to go back to the pool with the real shallow end, where the water was only waist high, where I could sit on the stairs in my swimsuit with the little ruffles and my swim cap with the pink fishies on it and take my time. Penelope sat by the side of the pool with her Rolleiflex camera dangling from her neck, her straw cowboy hat perched on her head to shade her from the sun, and told me I could hold on to the side as much as I wanted. She encouraged me to experiment and see what happened if I only held on with one hand or turned onto my back while holding on with one hand. When I finally decided to let go and float, it was *my* miracle to discover that I could.

4
CATCH ME

WHEN I WAS THREE, I HAD a red tricycle that transported me from one end of the porch to the other. Our porch was high off the ground, supported by pilings, the openings between the railings covered by chicken wire so that my extraordinary speed would not result in a fatal tricycle accident. Reliable, sturdy, and easy to handle, my tricycle could turn on a dime and park and stop at will. I liked to make automobile noises when I rode my tricycle. Penelope drove a red Porsche, and I liked the sound it made when she revved the engine, so I made those kinds of noises. And I always made a screeching noise when I stopped. I counted myself among the most competent and capable of tricycle riders.

I was not allowed to relax in my three-wheeled comfort and competence for long. All too quickly, the day arrived when Gardiner decided I ought to learn to ride a bicycle. Eyeing my beloved red tricycle parked in its space at the corner of our porch under a pine tree, I thought it an ideal time to bargain and told him I would only ride a blue bike with a bell and pretty basket with flowers on it on the handlebars. I was six when he presented me with a blue Schwinn girl's bicycle. It had a white wicker basket on the handlebars, a bell, and very pretty white stripes on the front and back fenders; it had a kickstand and a pair of training wheels on the back. It weighed one thousand pounds.

The first thing he did was to retrieve his wrench from his toolbox, with which he removed the training wheels. "No need for these. The only way to learn is to just get on and go!"

And with that, he loaded the blue Schwinn into the back of the VW Beetle, and off we went to the parking lot in front of the Blyth Arena, a huge, orange-painted, steel and glass structure, site of the 1960 Winter Olympic skating events, which was within walking distance of Papoose and the Squaw Valley Lodge swimming pool, the site of previous traumatic experiences. It was summertime, so there weren't any cars in the parking lot—a good thing for me—and we were close to his office where first-aid supplies were in abundance.

He gave his usual cursory instructions: "Now . . . I'm going to have a hold of your handlebars, and I'm going to run alongside while you pedal, and when you have enough speed, I'm going to let go, and you'll be on your own. Just remember . . . keep pedaling. That's what helps you balance."

Of course the second he let go, I stopped pedaling and froze, unable to comprehend how balance was possible with only two wheels. I began to scream, and Gardiner ran toward me to arrest what would have been a bloody crash onto the pavement. "Goddammit, Kacey! I told you to keep pedaling!" And then he held me close until I stopped shaking and said, "C'mon, Kace, let's try this again, only this time, we'll try a smaller hill." At least he called me by the nickname that only he and Penelope shared for me, so I knew he couldn't really have been that frustrated with me. They called me "Kacey" or "Kace," an amalgam of my first and middle initials, "K" for Kimball, and "C" for Converse. They called me Kimball when they were mad at me, for example, when I stole a ring from the drug store, or when I cleaned my room by shoving everything under the bed.

I was fuming; my resistance and resentment obliterating any desire I had to learn. With my brows knit and my mouth in a rigid frown, I obeyed his command to get on and try again, only because I knew he would have me pulling thistles as punishment if I refused to comply.

Over the next several hours, I learned to find my balance, but only after I told him to stop telling me what to do. Soon, I was pedaling across the parking lot with grace and ease. He told me he was proud of me, but I was still angry with him and couldn't be grateful that he was proud of me. When

I had gained confidence riding on the flat pavement of the parking lot, he put the Schwinn in the back of the VW and said, "Now you're going to learn to go downhill."

Sandy Way, our street in Squaw Valley, had long, steep hills at least as difficult as a road over the Swiss Alps. Just running down the hills was life threatening when I got going too fast, and riding the blue Schwinn would certainly require an ambulance to be on standby. There were no bike helmets for kids in the sixties, or if there were, Gardiner must have thought them unnecessary, as he thought most protective or preventative devices unnecessary, including seatbelts, sunscreen, and, of course, training wheels.

We started on a fairly small downhill, but, to me, it might as well have been Mount Everest. He instructed me to press back on the pedal to stop the bike, promising that simple action would slow me down. It seemed unlikely that such a simple move would stop the thousand-pound bicycle. First of all, it was a Herculean chore to push it up the hill to my starting point. He was a speck on the horizon as I stood at the top of the Road of Death awaiting his signal to start.

Now, most children would follow the instruction to press back on a brake, a simple enough piece of advice to follow. I remembered how he'd not disclosed vital information about being able to touch the bottom at the Squaw Valley Lodge pool that day, so I did not now believe that it would be that simple to stop my bike and would not even try. Once I got going, I became paralyzed with fear, all instruction erased from my memory, and screamed for Gardiner to stop me. "Catch me, Daddy! Catch me!" I screamed.

And he did. Poising himself with legs bent and spread in a hero's posture, he extended his arms and caught me, somehow managing to stay upright himself. "Goddammit, Kacey! I told you to press back with your foot to brake!"

Amazing that I didn't think my name was Goddammitkacey.

5
HORSES

PENELOPE LOVED HORSES, AND THEREFORE I loved horses too. She had taught me to ride even before Gardiner forced me to learn to ski. J. P. was a chestnut Morgan with a white blaze down his face, fifteen hands high and completely in love with Penelope, as most men were. She obtained the best spot for his corral at the Squaw Valley Stables and had it custom built for him so that he would have his own pine tree for shade and a nice view of the meadow. She kept saddles, bridles, brushes, and J. P.'s feedbag in a specially made tack shed right in the corral. About a half mile away from the stables, she tooted the red Porsche's horn to let J. P. know she was close, and he would prick his ears up and begin to pace the corral near the fence, whinnying with desire in anticipation of his beautiful Penelope's arrival.

She wouldn't let Gardiner ride J. P., and J. P. would likely have thrown him off anyway, but she let me ride him. I saw her whisper in his ear that I was special and that he should be extra careful with me on his back. She patted his neck, and he turned to look in her eyes. "There's a good boy," she said and kissed his nose.

I liked to wear my straw cowboy hat just like hers, and I had a red cowboy vest with a white fringe that Penelope had purchased just for me at the feed and tack store in Reno. I straddled the fence and listened to her instructions, clear and gentle, as she told me how to turn the stirrup, use my left foot, and face J. P.'s rear to mount. She brought J. P. close to the fence so I could stand on the bottom rail to reach the stirrup. "Now, tuck up on the reins, and take some of his mane into your hands," she instructed.

"But, Mummy, won't it hurt if I pull his hair?"

"No, it won't hurt him. Now grab the saddle horn with your right hand . . . that's it. Now swing your right leg over the saddle. Good girl!"

I was up high on J. P.'s back, and I became Penelope for a minute or so. She removed his halter and told me to give him a gentle squeeze with my legs, but my legs were so short he didn't feel a thing. She made kissing noises and began to walk, coaxing him along with her voice, and he followed. "Give him a little kick," she said. "These are called Rommel reins." I looked at the braided leather reins knotted with long tails at the ends. "Hold the reins loosely in your left hand, and use your right hand to hold the tails. Now rest your right hand on your right leg, sit up nice and straight . . . that's my girl! When he trots, squeeze in with your legs and sit to your horse."

It wasn't long before I could ride without instruction. When Penelope taught other kids how to ride, she spoke to them as if they were grown-ups, not the five-year-olds they were. And they loved her. But Penelope had no patience for whining and would send them home to their mothers immediately if they did. She expected them to explain to her what the problem was and then to solve it.

"Mrs. Pier, I'm hot."

"There's the creek," she would say. "Take your horse in for a swim. Then you'll both be cooler. Now let's have no more whining, shall we?"

When Penelope and I went riding alone, I had to ride one of the stable's dude horses, but I usually got the one I wanted. Penelope taught me to ask for what I wanted in a clear voice without any whining. "I want that one," I instructed the cowhand as I pointed to a chestnut with a long mane and tail. That horse wouldn't just lumber along; he had some mischief in him, but just enough to make the ride exciting. There were several I refused to ride because they were stubborn and slow. And I wanted one that looked like J. P. We would load up a picnic into the saddlebags and take off for the lakes nestled high in the mountains above Squaw Valley. When we arrived, Penelope set out her lunch of Gruyère cheese, Pepperidge Farm wheat bread, a few strawberries, and Wente Brothers wine, which she carried in a bota bag and squirted into her mouth. I had a peanut butter sandwich, three Fig Newtons, and all the water I could drink from the lake. Penelope always rode with brown gloves to protect her hands and her fingernails, which were cut short and always painted bright red.

We were quiet mostly. Penelope didn't like chatter and found talking unnecessary much of the time. "Let's just be quiet and enjoy the sound of the wind, shall we?" she said. Sometimes I wondered if she got tired of me. In the afternoons, she withdrew into her bedroom and told me she was not to be disturbed, that it was her rest time. I waited outside her door, drawing pictures of horses and trying not to make a sound until she opened the door and discovered me sitting there. "Hi, Mummy," I would say hopefully.

"Hello little Kacey," she replied. "Shall we take the dogs for a walk?" I rose up and floated along behind her.

6

SICKNESS

GARDINER NEVER MINDED MY CHIT-CHAT. I could have access to his lap or his attention. I went with him everywhere in the VW Beetle, and we sang rounds of "I've Been Working on the Railroad" or Christmas carols, even if it was July. Penelope was more elusive, uncertain, as if motherhood were a question mark lingering on the threshold of a doorway. I was afraid to disturb her when her door was closed, but I was willing to sit quietly with a book for as long as it took for her to be ready to have me with her on her bed.

When I was sick in the middle of the night, I didn't worry too much that I was bothering Gardiner when I woke him up. My room was downstairs, and the house was big; it was a long way to get upstairs to his bedside to wake him and I had to consider the danger, what with the wolf that lived in the dark place under the stairs. When I was sick, I tried so hard not to throw up that I waited until the last second. I hollered for him, then threw up all over the record player by my bed. Poor Gardiner cleaned up after me, got me a fresh nightie, then read me stories until I threw up again (this time into a strategically placed wastebasket). He stayed with me, reading me *The Churchmouse Stories* until I fell asleep, and he was right there when I awoke again. Even though he got up for work early the next morning while Penelope slept, he never complained. And he never woke Penelope to take over for him.

We got up early, Gardiner and me. I liked to sit over the heater vents by the big windows, letting the warm air make my nightie billow out like a flannel tent. He whispered when breakfast was ready. We always had to whisper, knowing what would happen if we woke Penelope. She would fling the door open to the bedroom and hiss, "Be *quiet*! For God's *sake*, Gardy! You've woken me *up*!" and then slam her door. He buried the phone under pillows on the sofa to muffle the ringing in the morning. When he was on call, he slept right next to it on the sofa, and he laid out all his clothes for the next day on a chair in the living room, so he wouldn't have to go into the bedroom at all. And he didn't flush the toilet, even if he'd left a turd from his morning ritual. Instead, he would leave a bottle of shampoo on the lid so she would know to flush first. We had to talk in low voices in the kitchen and not slam doors. It was too hard attaining forgiveness.

He rarely got sick, but when he did, I was so terrified that I couldn't stand being anywhere near him. He was the anchor, and if he was disabled by illness, I became unmoored. Penelope also depended upon him to be the healthy one, as her various aches and pains had to take precedence. He was not permitted to be weak or infirm in any way. If he got sick, especially if he was throwing up, she would play Wagner's "Die Walkure" on her Victrola and crank up the volume to drown out his heaving. I went to sleep outside in my tent just to get away from Wagner.

Holding his head when he was throwing up was out of the question, but Penelope was gifted in her way of protecting him from unwanted telephone calls and listening to him talk about his day, especially about that pain-in-the-ass Alex Cushing, the owner of the Squaw Valley ski area.

"Hello? Who is calling, please? What? Oh dear. Oh yes . . . just a minute, please." She would cover the receiver and whisper, "Are you here for Betty? Apparently, Brad has a pea up his nose, and she can't seem to get it out."

Occasionally, she would return to the phone and say, "I'm sorry, he's just left. May I have him call you back?" She was always polite until she got off the phone, and then she'd say, "Goddammit, why don't they ever get sick during the day, for Christ's sake?"

They had conversations about his day as he sipped his cocktail by the fire, and she cooked supper in the big open space that was the living room, kitchen, and dining area. She put his slippers on the stone hearth to warm by the fire and pulled his favorite chair in front.

He never seemed to run out of energy to care for his patients. I loved that my friends went to see him. He could tame the most unruly and frightened child with his voice and his humor. I overheard when one of my friends needed a shot of penicillin; Gardiner called for the nurse, "Bunny, come on in here, I need you to yank his drawers down while I hold him! Then I'll hand you the syringe. Ready? Now!" And then I heard the piercing scream as the needle was plunged into the boy's clenched buttocks. Afterward, Gardiner said, "You're a damn brave kid! That needle was one of my longest." The kid came out holding the empty syringe without the needle as a souvenir of his ordeal.

He was lonesome during Penelope's long hospital stays, which began when I was eight. We didn't play hide and seek anymore. I was worried she was going to die, and I was too afraid to ask any questions—I just swallowed them until they formed a heavy black ball inside my stomach. When she was home from the hospital, I tiptoed around the house feeling as if the spell would break if I made any noise. The dog tiptoed too, every step, her paw poised in midstride, trying to make her toenails hit the cork floor tiles quietly. The house felt so hollow without Penelope. I became even more afraid of dark places and tried not to sleep.

7

BEREFT

WHEN I WAS TWENTY-SEVEN, GARDINER AND I went to see our old house in Belvedere, a cozy little bedroom community in Marin County, California, where he and Penelope had lived after he'd abandoned his first family.

"When you were a tiny baby, we used to put you in the car up here when you cried, so you wouldn't interrupt our dinner," he said, pointing to the driveway above the house. Suddenly, all the years of feeling unwelcome made sense. In another life, before I came along, Penelope had traveled the world with her camera bags and her dachshund, Pretzel, in a little backpack.

She rode a scooter in Italy and stayed with her rich lesbian lover, Helene, in a chalet in Davos. Helene, whom Gardiner called "Fishballs," mentored a very naïve young Penelope into the world of photography and glamour. Penelope's parents had wanted her to have the proper Bostonian debutante life, with teas and socials at the Duxbury Yacht Club and a coming-out party where there were plenty of young Harvard boys to choose from. Penelope had eschewed the uncomfortable high heels and dresses and caught a train to Vermont, where she'd waited tables and drove a taxi just so she could afford to ski. That's where she had met Fishballs, who had been on assignment for some German skiing magazine. Soon, Penelope found herself trotting along in Helene's shadow, carrying gun cases, camera bags, and suitcases full of Kirsch, making magazine covers as a model for women's outdoor wear and as a photographer for men's hunting and fishing magazines. She rode horses in the canyons of Utah and ate beans out of a can; she hung out of airplanes in Alaska, shooting pictures of grizzly bears in Kodiak, and went deep-sea fishing in Acapulco.

The Rolleiflex cameras that I so often saw hanging round her neck served as reminders of her old life of high adventure once she had settled down with Gardiner in Squaw Valley. Our house was decorated with duck decoys from Abercrombie & Fitch, the walls adorned with the photographs she'd taken of famous skiers in the Swiss Alps; shotguns tucked lovingly away in velvet-lined cases in her closets, and the Smith & Wesson .38 with the carved bone grip was kept in its leather holster in her bedside table drawer. She didn't go for the women in Squaw, other than maybe one or two that she considered friends. "They bore me," she would say. "All they do is chit-chat."

When she was away in Davos with Fishballs, Penelope hired one of a succession of young German girls to be my live-in nanny. The third time Penelope left, I was three, and she told Gardiner that she would only be gone for two weeks, but she'd stayed away two months when he put his foot down. My first memory is of feeling an aching heart, like a rush of cold liquid silver bursting from my heart, spreading down my arms all the way to my fingers. The German girls didn't like me; I remember that, too. There were other German nannies in Squaw Valley, and they spoke in German to each other while we kids wondered what they were going to do to us next. We tried to be good, but it didn't matter: We still got the beatings. Gardiner didn't like having live-in nannies. He was accustomed to having his home to himself, where he could walk around naked in the morning wearing nothing but his slippers, whistling "With a Little Bit of Luck" from *My Fair Lady*.

I wanted a sister. I asked Penelope if I could have one, but she said it would be impossible. The instant I was born, she'd had her uterus taken out. She said she'd never wanted to go through the horror of birthing ever again.

She made another trip to Switzerland when I was four, leaving me with a different German girl who had fat little fingers like knackwursts. Renata yanked my arm when I couldn't keep her pace. We usually walked to see her friend Helga, who was Tiger and Chipper Atwater's nanny. Nannies were for mothers like Penelope, who needed time for riding, socializing, or zipping to Switzerland for a few weeks. Renata looked forward to her afternoon ritual of walking down Sandy Way to Helga's house, yanking me along, and cursing in German. There were lots of willow bushes along the way. She would stop and cut switches, braiding the slender branches together using several Milky Way chocolate bar wrappers to bind them at the ends. Renata loved Milky Way bars, which, after digested, would drift down to her butt and add to the expanding landscape. I was afraid Renata would tell Penelope I was bad—so bad that I deserved a spanking almost every day. And not spankings with her hands—spankings with willow branches.

Renata was sure I was young enough that I wouldn't later remember the beatings that left welts on my back and bottom. She must not have hit me hard enough, as the bruises faded after a few hours or a day. The longing for Penelope was almost unbearable, and it made me sick. But if I cried, I would be hit again and thrown into my crib.

I told Penelope on the day she finally arrived home, just as she was unpacking presents for me: a little blue traveling case from Lufthansa Airlines with a little bar of Lufthansa soap, a little yellow washcloth, Lufthansa toothbrush and toothpaste, some Lufthansa slippers, and lederhosen from Switzerland. I told her about the willow branch spankings. Within hours, Renata was gone. I begged, please, no more German nannies who didn't like me, and there were no more German nannies from then on. Instead, I stayed with other people's families when Penelope went away.

8

FISHBALLS

GARDINER WAS TOLERANT OF PENELOPE'S WANDERLUST, but he made it clear that he didn't like Fishballs much. He hated it when she came to visit, but he hated it more when Penelope left for long visits to Davos to stay in Fishballs's elaborate chalet. "Why do you have to go and visit that Nazi in Switzerland, for Christ's sake?" he would argue as he climbed into the passenger side of her red Porsche. She wouldn't let him drive because, as she explained, he handled her car the way one would handle a pickaxe. I sat in the tiny back seat for the drive to the San Francisco airport, where she would board a Swissair flight to Zurich—first class, of course.

"Because I love Davos. And she's not German, she's Swiss," Penelope replied, easing her hands into her driving gloves.

"That's what *she* tells you," he said testily. "She certainly behaves like a Nazi."

"Now, Gardy, take it easy. I know she's loud and boorish, but she's not fond of men, as you know, and she's very protective of me."

"Penelope, make this the last time you go away. From now on, she comes here. We have a perfectly good guest room with a nice bed and a view," Gardiner said, impatiently.

"You know she'll refuse to occupy a room where she can't have room service and all the Scotch she can drink on demand," Penelope said.

And so it was. Fishballs would visit at least once a year, but she stayed at the Squaw Valley Lodge.

Fishballs was about six feet tall, the only evidence of her gender being her breasts, the Twin Matterhorns, as Penelope named them, which cast a shadow upon all body parts beneath them. Her legs were long and thin with huge knees, and she had feet like canoes. She had a habit of rubbing her flattened buttocks as if to see if anything had changed since the last time she'd checked. She always wore expensive, tailored slacks that strained over her belly, which was distended by years of overindulgence in expensive Scotch and Wiener schnitzel. She wore red lipstick and painted her toenails and fingernails to match, setting off perpetually tanned, pachyderm-like skin. Her gold jewelry swung from each wrist and cascaded down the slope of her chest as she walked, jangling and keeping time with each strident step. She was mostly deaf, probably due to all the gunfire she'd heard while spending so much time out in the wilds of Africa and the United States on hunting trips. She wheezed from many years of smoking filterless Pall Malls, which was made worse when she had to climb the sixty-four concrete steps up to our house—another reason she preferred a suite at the Squaw Valley Lodge.

"My little Peeeelleeee!" she would boom in her low-octave, estrogen-starved body. "Gif your Helenle a kiss, my sveet little shugi!" My tiny mother would succumb to a stifling hug and a Scotch-laden kiss while my father patiently looked on, realizing that his house was temporarily going to be taken over by a woman who was obviously madly in love with his wife.

Penelope kept a journal where she wrote about how she had met Fishballs in Manchester, Vermont:

I stopped in the middle of the slope to listen to the tranquility of the newly fallen snow on the mountain, when my reverie was broken by a loud snap, followed by a slew of foreign curses delivered with unmistakable venom. When I called out, "Are you all right?" the reply was an impatient, "Jawohl!"

Penelope assisted by digging her out of a snowdrift and flagging down the ski patrolman, who arrived on the scene with a toboggan. Helene could not take her eyes off the beautiful, diminutive girl and decided that Penelope would be hers forever. That night, alone in her tiny room, Penelope continued to write of her first encounter with Helene:

> *"Now I want for you to pose me for my pictures!" she bellowed in broken English from her toboggan, where she lay recovering from her fall, aided by hot whiskey. And, so, I entered a world of wild living, plane schedules, rifles, bows and arrows, bloodshed, blisters, and Kirsch. Tyrannical, dictatorial, and with infinite energy, Helene drove me up and down the mountain, heedless of blizzards, needing neither whip nor megaphone due to a voice that was made for herding goats. I was soon confined to my bed with a cold and a temperature of 103 degrees.*

Gardiner stocked up on liquor when Fishballs came to visit and did his best to be nice to her, despite her not-very-well-disguised contempt for him. He just wished Fishballs would stay in Davos and leave his wife alone. She did not do a very good job of hiding her contempt for him, and she didn't waste any opportunity to remind Penelope that she knew he was a *schweinhund*.

Many years later, when Gardiner was winding down, I asked him why he'd tolerated Fishballs when he'd known that her motive was to steal Penelope, if she could have just gotten him out of the way. "Well . . . I loved Penelope. And part of loving her was accepting her relationship with Fishballs." He sighed and furrowed his now-deeply wrinkled brow, as he'd always done when contemplative.

Penelope said she dreaded visits from Fishballs, knowing Gardiner felt he was being invaded. "She's boisterous and demanding. It's like trying to stand up to a hurricane," she sighed one afternoon while hiding in her bedroom after having told Fishballs she was going to take a nap. I had sneaked in quietly, wanting to steal some time with her. "But I know she means well. She's just jealous of anyone who loves me."

"Yes, and she *does* always bring me presents when she visits," I said, nodding in agreement. "The bathing suits are kind of ugly, though, and she brings me boys' shorts with matching shirts. My bathing suits look exactly like her bathing suits. I look like a boy in all the pictures she takes."

"It's probably her way of training you to be a lesbian," said Penelope, patting my head. "A miniature Fishballs in training." And we unraveled into hysterical laughter. Penelope explained that lesbians loved other women and left it at that.

9

BEING WITH PENELOPE

EACH DROP OF TIME I SPENT with Penelope was like a soft cashmere blanket on a winter afternoon. Her attention felt warming and soft and melted me into peace. My heart burst when we saddled up our horses and went riding, or when we went for the ritual morning and evening trail walks with the dogs, yet at those times I also felt the lump rise in my throat, knowing the Penelope moments would never be enough and that they would always end too soon. Squaw Valley summer mornings awakened the senses, making it impossible to be inside, weaving the sunrise song of the meadowlark with the smell of meadow grasses and pine kissed by the dew.

In the afternoons, after she rested or spent time with her typewriter, we went to Tahoe City to shop and get the mail. When I stopped hearing the clack-clack-clack-*ding* of her Smith Corona, I knew it was almost time, and I could jump into her presence again. In those handfuls of space in the car, we talked about horses or dogs; we went about errands to the butcher shop, the Safeway, and the post office. We would run into her friends who wanted to stop and chat in the aisles of the brand new Safeway store, and she would give me a nickel so I could ride the mechanical horse while she chatted, somewhat reluctantly and hoping for an opportunity to escape.

We took the dogs for walks behind the house on the hillside covered with wildflowers—purple lupines, red Indian paintbrushes, and thousands of yellow mule ears. The smell of flowers mixed with juniper and pine and earth, especially near the little brooks that made their way down to the meadow, made me want to stop and kneel down really close to the ground to smell and see everything up close. Sometimes we just read together on her bed or played Parcheesi, dogs curled up at the end of the bed as if nothing in the world could disturb us.

I wanted to be exactly like her.

Penelope loved her red Porsche and treated it as if it were a living creature, like her horse or her dogs. She wore khaki pants and Levi's; button-down shirts from Brooks Brothers, tucked in at her tiny hips; sandals or Top-Sider deck shoes in the summer and boots in winter; cowboy hats and silk scarves. She let her beautiful black, wavy hair tumble down her back, except on hot days when we went riding; then she put it in two braids. Other mothers wore skirts and high heels; trousers that zipped on the sides with matching sweaters; dresses and pointy-toed heels; blouses with fluffy borders and frilly collars; and hair with lots of curls that stayed put, even in the wind. Penelope had two beautiful party dresses and two pairs of black, velvet high heels—one pair with rounded toes that were so high I could hardly stand up in them, and one pair with pointed toes that had smooth, flat bows on top and heels that were lower and which I could actually walk around in. She had two Chanel suits, custom fitted from I. Magnin & Co., that she called her "airplane suits."

She never wore earrings. Her ears weren't pierced, and she hated clip-on earrings. She wore gold bracelets and necklaces and her gold wedding band. She didn't have long fingernails filed to a point with frosty nail polish. Hers were short and manicured, and if she wore nail polish, it was always bright red to match her red lipstick. When she dressed for riding horses, she wore a light, woven cowboy hat in the summer and a black one for colder weather. Her riding boots were always polished and matched her gloves.

She had a large fur hat with built-in ear muffs and an Eddie Bauer hunting jacket—red, which matched her lipstick almost perfectly. She wore Chanel No. 5 or Givenchy perfume. When I missed her, I went to her bureau drawer with the carefully folded scarves, all in colors to match her shirts and sweaters, and put one to my face to smell her perfume mixed with the lingering scent of her face.

When she took even short trips without me, I became sick with despair, terrified she wouldn't come back. I tried harder to please her so she wouldn't leave anymore. I worried that she missed her life with Fishballs or that it was me she needed escape from. After I turned eight, her trips to Switzerland ended, as did the trips we'd make to the seaside when she was mad at Gardiner, and the trips were mostly to the hospital, sometimes for several weeks or even months. Each of those absences felt like an endless dark night, without any glimpse of dawn. I did my best to pretend everything was normal. When other people's mothers saw me and asked how my mother was, I made my answers brief. I didn't really know how she was; nobody was telling me anything. Besides, it seemed people preferred it when I just said Penelope was fine, and I didn't want to let any tears out. Nobody couldn't disturb my veil if I was quick enough. A good strategy was to avoid eye contact, especially with grownups, and pretend I was in a hurry to be somewhere. I visited her in the hospital in Truckee when she was well enough to be there and not in Reno or San Francisco, but I had mixed feelings about going to see her. I just wanted everything to be normal, and going to see Penelope reminded me that normal was gone.

10
LANA

EVERYONE NEEDS A BEST FRIEND WHO doesn't leave you when life stinks and you're acting like a brat, like Ethel was for Lucy in *I Love Lucy*. No matter how many times Lucy threw Ethel under the bus, they still made up and went on with life wearing adorable hats and matching purses. Lana was my Ethel. I needed to be better than her and she let me, even though she rolled her eyes and stomped off, swearing she was never going to be my friend again, ever, ever.

With Penelope being sick and away so much and Gardiner being so pre-occupied with her, I clung to parts of my life that remained still and steady, like going to school and my best friend Lana. We were the misfits, outcasts among our peers. We first met in the post office waiting for the bus on the first day of school. I was going into second grade and was excited about having a desk with a slanted top instead of a flat top. A slanted top was much more mature. I had everything arranged in my new pencil box, and I had a brand new lunch pail with flowers on it and a matching Thermos. Lana looked scared. I saw her looking at me from under the fake-fur-lined hood of her jacket. "Hi. What's your name?" I asked.

She turned from inside her hood and looked at me with big, brown, worried eyes. "Lana," she said quietly. "What's yours?"

"It's Kim," I told her not wanting to tell her that my real name was Kimball, which I was sure nobody else in the entire world had. And I would never tell anyone that my parents called me "Kacey," which I thought of as a boy's name. "I like your jacket. Is that real fur around your hood or fake?"

"Fake," said Lana. "My nana gave it to me. It's a winter jacket."

We sat next to each other on the bus and were rarely apart from then on. At recess, we waited for each other by the drinking fountain. The girls' bathroom had no doors on the stalls, so we provided blockage for each other. We couldn't sit at the same table at lunchtime because each class had a separate table, but we were close enough to trade food. She could eat disgusting food like spaghetti or meatloaf. I took all her applesauce and green beans.

Over the next few years, we developed a secret language, ran and hid from the kids who bullied us after we got off the bus, and met right at the door of the girls' bathroom at recess so we wouldn't have to face the playground alone. We stuck together on the bus so we didn't have to share a seat with anyone else.

We dreamed of becoming famous ice skaters. When we got older, we lamented our flat-chestedness and compared our bodies in her mother's full-length mirror to evaluate our progress: "I think mine are bigger . . . look. Stand sideways right in front of me," Lana instructed.

"They are not! It's not fair to stick your whole chest out. Just stand normally . . . Now . . . see? We're exactly the same," I said. I couldn't let Lana be ahead of me, considering she was a year younger.

We were adventurous and got to know people from out of town. Once, we made friends with a couple of women at the ice arena. We were actually trying to steal tampons from the machine when they walked in on us. They asked us if we needed help, and we told them we had lost our money in the tampon machine. We hadn't had our periods yet, but we lied and said we had. It was fairly obvious that we weren't even close, but they believed us and bought us each a tampon. Our plan was to go behind the Catholic church, where the trees were thick, and try putting them in. We'd seen ads about tampons and pads in her mother's *Cosmopolitan* magazines. The ads said tampons were convenient and easy to use, promising that you could even go swimming without leaving a trail of blood in the pool, or wear white pants without fear of ending up with a map of Tasmania on your butt. And then we asked the two women if they'd had their periods. We got them to tell us how babies were made, even though we knew already. After this rite of passage into the tampon sisterhood in the ladies' bathroom at Blyth Arena, they bought us hot chocolate with whipped cream. After that, we went to the Queen of the Snows Catholic Church and hid behind the trees out back. We tried putting in the tampons, but after a while we gave up. We couldn't figure out which hole to stick them in, and it seemed like it might hurt anyway.

Our mothers didn't fit the Squaw Valley mold, and each of us was an only child. We lied to people and said we were sisters. Sometimes we faked British accents and told people we were orphans, born in England and adopted by rich people in America. Lana's mother was never seen with other mothers nor at the Squaw Valley parties. Madeline was a barmaid and kept late hours. Neither of our mothers attended PTA meetings or volunteered to be a Brownie troop leader. Madeline wasn't interested in being in places where there were no available men, and Penelope hated meetings of any kind, especially when it involved bringing some type of snack food.

Madeline was one of about three single mothers in Squaw Valley. Lana didn't know her father, and he never visited. People in Squaw Valley drew their own conclusions about Madeline. She was beautiful and voluptuous, right out of a *Playboy* centerfold. Squaw Valley mothers kept their breasts fully concealed under expensive cashmere après-ski sweaters. When Madeline was cocktailing after the ski lifts closed at the Squaw Valley Lodge Bar, she did not go unnoticed, even by the most wholesome of the Squaw Valley husbands, with her perfectly manicured nails and her low-cut blouses showing the soft bulges of her breasts, offered like fresh peaches through the black lace of her bras, taunting and teasing the fantasy lives of inebriated millionaires and horny ski instructors. Madeline was on the hunt, having migrated from the San Francisco area, where the competition for husbands, especially wealthy ones, was fierce. She and the young ski instructors prowled for the same game: mates with money and deep pockets, no matter the tonnage around the middle or receding hairlines. Reno, with its bouquet of pink wedding chapels and bars all within staggering distance, made a quick and legal fusion possible. Squaw Valley was a sensible hunting ground for matrimonial prey.

We watched Madeline prepare for her night's work, which began at approximately one o'clock in the afternoon, an hour after she arose from the previous night's sleep. Preparation took about two hours, and the bar opened at three-thirty, when the winter sun began to fade and people drifted in off the slopes ready for hot toddies and mediocre piano music. We were not allowed in Lana's apartment at all before noon. Lana spent the night at my house whenever Madeline was entertaining a prospective husband. Madeline would pull a large wad of cash from her cleavage and hand Lana a few bills to go to the movies or the store. "Now run along, dolly, I have company," she would say, blowing kisses through her perfectly lined lips.

When Madeline was in a good mood, she let us watch her ritual of applying her makeup and fixing her hair. She plucked her eyebrows until there was only a thin line of hair remaining, and she painted on the rest. Then she encircled her big brown eyes with eyeliner in a very thin line that curved upward at the outer corners. Next came the eyelashes, which were huge and thick, like fuzzy black caterpillars, and which she glued onto her eyelids. She finished off with white and pink eye shadow, several layers of pinkish frosty lipstick, and a drawn-on beauty mark.

Her hair was piled up on top of her head, and then she made long, coppery-red pigtails with the rest of her hair, with little curls at the ends. She used a lot of paraphernalia to make it look that way. She had rollers and pins and sprays and clips, none of which I had ever seen Penelope use. She didn't even own any curlers. Madeline dressed for work in a tight black miniskirt and some kind of form-fitting top, usually black with white in it, along with nylons or black fishnet stockings and white go-go boots. Lana was often alone at night until one a.m., when Madeline returned home, occasionally with a candidate for husbandhood, at which time, Lana would leave the bedroom and go sleep on the sofa. She got up early and walked to my house or got on the bus wearing a jumper with her undershirt sleeves showing, carrying a box of cereal.

"Oooh . . . Cap'n Crunch!" I said, patting the seat beside me on the bus. "Can I have some?" I only got Special K or Total, if I even got dry cereal for breakfast at all. Usually, Gardiner fixed soft-boiled eggs and Pepperidge Farm wheat toast.

Lana handed me the box. "Okay, but don't take the prize," she said grumpily. The prizes in her cereal were usually whistles or rub-on tattoos.

We spent a lot of time at Blyth Arena, especially during the summers, when elite skaters from all over the country came to train for the Olympics.

The coaches had been in the 1960 Winter Olympics and had come back to Squaw to develop up-and-coming Olympic skaters. Lana and I hung on the fringes of the elite crowd hoping for a chance to be in the ice shows. I begged Gardiner to buy me lessons and skates. He finally broke down and paid for three lessons with a fat woman named Joyce who didn't like me.

Madeline couldn't afford skates or lessons, but Lana was determined and wanted to skate more than anything, so the instructors donated their time, and Lana got hand-me-down skates from some of the older girls. We only had two skating outfits between us, which we frequently swapped. We were so jealous of the other girls who wore different dresses every day that we sneaked into the locker room and tried theirs on when nobody was around. We landed parts in the ice shows' chorus lines, wearing cowgirl outfits with plastic gun holsters.

Gardiner refused to buy me figure skates, too, even though he could afford to buy them. "Goddammit, Kacey! I bought you brand new skis and boots, and you're *going* to be like the other kids around here and be on the Squaw Valley sporting club team. Ice skating isn't even a *sport*, for Christ's sake." So I begged one of the skating instructors to give me a used pair. They were just regular old Hyde skates that made my ankles look like toothpicks stuck into my submarine-sandwich-sized feet, but I kept them in their box, as if they were treasured, handcrafted skates, and I used coat upon coat of white polish to cover all the scuff marks. Still, they seemed to be gray and dull compared with the beautiful skates the other girls wore.

On hot summer days, Lana and I went up the mountain trails to the waterfalls and deep pools of crystal clear water from the melting snow. In the winters, we spent long afternoons in my room playing, unless Gardiner forced me to ski with the race team. Lana's mother couldn't afford to buy ski equipment either, and I hated going anywhere without Lana. Each weekend morning, when I begged to play with her instead of going to the dreaded ski practices, Gardiner practically came unglued. "Goddammit, Kacey, I will not have you sitting around here playing with Lana and those Barbie dolls of yours. Now, get your ski pants on this minute!"

Lana put on her jacket and boots and walked home while I went out on the slopes to endure endless hours of falling down on the slalom courses. Lana would meet me at four o'clock by the snack bar. Then we would steal plastic lunch trays from the lodge and use them as sleds on the little hill. We laughed until we peed, bouncing down the hill and sliding to a stop at the bottom. Then we would ask Gardiner for money for hot chocolate.

On weekends, Lana almost always spent the night at my house. Weekend nights were big money nights for Madeline. When Gardiner was on call and Penelope was in the hospital, there wasn't anyone around to tell us it was time to go to sleep. We stayed up late and watched scary movies on television. Even with a big antenna on the roof, we only got one channel, but it was better than nothing. During the movies, we would pretend that we were Zsa Zsa and Eva Gabor. We mimicked their Hungarian accents and called each other "dahling."

"Dahling . . . vud you like some more Bosco and milk? I am zeemply dyyyying for zee chocolate!"

"Vy, of course, dahling . . . anysing for my vonderful seester!"

Gardiner didn't approve of my clinging to Lana, but he was very kind to her, especially when she called late at night. "Hello, Dr. Pier? It's Lana. I'm freezing cold cuz I'm down at the store at the phone booth. Is Kimmy there?"

"Lana, its ten o'clock at night. Where's your mother, and why aren't you home in bed?"

"My mom is working, and I'm scared. Can I stay overnight with you guys?"

Gardiner sighed. "All right, Lana. I'll come down and pick you up, so you stay right there by the post office, okay?"

"Okay, Dr. Pier. Thank you, Dr. Pier, very much. I sure am hungry."

I wished she could be my sister. Gardiner wished I would play with the resort kids. He didn't understand how unpopular I was with them. I loved skating and riding horses and playing by the creeks—all things I could do with Lana.

When I was eight, Gardiner decided it was time for me to learn to be in the wilderness by myself. My bravery on overnight stays alone in the wilderness had extended as far as a flat place on the hillside in back of our house, within sprinting distance of the porch. I figured I could outrun any wild animal. His plan was to take me about a mile up the trail I had ridden on my horse with Lana. On foot, it seemed much farther. He wanted me to experience this rite of passage alone, or it wouldn't count as a true wilderness experience, but I begged to bring Lana, and he only relented after Penelope shamed him.

He saw us packing our bathing suits to swim. "You don't need bathing suits, for Christ's sake," he said yanking them out of our backpacks. "You're in the wilderness, and you should just swim naked!"

"For God's sake, Gardy, stop forcing her to be Huckleberry Finn. *You* didn't spend a night out in the wilderness when *you* were eight. Unless you considered the backyard of your Long Island summer home *wilderness*. And not everyone likes to be naked all the time, either. You let those little girls wear their bathing suits to swim if they want to, even if it is a lake in the middle of the woods." I didn't understand what she meant, but Gardiner did.

We carried a tent, sleeping bags, and food to the campsite. He built a dam across a stream, making a little pool from which, he explained, we could draw drinking water. He showed us how to build a campfire and how to put it out. Then he told us to set up the tent that was laid on the ground, a mysterious blob of nylon and poles. As we blundered, he corrected, and the ordeal was finally complete.

"There!" he said. "Now you're all ready for a night in the wild! All you really need is a knife and a piece of string to survive in the wild, but you've got the whole kit and caboodle. Now you girls have fun!" He waved goodbye and disappeared down the trail.

We were glad he was gone. "Let's have dinner," Lana suggested. We had Spam, crackers, cheese, and peanut butter sandwiches. For dessert, we made "Ovaltine" from a mix Gardiner had created out of Carnation instant milk, so we could just add water. We warmed it over our campfire in the little aluminum pots and then floated the marshmallows on top, just as we'd learned to do at Brownie camp. As soon as darkness fell, our excitement waned, and with each creak and hoot coming from the woods, we discussed the possibility of being attacked by wolves or possibly lions. We thought about escape plans involving climbing trees, but none had branches low enough. We thought about stabbing the attacking animals, but we only had a very small pocket knife, the one Gardiner had told us was all we needed to survive in the wilderness (along with the piece of string).

We didn't last long in the tent once darkness fell. We were in our sleeping bags, shining our flashlights toward the zipped door of the tent. "We should make a run for it," I said. "We'll just come back for our stuff in the morning."

"What about your dad?" Lana asked, pulling on her sweatshirt over her frilly pink nightie.

"Oh, I don't care what he says. We'll just sneak into my room through the lower window. The lock doesn't work, and I can pry it open. He'll leave early in the morning for work. He won't even know," I whispered loudly.

As soon as we were out of the tent, we ran like the wind until we got to my house, where we sneaked through the window and slept undisturbed until nine the next morning

The ghost of the Olympic Games still haunted Blyth Arena. It was an open rink with one side facing the mountain. Long, thick ropes hung from the roofline, presumably to offer some protection from the wind and snow off of the mountainside, and huge speakers blared organ music from the corners of the ceiling. The music in the rink competed with the yodeling and accordion music from the Hofbrau across the parking lot, where Martha the cook served knackwurst and potatoes to hungry skiers. Blyth Arena smelled of rubber mats, hot cocoa, and the breath of ice. The Longines scoreboards were suspended from the expansive vaulted ceilings on either end, and flags of all participating countries from the 1960 Winter Olympic Games still waved outside next to the big plaster statues of a speed skater and a hockey player.

The bleachers mostly sat empty except when we had our weekly ice shows in the summer or hockey games in winter. Sometimes there were conventions, like the Radio Church of God, for which the ice was melted, leaving only the concrete floor. Once, there was a rodeo inside, and the floor was covered with sawdust. We could play hide and seek forever in those bleachers, sneaking in and out of the old press boxes and team rooms where players once celebrated victories or grieved losses, and figure skaters waited to be called to the ice for Olympic performances.

Now, the team rooms were for all the elite skaters Lana and I envied. I wandered inside when they'd all gone home to rest between the morning and afternoon training sessions. I gazed at the open suitcases along the walls. Each suitcase had several pairs of skates made especially for those skaters, and I looked longingly at the whitest pairs that were reserved just for the ice shows. Their custom-made skating outfits for the show hung on the racks along one wall, each with their names and the titles of their performances. The outfits for the group number Lana and I had managed to get into were in a cardboard box, indistinguishable from the rest. We weren't special at all, just the leftovers, not good enough to be in the opening or closing number. We were in the middle somewhere, at a time when the audience might need to get up for popcorn or to use the bathroom.

I woke myself up at dawn and walked to the rink every morning, laced up my not-very-white skates with their dull blades, and stepped onto the unblemished ice to practice my limited repertoire of spins and jumps. I practiced for hours. My determination and hunger to be noticed, to become something special, were inexhaustible, boundless, and intense. Lana and I settled for parts in the weekly shows as members of the group performances, but we acted as though we were stars. I often found ways to sneak away from the dreaded Squaw Valley sporting club ski racing practice to the skating rink, where I could twirl and fly and imagine that I was beautiful and good.

I tried to shine, hoping that I would be invited to perform as a soloist, but I never was. I always looked up into the gallery, hoping that Gardiner and Penelope would be there to watch me, but they never came, and Lana's mother was always working at night. We had to be cheerleaders for one another, always praising each other and criticizing all the other skaters as we sipped our hot chocolate after the show and walked home to my house. "You shoulda had the solo," Lana would say to me.

"Do you really think so?" I asked with my heart full of love.

"Yup," she replied.

"I think *you* should have had it," I said, trying to be generous, knowing she deserved it more than I did.

I needed Lana way more than she needed me, and when she didn't answer the phone or when she wasn't available to spend the night at my house, I felt panicky and completely alone in the world. We had promised each other we would be best friends forever, without considering that adults can make stupid decisions that we would just have to go along with, and that they would be oblivious to the fact that they had destroyed our lives.

We must have seen our longing for attention in one another's eyes. We had crushes on older men, like Davy Jones of *The Monkees*, and argued over which one of us he might pick. We flirted with skating instructors and spent hours putting on Madeline's makeup, trying to make ourselves look older than our ten years. I was attracted to the hero types, like ski patrolmen and police officers. Once I had flirted with a highway patrolman who had pulled Penelope over for speeding in her Porsche. I had crawled over Penelope's lap to the driver's side and told him I loved his badge. Penelope still got a speeding ticket.

11

The Girl Who Cried
Ski Patrol

I'M SURE THAT LIFE WOULD HAVE taken an entirely different course had my nursery school teacher, Elenita Dardi Sullivan, been sensible enough to cast me as Mary, the mother of Jesus, in our nursery school Christmas play. I worked hard to be her favorite, offering to pass out cookies and juice at snack time and get the paints out for art projects, but she chose Mandy Ballenger, and I got a bit part as one of the shepherds and had to wear one of Penelope's dishtowels on my head. I refused to smile for the cast photo and scowled so fiercely that I gave myself a cramp between my eyebrows. I gave excellent performances all the time when it was called for. I was an only child and had no sibling competition, but getting Gardiner's attention away from Penelope was a huge job. It was like Hilda Swensen competing with Katherine Hepburn. Who is Hilda Swensen, you ask? Exactly my point. I had to resort to drastic measures.

I was seven when Penelope broke her leg up on Siberia, one of Squaw Valley's more difficult runs and especially so during windy snowstorms. She was loaded onto a toboggan that the ski patrolman had to drag carefully behind him, navigating through the bumps and rivets in the snow, down the mountain to the entrance of Gardiner's office. The patrolman peeled off the icy, snowy layers of blankets to reveal a shivering Penelope, who, upon seeing Gardiner's concerned face, dissolved into tears. There was a flurry of attention as every other injured skier was left to bleed or freeze to death on the x-ray table with nothing on but a paper gown—all the attention was focused on Penelope. An ambulance took her to the hospital in Truckee, Gardiner racing along behind in the light-blue VW Beetle. Penelope had a lot of emergencies: appendicitis, a broken tailbone from being thrown off her horse, and now this. And she never had simple ones, either. She couldn't just have regular old appendicitis—she had to have a perforated appendix and a dramatic ambulance trip followed by emergency surgery. She couldn't just have a bruise; she had to have a broken bone that involved crutches, surgery, and breakfast in bed for weeks afterward. Nothing was ever wrong with me other than tonsillitis, and all I got for it was a huge needle in my butt followed by the burn of penicillin and a command from Gardiner to stop my melodramatic crying immediately.

My first love was Wes Schimmelpfenig, one of Squaw Valley's tallest and most adorable ski patrolmen. Whenever he brought an injured skier into Gardiner's office, I always made myself available to help him, all the while hoping that he would notice my new ski pants or my pigtails with pink ribbons.

I'd just had it with all of Gardiner's attention being soaked up by Penelope. The only way to resolve the problem was to make Wes mine. I'd show Gardiner that he'd made a big mistake by casting me aside like so much rubbish and debris. So one day, while skiing one of the more challenging aspects of Gold Coast (which was near enough to Siberia to be competitive with Penelope's site of disaster), I fell to the snow, gripped my knee, and cried out in agony for the ski patrolman—specifically, Wes Schimmelpfenig. Soon, I drew a crowd of concerned adults, one of whom said he would get the ski patrol. I called out wanly, "Please make sure you only get Wes."

Within minutes, Wes arrived with a toboggan and blankets to keep me warm. I whimpered and pointed to my right knee, explaining how I'd fallen and twisted it, thereby rendering myself unable to move. I was loaded onto the toboggan and carried off by my knight in shining ski pants with matching jacket. When we arrived at Gardiner's office, everyone made quite a fuss, including Gardiner, who was initially captivated by my performance. Upon examination, however, it was obvious to him that it was all a ruse. First of all, feigning such an injury requires some knowledge about the nature of ski injuries. Gardiner's examination of my knee did not produce the pain he'd expected. "Kimball Converse Pier, you get up this minute and walk!" he commanded as if casting out demons at a revival.

I was sheepish but determined to keep up my ruse, if for no other reason than to save face in front of my true love, who shook his head and cleaned up all the gauze he'd used to wrap my perfectly healthy knee. I limped pathetically toward the bathroom, sniffling and choking back sobs, and locked myself inside. After a short period, someone else needed to use the bathroom, and Gardiner coaxed me out using a gentler tone, the one I liked. It was the tone he used when we were driving together without Penelope in the car. She refused to ride in his VW Beetle anyway, preferring to drive her Porsche, so I took every opportunity to go along with him wherever he went. Then I could be the center of attention, where I felt I belonged.

"Now . . . here's a dollar. Run along and get yourself a hot chocolate and a cookie or something." I gave him a deeply dejected look but took the money and limped all the more pathetically out the door and toward the snack bar at the lodge. Back in those days, a hot chocolate at Squaw Valley didn't cost five dollars; it was fifty cents, and when Gardiner didn't ask for his change, I kept it for myself.

I clearly needed a new plan to engage Wes as my future husband. I waited a decent amount of time before I had another accident on the mountain. I thought I'd wait until the next weekend when there would be a lot of people out skiing and Wes would be working. And I chose a more advanced run on which to stage my accident. But Wes was onto me, and after my "fall," he somehow convinced me that I was better off not taking up his time and making my father angry again. And so it ended right there on the saddle of KT-22. Wes knelt at my side, speaking softly so the crowd that had gathered around the poor little injured girl could not hear. When he arose, all seven feet of him, he spoke to my audience: "She's all right, but, unfortunately, the performance must be cut short today. You may get refunds on your tickets for today's show at the ticket window."

Okay, he didn't really say that, but he did say that I was fine and that I had probably sustained no more than a bruise. So the audience dispersed and went about their day on the slopes of Squaw Valley.

I knew longing so well. It was the first feeling I'd ever had. I knew the ache of missing love, of feeling bereft; I knew the passion of wanting to matter to someone so much that he would drop anything to come to my rescue. I knew Gardiner would rescue Penelope from a burning building with his bare hands and that her tears would elicit his sweetest, most compassionate side. A few years later, I gladly stood aside and made no demands on Gardiner's attention as he carried Penelope up the sixty-four snow-covered concrete steps to our house, IV bottle and all, so she could spend Christmas Day at home and not in the hospital. As she got sicker, I regretted every jealous moment that I'd ever wished I could have my appendix out or a cast on my leg. There would come a day when the medicine she had to take caused ulcers in her mouth, making it too painful to eat anything except the custard he made and then fed to her. She cried when the food was too hot, the heat of the food piercing through the sores, so Gardiner made sure he blew on each bite to make sure it was nice and cool. I tried to make myself into a good girl, obedient and helpful, hoping it would be enough to cancel all my sins and that she would live.

Despite my efforts to overcome being a prima donna, my longing to be the princess who made every man kneel and beg her for her hand in marriage prevailed. I was nine when my father made me take guitar lessons from Slim Lickleiter. I don't think Slim had much money, but he had a lot of back pain, maybe from his rodeo days, and I liked to think Gardiner had made a trade: "I will give you my daughter's hand in marriage if you teach her to play 'Red River Valley' on the guitar. And I'll throw in some Percodan if you teach her to play 'On Top of Old Smokey' . . . all the verses."

As much as I hoped Slim might marry me, Gardiner had actually proposed a less exciting trade: guitar lessons for me in exchange for medical treatment and pain medication for him, because of his back but also perhaps because lessons with me required narcotics. I thought Slim would make a fine husband and that we could play and sing together wearing matching cowboy hats. When I sang off key or hit a wrong chord, he gave me the look of an aging rodeo cowboy who suffers from chronic pain. He would come to the ice arena to visit another girl who had captured his heart, and when I saw him from the ice, I spread my arms, imagining myself the most graceful bird, and my heart beat faster as I whirled and jumped in my skates, hoping he would watch only me. But my white skates were scuffed and my ankles so skinny that the laces could not hold the boots tightly enough. My one skating dress was a little stained, and my lipstick from the drugstore just a little too pink. Slim wasn't at the railing to watch me.

I pined for friends to gather around and ask me to play, to argue over whose house I would go to after school. I simply could not seem to shake this need to be adored by every kid in Squaw Valley, even if it meant having an injury. Natalie and her brother, Timmy, had broken their legs skiing, and Gardiner had casted their legs, which by now had been all decorated by other kids with colored markers. Their mothers had knitted toe-warming socks, and they had crutches, and everyone wanted to hang out with them. I was insanely envious and decided that this time I would just skip the step of staging an accident.

I'd watched Gardiner cast people's legs dozens of times and thought I could do a pretty good job of it myself, so I slipped into the supply closet one day and stole about six rolls of plaster casting material and some rolls of cotton to go underneath the cast. Then came the tricky part: stealing the crutches. I'd have to sneak them out the back door and then walk home the back way with them.

The last time I'd used crutches, I'd been in second grade and had managed to snag a pair from Gardiner's office and hidden them behind a tree. On the way to the bus stop, I'd retrieved them from their hiding place and begun to use them when I was within sight of all the kids. Our bus stop was also the post office and the grocery store, which was right along the main road. Gardiner had driven by on his way to his morning hospital rounds and seen me. The VW Beetle had made a sudden, screeching stop and then ground into reverse and stopped right in front of me and my adoring fans. He'd snatched my crutches from under my arms and left me without any means of escape or rational explanation for my trickery. It had taken about a year for everyone to calm down and quit calling me a faker. This time I would need a more robust plan.

Once home, I drew a bath and sank all six rolls of plaster into the warm water. Then I sat on the toilet, propped my leg up on a stool, and unrolled the cotton wrapping around my leg. I had just enough for a full-length cast almost up to my hip. Penelope came in the bathroom just as I was wringing out my first roll of plaster. "Kacey, what are you up to?" she asked, slightly amused. "Oh, hi, Mummy," I said, embarrassed at being caught in my charade. "I'm putting a cast on my leg. Please don't tell Daddy." This request was ridiculous, of course, because he would be home for dinner and I would be wearing a cast. "I will speak to your father," she said, leaving me in privacy to finish my project.

Penelope, in all her wisdom, must have spoken to Gardiner about the lesson that was available for me in all of this, if he would just let the whole thing unfold, rather than doing his usual thing of yelling at me for being a hypochondriac and a huge pain in the ass.

I managed to finish casting my leg, although I had not waited long enough for the plaster to dry, and there was a large crease right at my knee where I'd stood up and forgotten that I shouldn't bend it. It was lumpy and cracked, but it looked convincing enough to me, and I had the crutches, which would placate any doubters from my last experiment with crutches the year before.

"You know that's going to itch a lot," he said, looking at me over his spectacles that evening as I hobbled around on my stolen crutches. "I don't care," I said a little indignantly. "And you'll have to wear that thing for at least eight weeks because that's how long it takes for a broken bone to heal."

"That's okay," I said.

I went to school and got the attention I craved from everyone, but the idea of not being able to go out for recess or play dodge ball in PE was beginning to put a damper on the attention I was drunk on. How was I going to get myself out of this mess? After a few days, my cast was in tatters anyway because I kept forgetting I had it on when I got up to go to the bathroom at night and would bend it in half. I had to capitulate. There was no way I could go eight weeks of missing recess and dodge ball.

"Daddy, I've decided I don't want to have a broken leg anymore. Can you cut the cast off?"

"What are you going to tell the kids?" he asked.

"I don't know," I said, suddenly feeling very foolish and ashamed that my quest for attention and popularity had resulted in this seemingly irreconcilable predicament.

"You could just tell them your old man said it healed really quickly. Just limp for a while. You're pretty good at that."

12

CHRISTMAS

THANKSGIVING AND CHRISTMAS, WITH THEIR EARLY darkness, the quietness brought by heavy snowfall, and the fire in the Franklin stove, filled my whole chest with happiness. I always dressed up in my best clothes, even though it was just the three of us and our dogs. But Penelope and Gardiner usually invited people who had nowhere else to go, so we usually had company for dinner, and I coveted my job as hors d'oeuvres server. But more than any other time, Christmas remains in my memory as the one ritual I knew made us a real family. When it all fell apart, my memory spoke and reminded me that I had had this one time a year when the joy was so overwhelming that I could barely breathe. I took everything in with wonder and amazement: the snowflakes, the reflection of the porch light on the tree branches flocked with heavy Sierra snow, the way Gardiner smelled when he walked inside breathless from stringing the Christmas lights along the roof, the sound of the Mormon Tabernacle Choir and Handel's *Messiah* on Penelope's expensive stereo system. Each Christmas strengthened my certainty that my parents, and even our dogs, would always be together and nothing could ever break us apart.

And I'm sure it snowed more in Squaw Valley when I was a child than it does nowadays. The snow banks were so high on either side of our steps leading from the street to our front door that I could dig caves in them. Gardiner would spend at least an hour trying to stomp a pathway down to the garage and then another hour trying to clear the huge berm left by the snowplow in front of our garage.

There might have been one or two Christmases during the 1960s with very little or no snow; one year it rained so much that some of the streets washed out. But my preferred memory is that the snow covered the mountains by mid-December, and we kids brought dry shoes to school to change into, after getting our boots filled with snow on the way to the bus stop.

Gardiner had a wooden toboggan, which not only was used for zooming down the hillside in back of our house but also was pressed into service as a transport device, loaded up with groceries and other items, and then dragged up the hill to the front door for unloading. It was also the annual Christmas tree hauler. We would boot through the deep snow into the woods behind our house to search for our Christmas tree. It didn't take too long to find one among all the densely packed fir trees. When we'd selected our perfect tree, Gardiner would unshoulder his axe and lop off the top of a tree or chop a little tree that was crowded in by the other trees at its base.

"This one is going to be bullied by his brothers and sisters, and he won't get any nourishment anyway," he explained as he hacked away. Usually our trees, like little orphans or unwanted stepchildren, were a little bald on one side, crooked, or tilted with uneven branches, skinny and malnourished. When we hauled our tree to the house and got it onto the porch, he cut the bottom of the trunk straight and then nailed two boards together to make a stand. It seemed it took forever before he finally said, "Well, Kacey . . . are you ready to put on the decorations?" And then we went down to the cellar to get the boxes and bags of Christmas decorations.

Our cellar was actually a sort of dungeon between the side of the mountain and the first floor of the house. The entrance to the dungeon was through my bedroom closet. Just inside the closet, on one side hung a dowel that had been mounted to the wall for hanging my clothes, and on the other side was the framed-in doorway leading to the cavern that Gardiner referred to as his workshop, where he kept all of his tools, lit only by a single naked light bulb. In *The Lion, the Witch and the Wardrobe* by C.S. Lewis, the wardrobe door led to a magical place called Narnia. My closet door opened into what looked like a mineshaft with mice living under the water heater and furnace. The rock walls glistened with seeping water from melted snow on one side, and on the other side, there was a wall with tools hanging from a peg board. My nightly entertainment was watching the mice scuttle out from under the water heater, traveling under the closet door to the dryer, which was in my bedroom with the washer because that's where the hook-ups were. Maybe it was just a mistake in the plans for the house. The mice would squeeze themselves underneath and collect lint and stray socks with which to fortify their nests.

Once we'd collected all the decorations from the cellar, for me, there was something about tinsel. There could never be enough of it. Once the tree was up, I was only interested in putting as much tinsel on the branches as my little hands could hold. We had colored lights and colored glass balls—red, green, and gold—and a few stray odds and ends to hang as well, but I had to be restrained from loading the branches with so much tinsel that none of the other decorations were visible. Once we were finished decorating, I thought nothing else could be more beautiful than that tree shining its lights out onto the snow-covered porch from the big floor-to-ceiling windows, which made our house unique among all the other houses in Squaw Valley. Each window was framed in green steel around each pane. Sixteen pane windows lined the western, eastern, and southern sides of the house so that the light shone in at all times of day. The top four frames and the bottom four frames cranked open like factory windows, so the wind could blow through in the summertime. Our tree shone out into the winter air, and I imagined all the animals in the forest would gather on the porch just to be close to it.

In the winter, we drew the curtains and shades to keep in the heat from the Franklin stove, which was stoked all day during the coldest days of winter. I was deeply concerned about Santa Claus being able to fit down the stovepipe, but Gardiner explained that Santa was a shape-shifter and could fit down pretty much anything. If there was no chimney or stovepipe, he could always use the door. The tree was directly across the living room from the Franklin stove, where I was instructed to hang my heavy woolen sock on Christmas Eve. Gardiner would set out newspaper leading from the granite hearth to the tree across the room. "Why are you putting out newspaper, Daddy?" I inquired. He'd only put newspaper on our braided rag rug when our dogs had been puppies.

"We can't let Santa Claus's boots leave tracks of soot on the rug. Now, you have to make Santa Claus a sandwich and a glass of Ovaltine. He will be hungry when he arrives, and he always appreciates a little snack," he explained after laying out the newspaper.

I was given responsibility for the sandwich making when I was old enough to stand on a stool to reach the kitchen counter, where I made a sloppy peanut butter and raspberry jam sandwich on wheat bread. I then reached for the jar of chocolate-flavored Ovaltine and, with Gardiner's assistance, measured out three tablespoons of the mix, put it in a whiskey glass, and poured in some milk. Then I stirred until it was dissolved. But I knew that the best part would be when Santa Claus reached the bottom of the glass and found the sediment of thick chocolate Ovaltine. I placed the sandwich and the Ovaltine on the table next to the tree and clasped my hands in delight at the beautiful tree and all the presents underneath. I was so young but so awakened in each little moment of being in this house in winter, with the fat snowflakes falling outside the window, and the dogs sleeping by the fire, and Penelope, so beautiful, smiling at me from the kitchen.

When I awoke on my fourth Christmas, it was four o'clock a.m. I went upstairs, where all was still dark except for the tinsel reflecting the shimmering colored lights on the Christmas tree. I looked in awe at the piles of presents under the tree and dared to creep just a little closer to see if Santa Claus had eaten his sandwich, which would be clear evidence that he had in fact made it down the stovepipe. I still wondered how this was possible given Santa's girth and the narrowness of the stovepipe, but I decided just to accept the magic.

The sandwich was gone and the Ovaltine drunk down to its last drop of sediment. I saw his sooty boot tracks on the newspapers from the hearth to the tree. My heart pounded when I saw my woolen stocking bulging with Santa's bounty. I was unable to resist the temptation to open just one present and chose the biggest one I could find from under the tree. And then it was just one more, and maybe just one more after that. I opened presents that were not mine, thinking it wouldn't be as naughty as opening the ones from Santa Claus to me. I heard my father open the bedroom door and shuffle down the cork floor in his leather bedroom slippers. He stood with his arms folded in his plaid flannel bathrobe and looked at me with the same look he'd given me when he'd discovered me drawing a mural on my bedroom wall with my box of sixty-four Crayola crayons.

"Kacey, what the hell are you *doing!*" he whispered loudly, not wanting to awaken Penelope. Frozen in a sea of shredded Christmas wrapping paper, holding a giant toothbrush that was supposed to be a back-scrubber for Penelope and Gardiner, I began to cry, my inability to use restraint and patience revealed in this awful moment where there was simply no escape.

"Now get back to bed right this minute, and don't you move until I come and get you. You're just lucky you didn't interrupt Santa Claus; he would have gotten right back on his sleigh without filling your stocking. God*dammit,* Kacey! You must learn to be patient!"

I went back to bed and prayed that I would be forgiven. When the light of morning made its way through the winter snowstorm that had blanketed Squaw Valley with two or three feet of new snow, I opened my bedroom door and listened for the sound of my father whistling, "With a Little Bit of Luck." He always whistled as he prepared his morning beverage of coffee mixed with Ovaltine and milk. "Daddy?" I whispered as loudly as possible without actually speaking. "Can I get up now?"

"You bet," he said from the top of the stairs. "Don't forget to wear your slippers and your bathrobe." Despite my naughtiness, I was presented with my very first pair of skis, as well as boots and poles, a gift I hadn't seen in my predawn act of debauchery. I wallowed and rolled in my joy. The Christmas rituals were among so many rituals that gave my life shape and meaning. I grasped and clung to each one as they began to disappear, one by one.

13
Brown Suitcase

In my ninth year, Gardiner and Penelope made many trips to San Francisco to see doctors and didn't take me along. Over the past year, she'd increasingly had trouble walking up the dirt driveway and then the sixty-four steps leading to our front door. She had never had to stop to rest before, but now she said her body hurt. She ran a fever and couldn't lift her arms to saddle J. P.

When they were gone, I stayed with other families—some I knew well, and some I didn't. The homesickness was unbearable, and the days were endless. Penelope gave me a brown suitcase to use, and we packed it together. She taught me how to pack it with everything I would need, sometimes for two whole weeks. She was concerned about clean underpants. I was concerned about how to pack all my treasures so I wouldn't be homesick. At other people's houses, I'd put away all the knick-knacks that were on their dressers and replace them with my little collection of essential items from my own dresser. It was something I always did when I stayed anywhere. Even in motels.

I learned how to wait. I waited by the main road, counting the cars and waving to people I knew as if I were just out enjoying myself and just happened to have my brown suitcase along to sit on. I listened for the unmistakable sound of my Penelope's red Porsche; I waited for the telephone to ring, and when it did, I waited for someone to answer, growing more frantic with every unanswered ring. It wasn't polite to answer someone else's phone.

When I stayed with families I didn't know very well, I was afraid to eat the food, and even more afraid to go to sleep. I had to stay with my Squench camp leader once.

She liked to be called Mrs. Squench, but her real name was Barbara. Squenches were creatures she'd made up, and we were Squenches from Squaw Valley who went to Squench camp in the summer. A Squench was a cross between a seahorse and a little fairy, like Tinker Bell. We Squench campers spent summer days out on the beach at Lake Tahoe swimming and being Squenches in the water.

Mrs. Squench's daughter, Chris, was a high school girl whose teased-up brown hair puffed up really high in the back and was formed into spit curls in front of her ears that she taped and sprayed with Aqua Net before bed every night. She wore frosty lipstick and a lot of black eyeliner and chewed Wrigley's spearmint gum. Once she offered me a half a piece, and it was so tiny that I swallowed it. When Gardiner asked Mrs. Squench if I could stay with her while he was away at whatever hospital Penelope was in, she often had Chris babysit me. Chris would have to drag me along on her dates with her boyfriend, who drove too fast in his Ford Fairlane. They made out in the front seat, and the car swerved all over the road, and I just had to hang on to the door handle and hope for the best. Mrs. Squench's son was fourteen and had a *MAD Magazine* collection. He told me I'd better watch it because he'd set a booby trap in his room in case I tried to sneak in, which I wouldn't have done because it smelled awful in there.

Finally, after what seemed like a year, the day came when Gardiner and Penelope were scheduled to come home, and I took my usual place out along the main road and waited with Brown Suitcase. I got off the bus that afternoon, rushed into Mrs. Squench's house, stuffed all my things inside my suitcase, and tidied up the guest room as if I'd never been there and would never go back.

I waited for hours and hours until the sun was about to set and finally gave up when it got dark. I sat down again on Brown Suitcase by the road. I couldn't return to Mrs. Squench's house now. All their knick-knacks were back on the dresser, and there was no sign of me anywhere in that room. I had to be gone and stay gone. It wasn't that far to my house, really—only one big hill and then a little one. The hard part would be walking the mile along the main road with Brown Suitcase and being spotted before I could turn up the road to my house. Someone's mother was bound to see me and ask what I was doing walking on the main road with a suitcase. I would just tell a lie.

Ever since I'd heard the story of Little Red Riding Hood, I'd been sure that the Big Bad Wolf lived under the stairs in my house, just outside my bedroom door. It was a spiral staircase with a dark place right underneath the first few stairs, and that was where he lived. I always took a running leap to get up the first few stairs and then ran as fast as I could up the rest until I reached the top. As I walked along, I worried that he also might be lurking in the bushes beside the road. Singing Christmas songs would help, as it usually did when I was afraid of the dark. Gardiner had taught me how to sing in harmony. Penelope had played the accordion, he had sung and played the harmonica, and the dogs had howled, and we had sung every folk song we'd known from the Kingston Trio albums. I'd begged to sing "O Come All Ye Faithful," even though it was months before Christmas. It had sounded so pretty when we'd sung it together accompanied by the accordion and the howling dogs.

I made it up both hills, switching Brown Suitcase from one hand to the other when my arm grew tired, and went around the lower part of the house to my bedroom window. I could pry the lower window open enough to reach inside for the crank to get into my room. It was dark in the house, and I made for the light switch in my room and then groped my way up the stairs to the kitchen, then turned on every light in the house. I felt safe in the kitchen. I needed Ovaltine. I needed sound, so I turned on the radio. I fell asleep on the living room sofa with Penelope's black cashmere sweater wrapped around my face and slept until Gardiner gently shook me awake. He had come home very late, and had covered me with a sleeping bag not wanting to make me get up and go down to my cold bedroom.

After Penelope got sick, Brown Suitcase became part of my identity. It was brindle brown, a little worn-out and crumpled on the corners from being thrown in the backs of dark closets or in the trunks of cars. It was never sure where it was going to end up. The stitching was pretty strong; the stitches were evenly spaced and each one certain of its ability to hold everything together, even if a thread or two was frayed.

It had two shiny, brass-colored clasps that made resonant clicks when I managed to get the teeth of the clasps to bite properly, which often required climbing on top and insisting upon closure. The leather would squeak in protest as I stuffed everything essential to maintaining a predictable life inside and then climbed aboard, kneeling on its lid and restuffing the hemorrhaging contents with my fingers, tongue out, eyes fixated on the clasps, ready to pounce when the teeth finally surrendered under my persistent pressure and reluctantly clicked. Brown Suitcase had tremendous resolve.

Inside Brown Suitcase, there were two compartments, each with several pockets along the side. One side had a semiflexible flap with two eyes, one on either end, which were meant to mate with two buttons opposite in order to secure the flap. The other compartment had a nice, soft, satiny cover, which was much more flexible with elastic around its edges. The semiflexible side required that the contents be folded flat and neatly stacked, or it would refuse to close. But the flexible side allowed for some slovenliness and lumpiness in the selection of essential items and the manner of packing.

I needed my special things in order to make my altar, no matter whose house I ended up in. I never knew. I made room for the practical things—the underpants, the socks, the sweaters—but I made more room for one of my mother's favorite scarves, stolen from her top bureau drawer. She'd never known I'd taken it. Each time, I'd fold it carefully and put it back before she was even home from the hospital. It smelled just like her, and I could always put my face into it whenever I missed her. I packed my bottle of Muguet cologne that Gardiner had given me for Christmas. I only used tiny little dabs in order to make it last. And I always brought my ceramic Cinderella figurine, which had come with the Cinderella watch I never took off except to take a bath or go swimming; my hairbrush; my jewelry box with a Tinker Bell that, when I opened it, popped up and twirled to the song "Your Mother and Mine" from the movie *Peter Pan*; and my rag doll with one eye and orange yarn pigtails. I packed my prettier pairs of undies, the ones that weren't stained by the medicine I had to take for chronic bladder infections; my favorite frilly dresses; my black patent-leather party shoes with the straps and bows on the top; and my ugly school shoes. All of it was stuffed into

Brown Suitcase and went with me on an endless and unpredictable journey of nesting, un-nesting, and re-nesting. It got to the point where Brown Suitcase didn't trust being unpacked completely and never went back under the bed. It just sat in the corner, all opened up and uncertain of what needed to be put away or laundered. Like me.

14

HOSPITALS

WHEN GARDINER CAME BACK FROM THE hospital in San Francisco, Penelope was not with him. He stopped by Mrs. Squench's where he'd left me while he went away, and she told him I'd left a note saying I was going home and that he and Penelope were going to pick me up at the main road. He didn't care that I'd lied to Mrs. Squench. He'd only come back to get me and bring me back with him to San Francisco. It was going to be a few days, he said. They had to do a biopsy of Penelope's muscle tissue. I was too excited about going to San Francisco even to ask what a biopsy was. Nothing could be better than riding in the car with Gardiner. We would talk about things, important things, like what telephones would be like in the future and why they didn't pull wrecked cars out of the Truckee River when they crashed, and we would stop at the Nut Tree for a treat.

We stayed at John and Buck's house on Buchanan Street in San Francisco. The house smelled so good, and there was a little garden in the back with a cupid that had water coming out of his penis. I visited him often and just stared. Penelope had appointed John my godfather when I was a year old. Buck was his boyfriend, and they'd come to my Christening ceremony dressed in Brooks Brothers suits and ties. Penelope had a lot of friends that she said were "gay as Dick's hatband." John and Buck were two of her closest friends.

She called some of her female friends "roaring dykes." She told me that John and Buck loved each other like married people, and that's why they lived together and didn't have any children, just Noel, Buck's poodle. Each day, I would wait patiently for Buck to get up (which was never until lunchtime) so I could go to the park and walk Noel with him. Buck drove a black Lincoln Continental convertible and always dressed as if he'd just stepped out of an ad for Brooks Brothers, even for morning walks. Their house smelled of old walls, roses, and velvet sofas imbued with Chanel No. 5. It was quiet and neat, with its perfectly matched, upholstered furniture and the quiet, comfy bedrooms with fluffy comforters.

The only other person in their house during the day was Rose, John and Buck's housekeeper. Rose's skin was so black that her smile lit up her whole face. Her teeth were bone white except for the gold ones in the back, and she made the most delicious turkey sandwiches in the world. She called me "chile" in a Southern accent and taught me how to snap my chewing gum. She smelled so good I just wanted to lie down in her lap and bury my face in her big flowered apron.

In the afternoons, Gardiner took me to Children's Hospital in San Francisco to see Penelope. Everything about San Francisco was so big and exciting, I never wanted to leave, but the hospital scared me, and even though it was called "Children's Hospital," there weren't any children that I could see. This hospital was enormous, nothing like the little hospital up in Truckee where Gardiner worked. The hospital in Truckee was only one building, and this place had at least four buildings, all of them tall, and each with an elevator. I had never been in an elevator, just escalators in department stores. I rode up and down, pressing the button for each floor just like in *Eloise*, a book about a girl who rode the elevators of the Plaza Hotel in New York.

I only saw Penelope briefly before she went in for the biopsy. After they wheeled her away in a paper shower cap, I decided to go exploring. Gardiner gave me five dollars to go to the gift shop and buy her a gift. I wandered the endless hallways looking for a thread of connection between this big hospital and the Tahoe Forest Hospital in Truckee. In the Truckee hospital, everyone knew me. I went with Gardiner whenever I could on his morning hospital rounds. While he went to see his patients, I made my own rounds.

There, my first stop was always the kitchen. In the mornings, the whole hospital smelled like breakfast, and I could help myself to whatever Maxie, the cook, had prepared. Usually, I chose red Jell-O, which I never got at home, and maybe some white toast with lots of butter and jam melted into it. Then I would visit Evelyn, the lab technician, who sat on a stool and looked through her microscope all day while her dachshund, Freidl, slept underneath on his blanket. Jars containing pieces of human tissue and parts of diseased organs sat on her shelves. Monica, the radiologist, had a whole human skeleton hanging on a stand by the x-ray machine. I'd learned the names of the bones, all yellowish-brown; the brown teeth, fixed in a permanent grin, looked as though they'd never been brushed, and little bits of fuzz still clung to her skull. Once, this had been a woman. Monica showed me how her hipbones flared like a butterfly to make room for babies.

At the very end of my route, I would stop at the nurse's station and play nurse until my dad was finished. Lois, the head nurse, taught me how to make a nurse's hat out of paper and pinned it to my head with paper clips. Sometimes I would bring my doctor's kit and beg the nurses to be my patients. I put M&M's in the pill bottles for medicine and let them choose the colors they wanted.

But nobody knew me here, and I wasn't allowed to wander into x-ray departments and nurse's stations. They shooed me out like a stray dog.

I finally located the gift shop in the huge, cavernous lobby of the biggest hospital in San Francisco and paid five dollars for a stuffed lion. I asked the lady for a red ribbon, which I tied around his neck, and then made my way back to Penelope's room, where I tucked him into the empty bed. And I waited and watched, occasionally wandering down the long hallway to see if I could see attendants pushing a gurney with Penelope on it. The nurses told me I wasn't allowed in the halls, that I really ought to be in the waiting room. But since my father was a doctor, they'd make an exception if I promised not to run down the hallway anymore. They told me to wait quietly in the room. And then the nurse gave me the greatest thing I'd ever seen. It was a television remote control that made the television turn on. By pressing the button, I could flip through all five channels and stop when I saw something interesting. I stopped when I landed on a channel where there were two women trying to wrap chocolate candies on a speedy conveyor belt, and were unable to keep up, so they began stuffing the chocolates in their dresses, and into their hats and then into their mouths. I laughed so hard that my jaws ached, and from then on, I watched *I Love Lucy* when ever I could or *The Fugitive*. We had a television, but we only got one channel, and *I Love Lucy* wasn't among the choices for television shows. Nothing for kids except *Disney's Wonderful World of Color*, and *Tarzan*.

I climbed up on the bed next to the stuffed lion and pressed the channel button until I landed on *I Love Lucy*. I was mesmerized, transfixed by Lucy and Ethel, and I wished I could wear dresses like theirs with matching purses and hats.

Penelope was finally diagnosed with polymyositis, a disease that nobody knew much about in 1968. All the doctors knew was that the body turned against healthy muscle tissue and devoured it faster than any medicine could stop it. We went home to Squaw Valley, but it was only a matter of weeks before something else happened, and she went back to Children's Hospital again.

It was the dead of winter, and I went to school every day feeling like nothing was going to be okay ever again. I folded my math paper and unfolded it so there were sixteen perfect squares. In each square, I copied a math problem off the blackboard in my neatest printing, as my teacher had instructed us to do, but I couldn't remember how to solve them. I didn't ask for help, and I didn't care. Sickness had intruded into my family before, but nothing like this. There had been the appendicitis and the broken leg, but this wasn't the same. This sickness was stealing her away from me for a long time, but I believed Gardiner could save her. I believed he could do anything. I believed he would never stop smiling and whistling "With a Little Bit of Luck" when he was making breakfast or casting someone's broken leg. And he would always sing with me in the car. He was bottomless, and I kept drinking and drinking, never asking him if he was all right, never doubting my safety. He never complained about taking care of Penelope and me. He was not going to let her die. I could tell by the expression on his face.

But after a while, I could tell he was lonesome during my mother's long hospital stays, and it scared me, making me wish I didn't have to live with him. I needed him to stay the same smiling daddy. Fortunately, I had a surrogate family where I was always welcome. I went to the Chisholm's house every chance I could.

Besides Lana, Mrs. Chisholm's two daughters were like my sisters, and Mrs. Chisholm included me in family rituals like summer picnic dinners at the waterfalls, where we'd sit on the warm granite rocks and eat hot dogs roasted over the campfire and toasted marshmallows for dessert. Being at Mrs. Chisholm's house made me forget the heaviness of my worry for a little while.

I was afraid to ask Gardiner if Penelope was going to die, so I didn't. I just swallowed my worry until it felt like an iron ball inside my stomach. When she was home from the hospital, the dogs and I tiptoed around behind her, not allowing her out of our sight. The house felt so hollow without her. I was even more afraid of dark places, feeling the presence of something so big and sinister that I could not hide from it. When Penelope was home, I begged to sleep upstairs in the living room instead of downstairs in my room, where I had suddenly become of afraid of the mice and all the noises they made.

15

OTHER PEOPLE'S
HOUSES

SOME NIGHTS WHEN GARDINER WAS HOME, he was called away to an emergency at the hospital, so I would need a place to stay. Lana's house was not an option because her mother was gone until very late at night, and I couldn't always stay at the Chisholm's house. I had to stay with other families with normal kids who weren't afraid to eat pizza, which to me looked scary with all the green specks of unidentifiable vegetables and bits and pieces of salami and sausage, but to other kids, it was like "Yay for pizza!" They would eat casseroles that to me looked like something our dog had urped up on the carpet.

I brought the usual things in Brown Suitcase. Whenever I went to strange places, whether to someone's house or a hotel room, I always cleared a little space wherever I could find it, even if it was just a windowsill. There, I laid out the scarf taken from Penelope's bureau drawer and arranged my things on top like a little altar, a place where I kept a finger hold on who I was, through all the new beds, dark hallways, unfamiliar bathrooms, and food I couldn't bring myself to eat. I could look at my altar when I needed to feel a little safer, but during the nights, I would often awaken shaking and sweating, my heart pounding, and feeling sure I was going to vomit from the fear seizing my stomach. I had a phobia about throwing up.

My worst fear was throwing up in a strange house without my father there. I imagined being lost in a dark house, unable to find the bathroom and throwing up all over the carpet, or in the bed, too frozen in fear to move. When I had these thoughts, I tried to calm down by whispering stories to myself. I played a game with myself that I called "Friendly Night, Bad Night." Every other night was a Friendly Night, when nothing bad could happen to me. On a Friendly Night, I could eat some dinner, and I could even allow myself to have fun with the kids in whatever house I was staying in. On Friendly Nights, I was protected against bad things happening during the night by thinking of Santa Claus and butterflies.

But somewhere inside me, there was a powerful demon that made me pay penance for Friendly Nights. And that's why Bad Nights existed on those in-between nights. I believed I deserved to have horrible things happen to me, but that the demon let me have breaks in between my fear-filled nights. I greeted these nighttime beasts in my white flannel nighties, beseeching them not to kill me or Penelope, and to please let us live. I was a watchful warrior sleeping lightly by her campfire, never allowing both eyes to close.

On Bad Nights, I didn't eat. That way, I wouldn't have anything to throw up. I lay in the dark, letting the fear envelope me, and I hung on, hoping I could endure the terror. Until I saw the edge of dawn, I ruminated about getting sick or Penelope dying. The fear was so intense that I shook all over and my teeth chattered. Catching the first glimpse of daybreak meant all the fear would go away, and the next night would be a Friendly Night.

Other mothers saw me walking home from school and stopped their cars to look at me with that "I'm so concerned" expression. I began taking the shortcuts home, even if it meant I had to climb the trail in thigh-deep snow to avoid questions like, "How's your mother, dear?"

If they managed to catch up to me, I would say, "Oh fine," all the while hoping I could slither out from underneath their lipsticked smiles. They would find out anyway at one of the many wine and cheese parties that Gardiner attended, where the wine gave everyone compassion.

I alternated among different families, mostly the Klaussen's house or the Chisholm's house, but I always hoped I would end up at the Chisholm's house. Mrs. Chisholm was warm and snuggly, and I wasn't afraid to be held close, even when the tears choked in my throat and I couldn't hold them back. She didn't say anything, and I didn't want her to; I just needed to be rocked in her lap and feel her breath moving in and out right next to me. Her skin smelled like it was the skin of an ancient mother's—sweet, warm, and safe. If other mothers tried to do the same, I felt that I was giving up or being disloyal to Penelope.

My favorite place at Mrs. Chisholm's house was the kitchen. Delicious food was always being prepared in her kitchen, especially at breakfast, when the smells of bacon and eggs mingled with the sweet smell of oatmeal cooked with raisins and coffee brewing. My second favorite place was the library upstairs, which looked out over the treetops and mountains. The carpet was soft and deep, and I could spread out cushions and read all the *Time Life* books, losing myself in all the pictures of faraway places. When I couldn't sleep, I tiptoed upstairs to the library to look at books until sleepiness overcame me. Mrs. Chisholm would often hear me and come into the library. "There's my little ghost," she would say with a gentle laugh. Sometimes she took me into her bed, where I would fall asleep in her arms while she told me stories in her soft voice. In her ancient embrace, I found the rest I longed for. I thought it might be fine to die in those moments. Awakening only brought back all the fear and my inner need to remain vigilant, taking up my burden of keeping Penelope alive, every intake of breath given to her life, every exhale not quite complete.

The Chisholm's house was only a few minutes away if I ran down the trail that was on the way to the bus stop. In the mornings, I met up with Brad, who lived across the street. I liked to go to his house because his mother always had Mallomars or Oreos, and they had a television that got two channels instead of only one like our television, so I could enjoy my sinful cookies while watching *Batman*. Brad was a misfit like I was, and he preferred playing school and house with Lana and me to playing with boys. He was overweight and insecure, and we loved playing with him. When we played school, he went straight for Penelope's black velvet high heels with the bows on top that she'd given me for dress-up and playing school. We traded the roles of "bad student" and "teacher," giving each other swats with my wooden paddle that had lost its little red ball on the elastic string.

I'd run as fast as I could to the Chisholm's house with Brad running behind me as fast as his chubby legs could carry him, down to the back stairs of their porch. With a full head of steam, we tried to leap all five steps onto the porch, but Brad's pants were too tight to allow for more than three. Mrs. Chisholm always had enough breakfast for us, and we ate the rice pancakes with syrup and the oatmeal with raisins even if we'd already eaten. Mrs. Chisholm made her daughters, Heidi and Michelle, take cod liver oil and brewer's yeast, which they managed to gag down with apple juice chasers. I joined that ritual too, and wished I was Mrs. Chisholm's real daughter. I felt ashamed that I didn't want to go home, and that I wished the Chisholm's would adopt me. My home wasn't the same anymore—not without Penelope.

16

MY HIPPIE PHASE

IT WAS 1968, AND I WAS in fourth grade. In March, I turned ten, and the world around me was changing. Gardiner grew his sideburns long, and his VW Beetle was suddenly the coolest car in Squaw Valley. He decided to get another television so Penelope could watch her favorite shows from her bed. It was a black-and-white Zenith with two antennas in the back, much less bulky then our old one, which now lived in my room. He put a bigger antenna on the roof of the house, too. We only got the NBC channel in Squaw Valley, but my world was changed by the peacock and the deep voice announcing that I was watching the NBC Television Network. The regularity of the *Huntley-Brinkley Report* and the way that Chet Huntley and David Brinkley announced themselves in the same voices every evening at six-thirty were comforting:

"Goodnight, Chet."

"Goodnight, David."

I was up at dawn on Saturdays waiting for my favorite cartoons. I had to endure a half hour of *Agriculture USA* before *Atom Ant* and *Secret Squirrel* came on. After that, it was *The Hillbilly Bears* and then Bullwinkle.

When Gardiner turned on *NBC News* and I heard the sound of bombs and gunfire, the screen showed black-and-white footage of soldiers running through swamps and helicopters flying through smoke. The war was in Vietnam, thousands of miles away, but the television showed thousands of people marching, yelling, and chanting, "One-two-three-four, we don't want your fucking war!" They put a *bleep* in where the swear words were. There were a lot of bleeps.

In tiny little Squaw Valley, the antiwar demonstrations were expressed in quieter ways—drawing peace signs on tennis shoes or painting them on the sides of VW vans; playing antiwar songs by Bob Dylan, or Jimi Hendrix and Janis Joplin, who screamed out the poetics of the culture. The Berkeley activists came by the thousands to Squaw Valley when the Maharishi Mahesh Yogi came to offer initiation into Transcendental Meditation. The air was heavy with the smell of marijuana, patchouli, and body odor.

Squaw Valley was a mountain retreat for peace activists from Marin County and Berkeley, who came during the summer and danced naked in the waterfalls. I bought stickers at Sunshine's gift shop in Squaw Valley. Sunshine owned the shop, and even though she was Penelope's age, she dressed and smelled like a hippie, with her tie-died skirts; long, white-blond hair; and tinted sunglasses. She played Jefferson Airplane records and sold beads and dangly earrings, posters of The Doors and The Beatles, Indian-print bedspreads, incense, and stickers that said, "Make Love Not War." I had to become a hippie; it was way cooler than being a regular ten-year-old. None of the young men were clean-shaven; they bound up their long hair with bandanas, and the women wore theirs long—either kinky or straight, and always parted in the middle. They didn't shave their armpits or legs, and if they wore bathing suits, the pubic hair crept out of the sides and blended in with unshaven leg hair.

I shed my little-girl ways when I mingled in the crowds down on the lawns, cooling in the slow drumbeat of evening. A bridge suddenly beckoned, and I crossed over, leaving part of my old self behind. When I went home, I rummaged around the cellar for a cardboard box, and when I found one, I set it down in the middle of my bedroom. Into the box went most of my Barbie collection, my Chatty Cathy doll, and many toys I felt no longer fit me. I saved the newest Barbie because Mattel, in its marketing genius, had made a hippie Barbie with curly blond hair, purple bandana, and tie-dyed, bell-bottom pants. When the box was full, I looked around my room, now bereft of toys, and pushed it down the hall into a closet where my father kept all his old army clothes. I begged him to pierce my ears, which then became constantly infected because I went swimming every day in the Squaw Valley Lodge pool, which, although dirty and buggy, had the best diving board of all the three pools in Squaw Valley. I could never leave the gold posts in long enough to let them heal. I put my Levi's through the wash tied in knots with a lot of Clorox, so they would be tie-dyed, and I wore Indian-print scarves loosely tied over my chest instead of T-shirts. Lana and I checked each other's outfits before heading to the village to mingle. "Looks pretty hippie-ish to me," Lana said, and off we went. We went to Sunshine's gift shop and bought pairs of sunglasses with blue or purple lenses and said "man" and "far out" a lot. We swam in Squaw Creek naked and camped in my tent out in the meadow.

Occasionally, there would be hours or maybe even a whole day when I didn't worry about when Penelope would have to go to the hospital again or when she would come home. Gardiner had hired a live-in nanny from Marin County, a nineteen-year-old hippie girl named Linda. She said, "far *out*," and had a VW Beetle with images of the Zig-Zag cigarette rolling papers guy painted on the doors. She lived in the downstairs guest room with her incense, patchouli oil, and a lot of Joni Mitchell records. Linda was a little on the fleshy side and loved to eat. I thought her cooking was disgusting, and Gardiner couldn't understand why. I missed the plain food that Penelope had made, which was all separated: hamburger, baked potato, and spinach, each in its own place on the plate, not all mixed together like the food Linda made, floating in sauce and all mixed together, reminding me of throw-up. I hated Linda's food, but Gardiner ate it with great gusto, wiping the plate clean and licking his chops.

When my Penelope was home, I would clasp my hands around her neck and make her promise she wouldn't go away: "Do you promise me you won't leave again, Mummy Mummy Mummmmmyyy?"

"Yes, I promise you," she'd say. As long as she promised, I could sleep.

"Am I going to throw up?"

"No, you won't throw up . . . everything is going to be super-superb," she reassured me.

I made her go through that ritual on a nightly basis, thinking it would prevent the frequent episodes in which I would awaken in a sweat, shaking violently and on the edge of vomiting. I circled my arms around her neck and smelled her beautiful, soft hair. "There, I have you now and you can never get away." I nuzzled her neck. She slipped so easily from my arms.

Linda's usual pile of food, beef stroganoff or tamale pie, landed in front of me at the table, and again I refused to eat it. And the same ordeal ensued: "Goddammit, Kacey! It's perfectly good food, and you will sit here until you finish it!"

"Fine . . . I'll sit here, but I'm *not* eating *this*. I'm afraid of it." Gardiner glowered at me and told me to stop being so ridiculous.

Linda had breasts that swung as they pleased inside her peasant blouses, like bags of Jell-O. A lot of women in Squaw Valley were going with the braless look these days, and Bohemian prints were the choice for the long skirts and loosely flowing tops. The fathers who once had closely cropped hair were allowing it to grow over their ears, and sideburns crept down their cheeks. Gardiner had curly reddish hair, or "rusting bedsprings," as Penelope called it, and he let it grow. He was balding, so it looked a little Bozo-ish, and I told him he should cut it.

Linda liked to make things out of dried flowers and put them all over her room. She told me my room was cluttered, but I was pleased with my arrangements of Barbie dolls whose hair I'd shaved, my Creepy Crawlers set, and all my crayons and watercolor boxes with dried out paintbrushes. I hated her even more for criticizing my sacred space, so I cluttered it even more by putting stick-on flowers all over the place that said "peace" and "love" and "flower power."

I was mean to Linda for being in my house where Penelope should have been. It was almost like Gardiner had given up when he had nannies come and live in our other downstairs bedroom. Linda's presence ruptured my vigilant hold on the dream that my Penelope would come home any day—if only Linda weren't there. I caught her in Penelope's closet once, her fat butt bent over as she examined the shelves where Penelope kept all her party shoes. "Hey! What are *you* doing in there?" I demanded.

Linda startled and raised her fat head with its stupid tie-dyed scarf wrapped around it. "For your information, missy, your mother asked me to get her camera out so your dad could bring it to the hospital."

I felt like tearing her eyeballs out. "Well, *I'll* bring them to her. And my name isn't *Missy*," I spat. I wasn't afraid of Linda. But Linda was afraid of me, and I liked it that way. "Now get out of my mother's room."

Linda looked shocked. I was only ten. And skinny. She outweighed me by about two hundred pounds, I imagined. "I'm telling your dad that you were being a brat to me," she said, shaking her finger at me.

"Go ahead," I sneered, leaning into my rage. I was blinded by it, and it took me hours of swinging on the willow branches out back to calm down. Tears stung my eyes as I thought about someone other than me being in Penelope's closet, and especially messing with her cameras.

17

BOLINAS

THE COMFORT OF THE ROUTINE AND structure I had known since kindergarten at Tahoe Lake Elementary School soothed me, and I didn't chew on my hair as much as I had done when it had first grown long enough to put in my mouth when I was around five. But soon after school started, Gardiner said we would be moving to Bolinas for a few months. He was in the Air Force Reserve and had been called into active duty. He needed to be close to Hamilton Air Force Base, near San Rafael, California, where I was born. Penelope's army of doctors were in San Francisco, and in Bolinas, she could be near the ocean and much closer to her doctors.

She used to bring me to Stinson Beach near Bolinas whenever she was mad at Gardiner. Usually she got mad at him when he wanted to bring his other three children, from his previous marriage, up to Squaw Valley for a visit. The boy, Mike, was deaf and autistic. He'd rubbed his erect penis against me when I was four, and Penelope had refused to allow him to the house ever again after that incident. She got mad at Gardiner for other things, too, like lying about where he was or coming home late. Once, when she'd had a broken leg, she got so mad at him for lying about where he was that she swung at him with her crutch and broke his ribs.

Penelope and I always left and went to a motel by the ocean when they fought. There were many cute motels in my early years—motels painted pink or pastel blue, with kitchenettes and windows looking out onto the ocean. There were coffee makers mounted on the walls with little packets of instant coffee, Coffeemate, and sugar. I made sugar water and begged Penelope to play tea party with me. If she refused, I dressed Vicky, our Vizsla, in my pajamas and we had a tea and dog-water party. And there were many long phone conversations between Penelope and Gardiner during these escapes. Once Penelope decided to forgive Gardiner for whatever he'd done, we would drive back home in the red Porsche.

Gardiner's former medical partner from San Rafael lived in a house built on pilings in Bolinas, so it was almost like living on a houseboat. I was put in the fourth/fifth-grade classroom at the little Bolinas school that looked like a church. Gardiner would drive over the winding mountain roads to the air force base in San Rafael and stay for three or four days, during which time I would be alone with Penelope. I'd thought it would be sheer bliss to have her all to myself, but she was different now. She was thin, the bones poking through her flesh, which was black and blue from of all the needles. She seemed lost, and she said things that didn't make any sense.

Sickness possessed her. It devoured her muscle tissue like dessert. The medicine to stop the disease only made it worse. Steroids made her crazy, and none of the sores all over her body would heal. Her face was bloated and hairy, and she hardly slept at all.

Years later, when I was old enough to understand, I learned that the theory behind using synthetic cortisol to treat an autoimmune disease like polymyositis was that it slows the autoimmune response by suppressing the immune system, giving the body a chance to regenerate muscle tissue. The problem is that the brain sees cortisol from some outside source and signals the adrenal glands to stop producing it. The massive injections of cortisone into the body create havoc in all the delicate systems, and chaos ensues. The body suspects trickery and engages its defenses, but it is no match for the syringe that infuses from without. The cortisol floods the brain and transforms natural aggression into madness, suspicion, and delirium. Cortisone, a natural hormone, activates a fight-or-flight response when the brain detects danger. But pharmaceutical cortisone in excessive amounts overwhelms the nervous system and blows the door to the unconscious off of its hinges, unclothing the goddesses of the secretive underworld and forcing them into the light of day. Their language is unclothed, uncensored, crazy and delusional.

Once, the voices from the underworld in which she dwelled told her to go out into the streets of San Francisco because her dogs were lost. She ran from Children's Hospital, wearing nothing but her thin hospital gown and her robe printed with little blue snowflakes, and kept running, down California Street, whistling and calling for her dogs, the echoes bouncing off the tall buildings, concrete beneath her bare feet.

Her confused immune system, deadened by immunity-suppressing cortisone, surrendered to the most benign of infections. Little sores turned into angry, festering wounds that refused to heal. One of my jobs while Gardiner was away from Bolinas was to coat the bedsores on her backside with Furacin powder and cover them with fresh dressings. The sores were so huge that she could not sit or lie without inflated rubber doughnuts and sheepskin to ease the pressure on the bones that were covered only by a thin layer of rotting flesh. I'd watched him give injections dozens of times, so learning to do it was easy. "Just tip the bottle up and suck the medicine in to the number I wrote down for you. Always push the plunger a little to get the air bubbles out. Then, find a place just above her butt that isn't too hard to the touch; you may have to give the shot in her thigh. Don't jam it in too hard or you'll bruise her, but don't waste any time either . . . just quick, like this." And he quickly stuck the needle in, pushed the plunger down, and took it out, holding a gauze pad over the site. Much of her major muscle tissue had deteriorated, making it hard to find a place where the skin wasn't bruised or the underlying tissue matted and hardened by scarring and degeneration. Most people can't reach their own buttocks very well, but she was further compromised by advancing osteoporosis brought about by premature onset of menopause. Sometimes, the needle just stopped dead as if it had run into a steel wall.

The doses of cortisone and Demerol were premeasured for her, so all I had to do was uncap the syringe, clean the site with alcohol, and tell her to count to ten while I administered the injection. "*Shit,*" she said as the needle plunged into her very bony backside. "I can't stand it there anymore . . . put it into my thigh, where there's some flesh left." The tears welled in her eyes and then she said. "I'm sorry."

"It's okay, Mummy." I didn't feel brave.

Life in Bolinas was oppressive, matching the fog that veiled the cliffs and shoreline each day. I tried to make the most of whatever independence I had in this tiny town, where there were three bars: Smiley's, Scowlie's, and Snarley's. There was one grocery store, a drugstore, and some surfboard shops. I did the grocery shopping and took the opportunity to purchase food items that I never saw in my mother's shopping cart. Back in Squaw Valley, I'd had to beg her to buy the things that other kids had in their school lunches—the Mallomars, Hostess cupcakes, and Oreo cookies. "Oh, now, stop begging for all this junk. All one has to do is look at the ingredients to understand that these items have no redeeming nutritional quality whatsoever. Now put the Mallomars back and replace them with some Fig Newtons, please."

Now that I was in charge of shopping, I could sneak in some of the naughtiest choices. I found Shake-a-Puddin' and Ding Dongs, Hostess fruit pies and Lay's potato chips, Sugar Smacks and Cocoa Puffs: all items I'd seen advertised on television and felt I must have in order to be a normal kid. I looked at the directions on the Shake-a-Puddin' box that said, "Just add water and shake," which was so easy compared to the pudding Penelope had had to mix and then wait hours and hours for it to congeal. I wanted her to eat my invention of vanilla mixed with chocolate pudding. But she said she'd eat dog food before she ate that crap.

The television in Bolinas had three channels, not just one. I was mesmerized by the choices but I was still particularly enamored with *I Love Lucy* and ran home from the bus stop in time for the opening song.

Bolinas Elementary School and its church-like building suggested it was a place of innocence and welcoming. There was one big white building with a belfry and a real bell inside it, along with two other buildings behind it, each of which had four classrooms. It seemed as if going to school in such a building would be sacred, like going to church. But on the inside, it wasn't sacred; it was cruel and hard. I was in a mixed fourth- and fifth-grade classroom for all my classes because there weren't more than twenty kids combined in each grade. It was in Bolinas that my love for school faded, and I fell, slipping and clawing down the unpredictable terrain of my life. I was homesick for Squaw Valley and avoided going back to the place I shared with Penelope after school. Once, I'd longed for Penelope. Not wanting to waste a moment, I'd run as fast as I could home from the bus stop. Now, I walked home slowly, fearing what I might find. She was gaunt and gray, her eyes puffy and purple from drugs. She was a skeleton, and I was stuck with her. I was afraid to sleep. Afraid to eat. Afraid to play or breathe. If I'd been home in Squaw Valley, I would have escaped to Mrs. Chisholm's house.

I'd thought maybe changing locations would have turned me into a popular kid. But I was scrawny, nervous, and defensive, easy prey for the bullies, and they pounced. So I went back to dressing up my dog and having tea parties with her. I might have enjoyed a nickname other than Toothpick, but it wasn't as bad as some of my other nicknames. It's a big lie that ignoring bullies works, and it's an even bigger lie that only sticks and stones can break your bones, but names can never hurt you. I let my mind wander far away from school. It used to be important to me to be the best at spelling and reading. The Bolinas fog could hide me now. I sat in math class and heard nothing but gibberish. The teacher, with his dandruff piling up in drifts on the shoulders of his polyester blazer and his yellowing buck teeth, did not notice me as I slumped in the back of the room at my metal desk. I didn't want help with math; I wanted to go home and stay at Mrs. Chisholm's house. I wanted to be pulled under by the fog and just disappear.

The bladder infections became more frequent, and I had to pee a lot. But in this school, I was too embarrassed to ask to go to the bathroom, and this resulted in a leakage problem. It wasn't long before I ran out of clean clothes. I wasn't sure how to wash them, because the washing machine in the house where we were staying had different buttons and dials than our old Kenmore in my bedroom in Squaw. I tried washing them in the kitchen sink with dish soap. Once, having run out of clean dresses, I wore pants instead of a dress to school and was sent home by the principal because girls were not allowed to wear pants to school.

Penelope wandered the house at night, muttering and raving at things that weren't there, and I learned to awaken when I heard the slightest noise, to steer her back to bed. She hissed at me, her tongue thickened by narcotics, "Stop telling me what to do. I am your mother." Waking up was so painful, and staying awake even more so.

Sometimes, I reluctantly crawled into bed next to her so she would stay there, at least until the next hallucination convinced her to wander the rooms again searching for imaginary people and monsters that existed in a realm only she inhabited. I lived in a state of watchfulness, aware of every sound, and my "sleep" actually fell somewhere between wakefulness and the threshold of sleep—a pattern that never resolved itself. I would often jolt awake to find her skeletal figure hovering over my bed. "You've been screwing boys, haven't you?" she demanded, hovering over my face.

"Mummy, remember, I'm only ten?" I whispered, frightened and uncertain as to what to do. There was nobody to call, not even Gardiner. It was just me and endless night.

If I had been at home, I would have been at Tahoe Lake Elementary, cutting snowflakes out of construction paper or becoming mesmerized by the feel and scent of the books in the library. I would have eaten lunch at the cafeteria from a brown plastic plate with three little sections that separated all the food, leaving most of it except for the french bread or maybe the applesauce. All this fog and grayness gave me headaches; I wanted the crisp, cold air and the sky that was so blue I thought it was a shell and that God's face had twinkling blue eyes and a gray beard, and that he would peer through the clouds to watch me.

After a few months in Bolinas, Gardiner said Penelope was too ill to be at home anymore, and he took her to San Francisco to the hospital again. I sat in the back of the car, feeling ashamed of being relieved, but the idea of going back home where I could fall asleep to the silence of snow falling and the sound of our forced air heater turning on at night almost helped me to overcome my shame.

I wore my sorrow in my suspicious frown; knitted brows; stringy, dirty hair that partially hid my face; and thin, dirty legs protruding from my light blue, pee-stained smock that kept slipping down over one thin shoulder.

After bottles and pacifiers, I'd discovered my thumb and sucked it until the skin was white and waterlogged. Finally, when I was five, I was brave enough to give it up. I marched upstairs, got the red plastic trash bin out from under the kitchen sink, and brought it into the living room where Gardiner and Penelope were having morning coffee. I stuffed my patchwork "biddy" into the can, abandoning my favorite object of comfort, the quilt with the little lambs sewn into the light-blue and white squares. "I don't need my biddy anymore, and I'm going to stop sucking my thumb,"

I announced. I might as well have told Gardiner that my life goal was to be an Olympic ski racer.

Now I wasn't so brave. I had no biddy, so I pulled the wool off my blankets and made little fuzzy balls that I could rub under my nose at night to comfort myself.

18

MRS. FARR'S
FIFTH GRADE

PENELOPE USED TO LOVE TO TAKE pictures, especially of me. It was difficult for her to cuddle me, preferring to cuddle her dogs more than any human. Maybe she felt safer loving me through the lens of her camera. It had been at least three years since she'd touched her cameras. Her Rolleiflex camera bags sat neglected in her closet in their worn and battered brown leather cases. She'd had them at the hospital for a while, but she changed hospitals so frequently that Gardiner brought them home, and there were no more pictures. I have no record and no idea of what I looked like between the ages of ten and eighteen. I stepped further and further back from the center of my family, trying to make room for my mother to live, regretting every bad thing I'd ever done.

I was happy to leave Bolinas and the school where I had no friends and was called Pee Girl and Toothpick. But even going back to Tahoe Lake didn't relieve the daily worry and fear that Penelope would be gone, back in the hospital with a sudden new emergency, or that she'd be dead. Now, none of the clocks seemed to say the same thing. I clung to the classroom, with its comforting routine and the dependable *tick* of the big hand before it moved forward another minute, punctuated by bells at the hour's end. I knew that at fifteen minutes to nine, the whole class would stand up and mumble and yawn through the Pledge of Allegiance, followed by a song. It was either "My Country, 'Tis of Thee" or "America the Beautiful." *Ohhh beauteeeful for spaaatious skies, for amber waves of graaaain . . .*

Then the student who was chosen to be the weekly lunch monitor took the count for hot lunch or milk only. I knew that at ten-thirty there would be morning recess for twenty minutes, and at noon the Tahoe City firehouse would sound the siren, and it would be time for lunch. The lunch menu, printed on blue paper smelling of the purple ink from the mimeograph machine, was handed out each Friday, along with notes to parents. I loved the smell of the ink and held the freshly printed menus to my nose on the bus home. I knew there would be spaghetti or pizza on Wednesdays, usually sloppy Joes on Mondays, chili and corn bread on Tuesdays or Thursdays, and fish sticks on Fridays. My fear of food was severely limiting my options. I only ate the cornbread or mixed fruit, on the brown, plastic, three-compartment plates, except on Fridays when I could eat the crispy fish sticks swimming in ketchup. On Fridays, I ate all my lunch and felt full—often for the first time in several days. I was afraid to be full. It felt better to be empty.

I also loved that the same kids and teachers were here every year. The best thing about being back home in Squaw was being in Mrs. Farr's fifth grade—a long-awaited honor.

Mrs. Farr never removed her dark glasses with the green lenses, for reasons we never asked her about. Her glasses were shaped in the sixties' exaggerated cat-eye style, with a little smattering of rhinestone at the outer corners, which were the only frivolous decoration in her ensemble. She wore light red lipstick, not the frosty pinky colors that were all the rage back then. She usually wore a skirt to mid-kneecap with a matching blouse, buttoned right up to the throat and pinned with a lovely pin or with a scarf, opaque hose, and flat, sensible shoes. She had gray hair that she brushed into a smooth, even oval framing her forehead and face. I adored her; it was my mission to please Mrs. Farr. I was quick to ask if I could stay after class to be the blackboard monitor, whose job it was to clean the green surface with the big eraser and draw fresh lines with a line maker that held three pieces of chalk, or to straighten all of the desks into perfect rows. She taught the class about things that meant a lot to her: the names of different types of trees indigenous to the Lake Tahoe area; perfect printing and cursive writing; and the two subjects about which she felt most passionately, the children of Mexico and Native American people.

She held great reverence for trees and defended them when they were under threat as if they were her children. A huge Jeffrey pine stood right in the middle of the street in Tahoe City, and on numerous occasions, it was proposed that the tree should be cut down because drunken tourists kept driving into it. Mrs. Farr won many a stay of execution for the tree, but after she died, they cut it down.

Mrs. Farr read to us each day after lunch recess—a calming respite from the frenetic games of tetherball, jump rope, and running from the boys. I settled into my desk—the same one every day, fourth one down in the row. I loved my desk, with its gently slanted top and the pencil holder at the bottom. I could lift the top and hold it up with my head as I searched for the right book or my Crayolas or a sharper pencil. Mostly, I loved to put my head down on my sweater and listen to Mrs. Farr read. She read Jack London stories and Robert Service poems; she read *Island of the Blue Dolphins* and, on some days, Pippi Longstocking or Mrs. Piggle-Wiggle, just for fun.

Sometimes she didn't read out of books; she told stories of her own about *her* summer adventures in Mexico with children who had no access to schools. She told stories about the Tahoe City buildings and how they'd changed shape and personality with each hopeful newcomer who'd had an idea for a business. Her voice lilted and swayed, and my imagination drifted happily along, lost in the stories and the smell of her hand lotion mixed with that of the crayon drawer.

I loved the school library, musty from the hundreds of little hands that had turned the pages. It seemed as if the library had its own language, spoken in a whisper that could only be heard in silence. I loved to finger through the index cards, so pleased that I'd learned the Dewey Decimal System in third grade. I could find any book by following the number written on the card and finding the matching numbers on the spines of the books. I brought my three allotted books per week to Mrs. Keen's desk, where she peered over her black, horn-rimmed glasses and stamped the cards, then filed them away in her little box of checked-out books. I checked out Trixie Belden books and books about horses. If library books were late, she sent a note home on Friday stapled to the lunch menus and the announcements for PTA meetings that my parents never attended.

Mrs. Keen was the playground monitor, too. In the library, she seemed almost nice, but at recess, she was terrifying. With her brows knitted, her whistle in her mouth at all times, like a faithful minion, she roamed the playground and watched vigilantly. At the first indication of a scuffle at the tetherball or cheating at hopscotch, she would inflate her cheeks and lunge, emitting the shrill blows from her whistle and issuing the command to stop immediately and go stand against the wall. Occasionally, the crime was severe enough to warrant reprimand from Mr. Smith, our principal. Mrs. Keen was not to be trifled with and tended to frown, even when approached with a bouquet of wilted dandelions for her desk. Such gestures would only arouse her suspicion of a bribe, and she would quickly run through her overdue book files before accepting any gifts.

In our after-lunch story time, Mrs. Farr read books that contained history lessons of some kind. She read us the book *Ishi: Last of His Tribe*, about a Yahi Indian whose tribe was eradicated, along with so many other tribes, by white gold seekers and devout believers in their inalienable right to the pursuit of life, liberty, and happiness no matter whose toes were stepped on or whose ancestry was erased. She also told the story of the Donner Party—of the starvation and death the travelers endured on the shores of Donner Lake. Mrs. Farr suggested that perhaps the early blizzards of 1848 had been nature's intervention to balance the horrid scale of genocide brought upon the indigenous tribes by white-skinned people in the Land of the Free and Home of the Brave.

I'd gone to Girl Scout Camp at Donner Lake in the summer. It was hard to imagine people starving and suffering in the same place where we scouts had sung songs and eaten s'mores until we were nauseated. Mrs. Farr told the stories of Native Americans and the Donner Party with great passion and stopped numerous times to answer questions, just as Gardiner did when he told stories. Mrs. Farr knew about my life at home, and her special attention gave me a reason to care about school. She cared for me in small ways, discreetly, so that other kids wouldn't think she was picking favorites. Once in a while on Saturdays, Mrs. Farr and her husband, Harold, took me to lunch at Pedro's Mexican Restaurant in Reno, but I couldn't eat the food, abiding by my policy never to eat anything where I could not identify the food groups or when there was sauce of any kind covering it up. Mrs. Farr also sent me cards in the mail, in which she wrote comforting messages in her perfect print and signed them, "From Your Secret Pal." I knew that my Secret Pal was Mrs. Farr. Nobody else on the planet could print that perfectly.

She let me go to the bathroom without raising my hand. I had to drink a lot of water to try to prevent more bladder or kidney infections—the latter of which I'd had twice, each time being so sick that Mrs. Klaussen had had to give me rubbing alcohol baths to bring my fever down—and holding my pee was impossible. We had a system, Mrs. Farr and me. All I had to do was catch her eye and wink. She would nod her head, and I would leave. I had to move my desk to the end row by the door so as not to disrupt class. The medicine I took made my pee turn orange. If I tried to hold it, too embarrassed to ask to go to the bathroom, I leaked, and there would be an orange map of pee on the seat of my pants or dress.

Mrs. Farr's loving attention made the thought of disappointing her unbearable. But I committed possibly the worst offense imaginable in Mrs. Farr's pristine classroom. Her room was a showplace, an expression of the sacredness of education. The blackboard was clean, the chalk tray stocked with sticks of white and colored chalk and her nice erasers all lined up perfectly. Mrs. Farr always went across the street to her house for lunch. The room was empty when I went to the classroom with two of my friends to get my jacket for recess. "I bet you don't know what a penis looks like," said one.

"Oh yes I do. My dad has a book with pictures in it," I said smugly, recalling Gardiner taking his *Gray's Anatomy* book off the shelf to give me an anatomy lesson after my friend Molly told me that people made babies by rubbing against each other and demonstrated by rubbing two stones together.

Then I proceeded to draw a larger-than-life but otherwise anatomically correct penis on her blackboard while narrating about and then labeling each part. They thought I was too much of a teacher's pet to render this particularly daring drawing on Mrs. Farr's blackboard right next to a perfectly printed Robert Service poem, and I felt it necessary to destroy their perception. I was hard at work when Mrs. Farr walked in unexpectedly from having her lunch across the street, I froze with my chalk in midstroke, having just put the finishing touches on my work. Mrs. Farr asked my friends to leave and then looked at me for a long time from behind her dark glasses. Her chin quivered ever so slightly, and then she reached into her bottom desk drawer for her wooden paddle. I was beside myself with shame as she escorted me out into the hallway and told me to bend over. The three swats to my buttocks with the pine paddle burned, but not as badly as my heart. I feared there would be no redemption and that I'd lost my one and only mainstay in the chaotic storm that was now my home and family. My punishment was to clean the blackboard with water each day for a week after school, and I had to take the late bus home, which ruined my plans to play with Lana. I cried and cried, ruminating on ways to earn back her love, believing I'd lost it forever that day.

There were people who came into my life for a single moment or for a period of a few months during this time in my life. I hardly ever saw Penelope other than for brief visits to the hospital, where I tried to cram too much talk into too little space. And Gardiner was frantic between trying to find a doctor who could diagnose her illness and trying to manage his own practice. Our house did not echo with her music anymore, and the dust balls gathered beneath the furniture.

Mrs. Farr fed my hunger for attention secretly and quietly. The breath of love was soft and sweet as she walked past my desk to look at my math work. I was so grateful for the familiarity of the afternoon sun shining on the playground, the ritual of cleaning our desks out on Fridays, and the simple sounds of pencils being sharpened, or the bell ringing for recess right at 10:30 and again after lunch at 12:30. I felt belonging in Mrs. Farr's classroom, where the papier-mâché volcanoes made with laundry starch stood neatly in a row, and it smelled like wet brown paper towels and cleanser mixed with the smells of paste and crayons. Sometimes, I took the sleeve of Mrs. Farr's soft wool sweater, which hung on the back of her chair, and held it to my cheek for a moment before leaving the classroom for lunch.

19
Girls

IT SEEMED EVERY GIRL WAS DEVELOPING breasts and growing pubic hair except me. A bunch of us compared our budding titties in the girls' bathroom during lunch recess one day, and there was no sign of puberty on my skinny eleven-year-old body. Donna, a girl with pimples and oily hair, said she'd started her period. I was so jealous I demanded to see evidence, so she showed me the pad with blood on it. Nature had seen fit to bestow two little perfect breast buds on Lana's chest that were visible even through loose-fitting dresses if she held her shoulders back. I accused her of stuffing, but she revealed herself in the bathroom. While we were in there, Lana's shirt held high to reveal her chest buds, numerous other girls chimed in with their stories about developing and having to shave their legs and wear bras with actual cups, not the training bras with no cup at all. Lana had betrayed me by developing breasts before I had, and I felt like an outsider. My chest was nothing but ribs and tiny little-girl nipples, my daily searches for pubic hair yielding nothing but bald, pink flesh.

But . . . I had a dress with two chest pockets perfectly placed over where I should have had breasts, so I wore it several times a week. I could shape Kleenex tissues into buds and put one in each pocket, pinching and puffing until they were perfectly balanced and not too pointy. I had to pay close attention about hanging upside down on the monkey bars or playing teth-erball too hard, to prevent losing the tissues on the playground. One day, Mrs. Farr made all the boys leave the classroom to show the girls a special movie sponsored by the people who made Kotex Sanitary Napkins. Each box for regulars was blue with a beautiful white rose on it, and the purple box was for super-sized pads, in case you bled like a river. I knew because I'd read the boxes in the supermarket when Gardiner wasn't looking. All the girls received little booklets put out by the Kotex people that showed how breasts and pubic hair appeared in stages until there was a fully developed woman with an hourglass shape, full breasts, and a big smile on her cartoon face. I was in love with her.

The movie showed a diagram of a vagina, a uterus, fallopian tubes, and ovaries. I sat mesmerized by the flowery way in which the narrator described the wonderful world of menstruation and becoming a woman. Everything about menstruation seemed so magical and wonderful because of the boxes of pads with roses on them, the little belts you had to wear to keep the napkins in place, the little bags you would carry to discreetly hold your pads at school, and the secret all girls would share about womanhood.

I begged Gardiner to take me to K-Mart in Reno and buy me all the necessary supplies right away, certain I would start menstruating very soon. He looked at my chest and my little tiny hips but agreed that I should be prepared. I longed for it to happen to me and checked my underpants multiple times every day. Some girls I knew said they thought it would be disgusting and boring not being able to swim when you got your period, and that they never wanted to get their periods, but I wanted something to happen to me—something just about me, not about Penelope. My whole life had been about her being sick, and nothing had ever happened to take Gardiner's attention away from that, except when I'd cut my finger open trying to use his razor to shave the nonexistent hair on my legs. He'd had to haul me down to his office on a Sunday, cursing all the way, to sew me up: "Goddammit, Kacey. What the hell were you doing with my razor, for Christ's sake! I wish you'd stop being such a pain in the ass."

20

LOSING CHRISTMAS

A NOTHER CHRISTMAS WAS APPROACHING WITHOUT ANY hope of
Penelope coming home from the hospital in San Francisco. Gardiner
forgot about Christmas and went to Chinatown at the last minute, where
he swept a few cheap toys into a brown bag. He bought a tree and stood
it up in its usual place in the living room. I decorated it by myself. There
were presents for Gardiner and Penelope that I put under the tree and a
couple for me from my grandparents. I took the woolen stocking out of
its box and looked at it, afraid to hang it up. Every Christmas, I hung it
on the knob of the Franklin stove, but I doubted that it would be filled
this year.

I awoke on Christmas morning afraid to go upstairs. I wanted to run
away to the Chisholm's house, where everything would be normal. But they
were probably sick of me, I thought. I wasn't part of that family.

The year before, Penelope had wanted to have Christmas Day at home,
so Gardiner had borrowed an ambulance from Jack DeRyke's Ambulance
Service and brought her home from the hospital in Truckee. He'd carried
her up the long driveway and up all sixty-four steps, IV bottle and all, and
put her on the sofa for a few hours at home. I was a ball of frenetic energy for
those few hours, dancing and singing and drawing pictures for her, wanting

to be the cure and make myself so incredibly wonderful that she would get well in one afternoon and never leave again.

I went over to the stocking. My father was drinking his coffee and looked at me over the top of his glasses. The stocking was full, but there were no newspapers with sooty boot tracks, and I hadn't bothered to make a sandwich or Ovaltine for Santa Claus.

"There really isn't any such a thing as Santa Claus, is there, Daddy." It was a statement, not a question.

"No . . . there is no Santa Claus," he said.

I took out each cheap little plastic toy collected at the last minute in Chinatown. "Thank you, Daddy," I said.

"Aren't you going to open the other presents?"

"Oh . . . yeah . . . I guess so. But can Lana come over?" I hated being alone with Gardiner now. It was so depressing and a little scary. He wanted me to sleep with him, so I did, but something made me want to sleep on the very edge of the bed on Penelope's side.

21
RUNNING OUT

Penelope's illness worsened that winter. She was flown to UCLA Medical Center for a trial of experimental medication. I saw her only once, and only from her hospital room window. The drugs caused sores that invaded her mouth, making it almost impossible for her to speak, and we couldn't have our phone conversations, which had always ended with her saying, "Don't forget me." And I would promise I wouldn't. The medicine had rotted all her teeth, which had then been surgically extracted; her bones were brittle; her hair was gone; and she was so thin that I was afraid to touch her. She said the medicine was like taking poison.

"The medicine is worse than the disease," she said hoarsely. She vomited constantly, sometimes even her own saliva; her nail beds became infected, and her fingernails, once smooth and perfectly shaped, grew back in misshapen ridges. Still, she would not relinquish the essential pieces of herself that made her Penelope. She asked Gardiner to bring her Victrola to the hospital so she could listen to her favorite operas. She filled her room with photos of me and J. P., who was pastured and, eventually, after several summers of not being ridden, sold to a cowboy who Penelope knew would love him and ride him. She surrounded herself with her favorite perfumes and wore soft, pretty bed jackets from I. Magnin's over her hospital gown. And Gardiner brought the dogs to visit once she was out of the ICU and could be wheeled outside the hospital all bundled up in blankets. One morning, before Gardiner and I left the house to visit her, she called.

"Hi Mummy!" I said, always excited when she called.

"Kacey, I want you to bring me my hockey skates," she instructed. "You'll find them in the hall closet. Boca Dam is frozen over, and I'm going to go skating as soon as they let me out of this dump."

It did not occur to me to argue about whether she could go skating when her hair had fallen out and she had to wear a hat to keep warm, and with her legs so thin that her socks wouldn't stay up. I just got them out and put them in the car. It was January, and it was so cold, the snow squeaked under my feet. I hadn't seen her at all since September, when school had started, except once just before Christmas when she'd come up to the Truckee hospital briefly.

But in late January, she developed pneumonia and was back in intensive care in the Reno hospital before she ever had a chance to go skating out at Boca Dam. They didn't allow kids in the ICU. "Too many germs," Gardiner said. Penelope weighed about eighty pounds. When I saw her through the window of the ICU, it frightened me. She had tubes coming out of her arms and an oxygen mask over her face.

I could see every single bone, and yet she still forced herself to try to walk the hallways because lying in bed was unbearable for her. Her body had always been small and lean and muscular before the disease had transformed her. She was so proud of herself the day she could walk all the way across her hospital room without resting.

Penelope must not have doubted Gardiner's devotion and loyalty to her. She had every reason to believe she was the love of his life. Why wouldn't she be? There was never a doubt in my mind, even when he started taking me over to Sammie's house. Sammie worked in his office as a receptionist, but she wore a nurse's uniform with the zipper undone down to her cleavage. She had come from Reno, where she dealt blackjack to make ends meet. She'd had three kids with different men: a used-car dealer, a trucker, and then a rodeo cowboy who'd disappeared when the pregnancy test was positive.

She must have gotten a fairly decent amount of alimony from the used-car dealer; no single mother of three could afford a house up at Lake Tahoe unless she was either a real estate agent or a lawyer. Her oldest daughter was sixteen. Her real name was Cherrie Lynn, but she preferred to spell it "Cheree," and to be called Cheree without the Lynn because it sounded more French, and she had a boyfriend in Vietnam named Frenchie. Each morning before school, I watched as Cheree ratted her hair up into a big nest in the back of her head and then sprayed and sprayed with Aqua Net, so that it looked like she was wearing a big helmet with spit curls by each ear, then drew thick black eyeliner across each eyelid and put on layer upon layer of frosted pink lipstick. The final touch was the dot she made on her cheek just like Mrs. Squench's daughter Chris had done.

"Why are you doing that?" I asked.

"It's a *beauty* mark," she said, rolling her big brown eyes and snapping her gum. She smoked, chewed a lot of gum, and made long chains out of gum wrappers. When I stayed the night, Cheree told stories about Frenchie and their plans to marry as soon as his tour was over. She smiled through her buck teeth and chewed her gum faster as she gazed at the picture he'd sent and went on and on about how sexy he was in his camouflage pants with no shirt on and the gun on his shoulder.

Sammie's younger daughter, Tammy Jo, was closer to my age. I knew her from hanging around the ice arena. She had managed to get a solo in the ice show. Lana and I had discussed this at length while watching her from the railing as she'd skated around in a little dress that was too tight and sawed her crotch in half like a camel's toe, the same way Sammie liked to wear her jeans. We figured Sammie must have had sex with the lead instructor, Jimmy, and that's how Tammy Jo had gotten the solo.

Sammie liked to ice dance, especially with Jimmy, who was married to his ice dance partner from the Olympics, where they'd won a bronze medal. Lana and I watched Sammie stick her ass out in her little skating skirt, smiling up at him and pressing her boobs into his chest. I wished I could stay home and play with Lana instead of being dragged to Sammie's house.

Sammie smoked a lot and called everyone "hun," and hearing Gardiner called "hun" made me feel like I was living in a different world, a world of coffee shops in casinos, wall-to-wall shag carpeting, flowered sofas with matching loveseats, ugly lamps, and air that was hazy with cigarette smoke from Sammie's brown, filtered Winstons. Penelope was the only one allowed to use terms of endearment with Gardiner, and none of them was never "hun," like the way waitresses at Harvey's in Reno talked. Sammie belonged in Reno, and I wanted her to go there.

"You're not a real nurse," I said under my breath when she was hanging around Gardiner's office one afternoon after school. Lana was standing behind me, clutching my hand.

"What, hun?" Sammie looked at me with a slightly irritated expression.

"I said you're not—"

Lana yanked my arm. "C'mon, let's go slide on the lunch trays," she said urgently. We went outside in the winter air and slogged toward the cafeteria in the lodge.

"I hate her. Why doesn't she just die."

"I know," said Lana. "Her kids are ugly, too."

Sammie had big pointy boobs. I told Lana that I'd sneaked into her room once and looked in her underwear drawer to see what size bra she had. "It's one of those Playtex Cross Your Heart bras, and they're pointy at the end. Some of 'em have foam inside to make 'em squish up more." I was giggling uncontrollably as Lana and I stumbled to the top of the Little KT ski hill with our stolen orange lunch trays. "And her butt is so wide . . ." I was now unable to stand up, and instead I rolled down between the moguls, Lana on top of me, laughing her billy goat laugh. "I bet her dress slides up when she sits down, and you probably even see her flaps . . ." We sprawled on the late afternoon snow and laughed until we peed.

When we stopped laughing, I thought of Penelope's narrow hips, small breasts, and long, strong legs. The image of her beautiful face was so fixed in my mind that I thought she never looked any different, even without hair or teeth.

My faith had been strong ever since I was eight and she'd first gone away to the hospital in San Francisco. It was always, "When Mummy comes home, then everything will be perfect." Now I was eleven, and I was exhausted from hoping.

Penelope was a master at crafting just the precise recipe of insulting words. She told Gardiner he'd truly outdone himself in selecting a creature that could probably fit an entire fleet of incoming sailors into her vagina, and she suggested a sort of homing device in case he lost his entire body in there.

She was felled by the apparent ease with which he'd told her he no longer loved her. She looked at him over the rim of her oxygen mask. "But . . ." he said, feeling comfortable with himself, "I will not divorce you. That way, you will have medical insurance."

And with that, he left her panting for breath in the Intensive Care Unit at Washoe Medical Center in Reno. That was when she called me, wheezing through the receiver. I listened to her strain to get words out, suffocating under the weight of another bout with pneumonia. "Kacey?" She wheezed into the phone. "Mummy?" I pressed the receiver closer to my ear. She wheezed the story out, and my heart beat one big, loud pound before racing as hard as it could back to Wonderland where everything was going to be super-superb.

"Kacey? Are you still there? Promise me you won't leave me. You're all I have left to live for."

"I won't," I promised, swallowing the bile rising in my throat. I sat down on the floor by the window where our Christmas tree usually went.

Penelope survived yet another bout of pneumonia and came home. It was springtime, and good things happened in spring. Her hair was growing back, and she thought perhaps he would change his mind. She wanted him to change his mind so she could tell him to go to hell. She wanted him to change his mind so she could feel this was her home. She had lived for this day when she was finally pronounced well enough to go home. She wanted him to change his mind because he had no sense and would ultimately regret his decision and possibly burn in hell for all eternity. She enjoyed thinking of him burning in hell and begging the devil for his penis to be spared.

Over the last four years, there had been moments when I'd forgotten to be anxious and had lost myself in play, but the heaviness of fear had always returned when at bedtime. I had waited for the sun to come out, for the day Penelope would come home to stay.

Gardiner couldn't be having an affair with Sammie, I thought. Penelope must have been hallucinating. But I had to ask him if it was true, and I finally mustered up my courage one day when he was driving me to Reno for an annual bladder procedure that involved filling my bladder with dye to maximum capacity and then peeing on the floor in front of an x-ray machine with the nurses cheering me on. After that, I underwent a cystoscopy under general anesthesia that felt so good I wanted to stay asleep where everything was soft. I was in love with my urologist. Dr. Nitz, who was married, which did not deter me in my mission to make him mine. After all, he'd seen every single nuance of my crotch, and I'd made sure I'd washed it thoroughly before each visit, remembering what Penelope had taught me about cleanliness. "Get right in between those flaps. One should never smell like a fish dock on an August afternoon."

I thought perhaps a cake would really impress him, and I found a recipe with a lot of chocolate in Penelope's *Fannie Farmer Cookbook*. When I pulled it out of the oven, it looked okay, but it tasted awful. Too much baking soda. I put on several layers of chocolate frosting, hoping to cover it up. The cake had been intended to show him that I was so much more than the bacteria colonizing in my bladder.

Gardiner was driving Penelope's Porsche. I knew she hated it when he drove her car, and I wanted to hit him. "He drives it the same way he handles a horse—yank, yank, pull, yank . . . no finesse whatsoever. All force. A sign of poor breeding." I giggled a little when I thought of Penelope saying this while we had driven together on her daily errands—now such a distant memory.

"What's so funny?" he asked me now.

"Nothing," I snapped. "Nothing *you* would understand." I felt the lump in my throat swell as I tried to formulate my question and pushed it out past the lump in my throat. "Mummy says you're having an affair with Sammie. It's not true, *is* it, Daddy?" The question wasn't really a question. I wanted him to affirm that the whole thing was so silly, just another one of Penelope's hallucinations. "Of course not! What a silly question!" I imagined he would say. But he was silent for a few seconds. My heart fluttered and waited like a frightened sparrow.

"Yes, it's true," he said. "Your mother is . . . well, she's very sick, and I *blah, blah, blah* . . ." Everything sounded like a mudslide, a mudslide he was spewing out of his mouth like the steel pipes alongside Interstate 80 that spewed muddy water from the Truckee River overflow.

I stopped breathing as he spoke about this woman who was so unlike Penelope, the only woman on earth I wanted to be. I gripped the little silver handle on the dashboard, willing my tears back. I pressed myself against the passenger side window as far away from him as I could get. Maybe if I pressed hard enough, the door would fly open and I would die when I hit the pavement at seventy miles per hour. We passed Boomtown, where people stopped to gamble one last time before crossing the state line into California. "Welcome to Nevada," the sign read. Suddenly, billboards appeared on both sides of the freeway with dancing girls wearing bras with blinking lights on them, beckoning travelers to gamble in Reno and eat ham and eggs for ninety-nine cents.

How could this be real? He'd always seemed to love Penelope. What about that Christmas when he'd carried her up the sixty-four stairs for just one day at home? What about all the stories he'd read aloud to her in a Scottish accent? He'd baked her custards to accommodate her sore mouth. She'd thrown them up as quickly as she'd gotten them down, most of the time. When I'd heard my mother retching and crying upstairs, I'd run outside or hidden under my blankets with my hands over my ears and cried for her suffering, angry that I couldn't suffer, too, angry that she couldn't come to Brownie meetings and pick me up from school when I got sick. I could not let this be real.

I could not tolerate the death of an ember I had so tenderly kept aglow for so long. My memories of them talking together by the fire as I'd peeked at them from their bedroom door made me brim with joy. He'd called her Moonbeam McSwine and she'd called him Lonesome Polecat after the L'il Abner characters. I'd planted myself between them, swimming in the paradise of being their only child, the one who would be between them for ever and ever, and I'd asked what my special name would be, and they'd told me it would be Moonshine McSwine. Together, they'd spoken of building a yacht so they could retire at sea when they were old. "Like the Owl and the Pussycat who sailed away in a beautiful pea-green boat," Penelope said. They had a blueprint of a Hinkley forty-eight-foot yacht on their bedroom wall.

When we arrived at Washoe Medical Center in Reno for the bladder procedure, the nurse took me to my bed in the pediatric unit. I just wanted Gardiner to leave. I refused to look at him or say goodbye. I hoped they would find a huge tumor that would require major surgery, and then I could stay there and never go home. I could move into Penelope's room, and we would live in the hospital together eating hospital toast with jam, hospital eggs, and hospital Jell-O. And we would watch television in bed all day. Or maybe if

I was dying, Gardiner would come to his senses and tell Penelope he loved her after all. Then we could all go home again and be normal. I prayed and chanted, trying to produce a tumor as they put me to sleep and stuck the scope inside my bladder.

When I awoke from the anesthesia, I felt for a bandage on my belly and cried when I felt nothing. They would make me go home the next day. But there was no home for me anymore. I refused to leave. I begged Gardiner to let me stay with Penelope in her room upstairs in the ICU. I wanted to be the sick one. If I died, maybe Gardiner would forget about Sammie. I tried screaming and clung to the steel rails of my hospital bed. But Gardiner just got impatient and angry.

"Goddammit, Kacey! Knock it off, for Christ's sake! You're behaving like an idiot." And he dragged me kicking and screaming to the car.

22

ALMOST

IT WAS A SOFT MARCH AFTERNOON in 1970, and I was glad to be back at the ice arena to prepare for another summer of being in the chorus line with Lana and hoping for a solo. Lana told me she was moving away at the end of the school year. Madeline had met a man who lived on Cape Cod, and she would follow him there and get a job at a lobster restaurant serving cocktails.

Lana and I had parakeets, and she'd trained hers to say his own name, Honey, and whistle just like she did. Once, he flew out of her apartment and into a pine tree across the street. We both sobbed and called for him, Lana whistling their special whistle. Honey flew down from his perch in the pine tree and landed on her head.

We promised to write each other every day when she left, and we drew parakeets on the envelopes of the special flowery stationary we'd bought with our pooled allowance money.

The ice arena was all I had left of summers past. One day, when I was at school, Gardiner decided to put my horse to sleep. He had diarrhea all the time now, because he was so old, but I hadn't given up on him yet. I went to see him every day and brushed the fly eggs out of his coat. He was so bony that the curry comb hurt him, and he cringed when it bumped along his ribs.

I braided his mane and trimmed his shit-caked tail, but he still just looked like an old, tired horse who was only here because he wasn't dead yet.

I spent my time alone lying along the branch of a juniper tree that marked the end of the trail we'd walked so many evenings with the dogs. I rubbed the green needles between my fingers and held them to my nose. I let the wind blow through me and watched the enormous sky. I didn't want to go home, only to fall asleep in the arms of this tree forever.

It was a warm April afternoon and Penelope heard footsteps on the front porch. She heard the door open as she rested on her bed.

"Gardy? Is that you?" There was no answer. Then the door closed again. She went to the window and saw him walking down the sixty-four concrete steps he'd built in 1959 thinking he would always be here. He was carrying a paper bag full of some of his clothing. She went back to the bed and looked at their books on the shelf above it, all read in once-cozy bliss. She opened her bedside table drawer and unsnapped the leather holster. The Smith & Wesson .38 with the carved bone handle must have felt so heavy by then. As withered as her muscles were, she must have had to lift it with both hands and hold its cool metal barrel against her cheek and then slide it down to her mouth. Cold, soothing metal against her tongue. It would be so sweet. Quick. Final.

He walked upstairs again and into the bedroom and saw her there, with her Smith & Wesson in her hand pointed at her temple. He knew not to make any sudden movements. She could move her finger just a little and his life would be forever ruined. "Penny . . . please . . . think of your daughter. She needs you. *Please* Penny . . . give me the gun." Her hand began to quiver, and he crept up, grabbing her bony little hands and easily forcing the gun from her grip. She fell to her knees, heart pounding, sobbing. "Get away from me, you son of a bitch!" she sobbed, spitting in his face and clawing at his hands with fingernails gnarled from drugs. She growled in a voice that came from the roots of her heart. She groped for dignity, a bleeding doe trying to escape her predator.

The need for perfect darkness had come: a withering sorrow that couldn't stand light and could not tolerate joy, even in tiny drops. She'd been amputated. Junked for a piece of more succulent fruit where the dryness and tyranny of disease hadn't stolen feeling and desire. She'd tried to give it to him. Even when she'd felt like her body would crack and shatter into a billion pieces and the nausea waited at the back of her throat, she'd opened her legs. She'd gritted her teeth, wondering if her pelvis would shatter when she'd tried to open her hips enough to let him in, but he'd said he had to have it. She'd winced back tears as he had pushed himself inside her. She'd felt so tiny and brittle, and he'd felt so huge. She'd prayed it would be quick so she could go in the bathroom and throw up and put a warm cloth on her vulva. He would be nice and kind to her as long as she could do this one thing. *Just a few minutes*, she'd told herself. *I can do this for just a few minutes.*

Once, she had felt beautiful. She could put cream on her long, lean legs and wear her black lacy underpants with a matching soft brassiere that didn't exaggerate or reshape. She'd loved what was there and worn her clothes as if she'd loved every inch of herself. As the disease had eaten its way through her muscles, it had left her with delicate flesh stretched over fragile bones. A walk across the hospital room was a triumph, and the usefulness of her vagina was the last thing on her mind. Her mouth had been coated with sores for many months. She could manage custard or Jell-O without tears if she took a small mouthful and then quickly slipped a piece of ice inside afterward. Sometimes she just gave up and cried, pushing the rolling table aside with the booger-green water pitcher threatening to tip over. It was so rare to be hungry at all.

Now Gardiner called the sheriff while he held her down with one of his arms. "She was trying to commit suicide!" he said with desperate sort of irritation. Or was it really terror? Could he still feel fear that she would leave him behind? The blueprints of the Hinkley 48 weren't on the bedroom wall anymore.

He was supposed to go to Sammie's house for dinner, and this would change his plans.

The sheriff, Dave, was a friend. His wife Bunny, was still one of Gardiner's nurses, and I'd stayed with them sometimes when nobody else had been available to take care of me. Now, Dave took Penelope away while trying to soothe and calm her, even with the handcuffs on her.

"Dave, get these fucking things off me," she said, retrieving her dignity.

"All right, Penny. But I'm locking the car doors."

They got into his sheriff's car and drove down to DeWitt State Hospital, a psychiatric facility in Auburn. She needed to detox from her Demerol, but

96

she didn't want to. "It's the only fucking thing that makes me feel like living," she told the attending psychiatrist, daring him to argue with her. He had to agree. "Well, Demerol and my daughter," she added.

"In that order?" he asked.

"Yes," she said.

It wasn't about choice anymore. Having a reason to live was the goal at DeWitt for the next three months. I remembered my promise: "No, I will not leave you," I assured her. I didn't want to promise. I wanted everything to be the way it had used to be, with Gardiner at home where he belonged. I wanted our evenings of storytelling by the fire; I wanted my mornings with my daddy, when we talked in whispers so as not to disturb the sleeping Penelope. But I promised anyway.

And I remained steadfastly and bountifully full of hatred for Gardiner and his choice to ruin my life. I felt lifeless and homeless now that I knew there would never be a day when Penelope might finally be well enough to come home forever. I still longed for the happy reunion when I could exhale all the tension of wishing and hoping. I was irritated at everyone, even Lana. I became bottomless, my tears never reaching a watermark. I chewed my hair, and I chewed pencil erasers, and when those were gone, I chewed the metal band that held the erasers until I got down to the wood. I chewed my nails and the skin around them until I bled.

23

WAITING —

SPRING 1970

SPRING IS PATIENT, SLOWLY AWAKENING EVERYTHING after winter's long sleep. Spring uncovers and waits for tender things to reach up toward the light, nurturing the earth that smells of rot and new growth. Spring opens the invitation to start again, like the new mule-ear blossoms on the hillside behind our house. The creeks are full, and the water tumbles over the granite, ancient and knowing.

The earth smelled like water from snow mixed with death and new life. Waiting felt different now. I waited for the day Gardiner would change his mind and turn back toward our old life. As quickly as he opened the door to talk about how Penelope had almost ruined his medical career by forging narcotics triplicates, or how she had become hopelessly addicted to narcotics, I slammed it, blocking my ears and singing inside my head.

I remembered a summer day when I'd been playing down by the swing he'd built for me and I noticed a small pile of charred paper and sticks as if someone had tried to build a campfire. I pawed at the ashes, intrigued by the familiar sight of Demerol bottles, with their labels partially burned. A needle pricked my finger, and I discovered many more spent syringes underneath the ashes, and more empty Demerol and morphine bottles. Gardiner told me she'd staged a fake robbery, that she'd called him one day from her bed and told him someone had entered the house and stolen drugs from the bathroom. I felt like a traitor for even listening to him. I hated myself for enjoying being at Sammie's house now. Now I knew why we were over there so much. Before, I'd thought we were all just friends.

While Penelope was still at DeWitt, he made a plan to take her to one of their favorite spots at Tomales Bay. She probably thought it was going to be his attempt to redeem himself, one of his on-his-knees apologies where he would tell her he'd temporarily lost his mind and ask whether she would still consider retiring at sea in a beautiful pea-green boat. Then I heard him talking to Sammie in her ugly living room that smelled like creamed tuna on toast and stale Winstons.

"I'm going to see if I can get her to understand," Gardiner said in a low voice. "But I'm afraid of what she might do."

I watched him and Sammie talk about Penelope as if she were an unwanted, disobedient, stray dog. Sammie's thick, stupid lips left greasy, cheap-lipstick marks on the filters of her Winstons as she took long pulls and exhaled, rolling the cigarette between her fingers, with their long, pointy nails polished with cheap pink nail polish. She rolled her tongue around in her mouth before exhaling, so comfortable with herself as Gardiner confided in her. I wanted to hurt her, smash her boobs with a bat, and destroy that organ she pretended to play.

"Your mother is a drug addict," said Gardiner, furrowing his brow. "She isn't the same person. The drugs for the disease changed her personality, and she's addicted to Demerol. She forged my name on a narcotics triplicate, and I nearly lost my license. So the best thing for you to do is stay with Sammie and me."

Even though I was terrified of being alone with Penelope, the thought of leaving her was unbearable. "I'm *not* leaving her by her*self*! "I shouted, feeling like a traitor again for allowing myself to feel comfortable at Sammie's house even for a minute. "You're just *lying* about her so you can feel *better!*" Sammie looked at me through narrowed, mascara-caked eyes and then back at Gardiner, adjusting her posture so that she was pressed up against him.

"Well, if she causes any problems, I'll just hop a plane and come down, okay, hun?" Sammie poked at her teased-up hair the color of Gallo Vin Rose. I wanted to go home and be in my own room, even if I had to be alone without anyone in the house.

He didn't come home from Tomales Bay with Penelope. He took her back to DeWitt, where she would stay for another month.

The weeks seemed interminable, but the day finally arrived when we would bring Penelope home. Gardiner seemed irritated at the inconvenience of having to make the trip and that she was coming home at all. It had been almost two months since she'd held the gun to her head. I was intent on changing his mind about leaving Penelope in the sixty-six miles we would drive between Truckee and Auburn. I pulled out all my memories, throwing them in the sky like birds. Triscuits with melted cheese and paprika before the fire, and the stories . . . "Remember the stories of Fillmore and the lobster pots?" (She loved the way he could tell it in a Maine accent.) "And Daddy, remember Rufus, the little fawn, and how we bottle-fed him and he slept with the dogs in the bathroom?" I reminded him of the music we played. He could play the harmonica and she could play her accordion and I had my little zither harp. "We could play music again and the dogs will howl!" (I laughed, and he didn't). "We could have Christmases again . . . just like we used to." (He wasn't really listening). "And the mornings, Daddy. When we had to be sooooo quiet so we wouldn't wake Mummy. Remember how much fun we had?" On and on, I painted the scenes for him.

"Remember how you woke me up in the morning for school and fixed our breakfast while we listened to 'Paul Harvey News and Comment' on the radio? Remember, Daddy?" He told me to stop talking so he could hear the radio.

I was silent, lost in my reverie of breakfasts with Gardiner. Breakfast had been carefully constructed to balance protein with carbohydrates, usually soft-boiled eggs or oatmeal made with raisins and honey, whole grain toast and marmalade, and Ovaltine. But on Sundays, he made pancakes from his own mix, with maple syrup from his father's maple trees back in Massachusetts. Daddy Roy, as all the grandchildren called him, made sure everyone received at least three quarts of maple syrup at Christmas to last a year. I stood on a stool next to him while he taught me exactly when to flip them over. "Watch for the bubbles to stop, Kacey; then it's time to flip them.

Like this." And he would slide the spatula underneath and pop them over, revealing the fragrant brown pancake's belly. "Remember how we had to tiptoe around, Daddy? She would come out and whisper really loud telling us to be quiet. And you made me do sit-ups every morning."

He did not lift the brush to help me paint, so I painted harder, in more detail, with more colors and depth. Still he did not lift his brush to help me. And painting scenes of the perfect family by myself would become my life.

I couldn't count the times I longed to be with her, to sleep in the hospital bed next to her, to watch the television suspended from the ceiling and eat hospital food off the tray table with wheels that had a slide-out mirror. I loved the smell of hospital food, scrambled eggs and toast, bacon, and butter in little cubes covered with waxed paper. It reminded me of when Gardiner would take me with him to the hospital in Truckee where he did his rounds and I went to the cafeteria to have breakfast.

As we pulled up at the iron gates of DeWitt State Hospital to pick her up, the gates opened, and there she was. Waiting. She was waiting right by the gate. She smiled with that beautiful, perfect smile with that one tooth slightly overlapping the other. And the smell. Oh yes, that was the smell I buried my face in, when I wept in the closet among her cashmere sweaters. Her black hair, woven with silvery gray that had once cascaded down her back, was now shorn to a fuzzy quarter inch. She had been bald just a few months ago, and the hair had strained against all odds to grow back. She had new teeth that looked exactly like her real ones. The sores in her mouth had healed, and she could wear the new teeth all the time except when she slept. She was dressed just as I'd imagined: Levis, a turtleneck, and a soft, cashmere, Brooks Brothers sweater, forever embalmed with Givenchy perfume. So thin, but she was Penny again. She was Penelope.

When we arrived at our house in Squaw Valley in the late afternoon, they were quiet. Penelope went to her dogs, and her tears flowed. Penelope turned to look at me said, "Let's you and I go feed J. P., and then we'll go out for supper." She wiped her eyes and swept past Gardiner, who stood in the kitchen staring down at the cork floor. Maybe he was crying too. Penelope snatched the keys to the red Porsche, gathered her pocketbook and her cowboy hat, and whistled for the dogs, and I trotted after her down the sixty-four concrete steps to the garage.

Gardiner was gone when we came home. He came back the next day, "to get a few things," he said. And one hammer at a time, he moved his tools. Then one pair of pants, or maybe two; a jacket, and he needed a couple of clean shirts, some shoes; and soon his closet was empty, and Penelope's books on the bookshelf drifted over to where Gardiner's books used to be, like teeth looking to fill the empty spaces in an old person's mouth.

PART II

KIMBALL AND PENELOPE — MANY NEW LIVES
1970-1975

24
THE NEW LIFE

PENELOPE DECIDED WE SHOULD MOVE AWAY. We were playing Parcheesi on her bed. "Leave this Godforsaken shithole," she said. "For good. Move to Laguna Beach and start a new life." It sounded good to me, especially since Lana had moved away. Penelope had loaded up the Porsche many times in the past when she'd been mad at Gardiner, beginning with my conception, when she left for Carmel in her MG for a couple of weeks.

Throughout my childhood, there had been times when Penelope would suddenly pack up the Porsche and off we went, leaving skid marks on the asphalt in front of the house. And we'd spend a couple of weeks in Carmel or Laguna Beach before returning home again. This time, she said, it was a permanent move to Laguna Beach. She said something about not having a pot to pee in or a window to throw it out, and she got her piggy bank out and the wool sock she had in her bureau drawer with silver dollars in it.

"Here, you count the silver dollars," she said. "I'll count the money in my piggy bank. Your father will have to give us money because, if he doesn't, I'm going to take him to the cleaners. He won't have a leg to stand on." I imagined him standing on one leg in front of Fontana's Dry Cleaning in Truckee as punishment for his sins. She wasn't showing any sadness about him being with Sammie, only righteous indignation.

Penelope was a smoker, but not like Sammie, who smoked Marlboros with brown filters. Penelope was a Marlene Dietrich or a Greta Garbo-with-the-cigarette-holders smoker, and it was Kents or Benson & Hedges with white filters. I decided to start smoking too. I was looking at the eight packages of cigarettes she'd purchased so I could try them out, and I selected the one with the prettiest packaging. The Virginia Slims were feminine, but Eve cigarettes were the prettiest, more womanly, with the pretty design painted right below the filters.

Sammie-bashing was our nightly entertainment, along with *Bonanza* and *M.A.S.H.* I dressed up in the most disgusting combinations of clothing I could find, stuffing balls of socks in Penelope's teeny little bras and putting cushions in my stretch pants for butt cheeks and pulling them up so my labia were split like camel toes. I caked my face, eyes, and lips with makeup, teased my hair into a rat's nest, and performed for Penelope. "Ooooh, Gardy . . . I just *love* those polyester pants on you! Those white buck shoes are *real* classy!" I leaned into every word as if I were squeezing pasta through a pasta grinder. At least we had each other. Every five seconds, I wanted to ask her if she was feeling okay. "We need a new name for your father," Penelope said as we packed the red Porsche.

"He's not my father," I said.

Penelope had to have certain things with her on trips. Our one remaining dog was first on the list. Vicky had died of old age, and our miniature Dachshund, Tiggy, had died of stomach cancer. Patience was a very high-strung Vizsla and sat on the suitcases when she saw them come out of the closet. She was almost as skinny as Penelope. When Penelope had been on the brink of death, Patience had suddenly stopped eating. She'd throw up all her food and had gotten so weak she couldn't get up. Gardiner laid her on the sofa and put one of Penelope's cashmere Brooks Brothers sweaters on her and started an IV. As Penelope pulled herself back from death, Patience began to brighten and recover, but the ache of missing Penelope affected her in the same way it had affected me.

Penelope never trusted any tap water. On every trip, we took at least a gallon of bottled water. She brought the Nordmende radio so she wouldn't miss the Metropolitan Opera, her Rolleiflex cameras (because she was planning to restart her career as a photographer), her carpetbag full of pills, and the Smith and Wesson .38. I had my diary, my Donny Osmond records, and my parakeet, Ollie, whose cage had to fit between my feet.

25

TRYING NOT TO BE PENELOPE

EADED FOR LAGUNA BEACH, WE DROVE down Highway 395, paralleling the eastern slope of the Sierra Nevada Mountains. My life in those mountains, near Lake Tahoe, was ending, and at that moment, I didn't care. I couldn't miss my father; it was not allowed. And our house . . . well, it had bad memories now, I told myself. I'd never spent one single Christmas without snow, and in Laguna there would be no more skiing, but I really didn't like skiing that much anyway, I told myself, remembering the Squaw Valley Sporting Club and wearing the orange hat with no stripes that indicated I wasn't good enough to have made the racing team. I had worn the stripeless orange hat of shame only when Gardiner had forced me to go to ski-racing practice.

Laguna Beach was a large town with traffic lights, public transportation, and fast food places, none of which were in Tahoe City yet. Once we got settled in our beachfront apartment, which probably was part of Penelope's plan to "take him to the cleaners," I decided to explore the town. I dressed up in my ankle socks with slip-on loafers and a knee-length, paisley-print summer dress. I'd thought the knee-length dress code existed everywhere, until I looked around and saw the girls wearing shorts that barely reached below their butt cheeks and little halter tops. Girls had long hair and tans, and the boys all seemed to have saltwater blond hair, perpetually wet and matted from surfing. I sat on the beach and looked at guys getting ready to surf with their surf shorts barely hanging onto lean hips, revealing crests of firm buttocks and soft trails of hair leading from their navels to their crotches, an area my gaze was perpetually fixated upon. I couldn't tear my eyes away from beautiful, tanned indentations of abdominal muscles and the maleness embodied in the way they walked into the water and sat astride their surfboards waiting for the waves.

The women on the beaches made me long for womanhood, with their long hair streaked by the sun and the sea. Their bikinis were worn recklessly, the straps not caring to hold everything tightly, and the material only loosely caressing golden brown skin and young breasts like nectarines with upturned nipples. As they lay in the sun on their backs, their bikini bottoms rested on graceful hipbones revealing flat, feminine abdomens punctuated by gentle pubic mounds underneath. I felt my boyish shape and prayed harder that I would be transformed so that my butt would be shaped like an upside-down valentine, defined by a little waist and some nice luscious breasts to tuck into a bikini top. My stick-like body made me look like Scooter, Barbie's freckle-faced little sister who wore a one-piece bathing suit. I examined myself closely in the full-length mirror on the bathroom door in our apartment, trying to find a posture that made me look more like Barbie and less like Scooter, but it was no use without stuffing socks or tissues into my bikini top, which would never work unless I never went swimming. I decided that while on the beach, I would lie on my stomach all the time, with one leg flirtatiously bent and my bikini top untied to avoid a tan line, a safe position in which to hide my lack of feminine hipbones or breasts.

I had brought my guitar with me from Squaw Valley on the chance that I would be discovered by some big agent and become famous like Donny Osmond, whom I planned to marry. I brought it to the beach every day and sang "On Top of Old Smoky" and "Red River Valley," the only songs I knew. Whenever someone walked too closely, I stopped singing and just strummed.

I was now responsible for doing the majority of the household duties, more than I ever had done in Squaw Valley. It was actually fun to do the laundry at the laundromat, except for lugging the pillowcases full of laundry up the hill from the apartment and then over two blocks. I borrowed a grocery cart from Gene's Market, which made it a lot easier. After I put the laundry in the washer, I went next door to the market to do the grocery shopping.

Penelope gave me a list and a blank check, and I shopped with the other women, holding up jars of peanut butter, canned goods, and boxes of cereal to read the prices stamped in purple ink to comparison shop. I only bought brands I'd heard advertised on television—"Choosy mothers choose Jif" wasn't as appealing to me as "Peter Pan Peanut Butter is the p-nuttiest!" And I chose cereal that had never been allowed in our house at Squaw. Penelope didn't care anymore if I ate Sugar Pops or Sugar Smacks or Froot Loops. I liked to suck all the sugary flavoring out of the milk-soaked nuggets before swallowing. It made breakfast a celebration of color and sweetness. I always threw in a few trashy teeny-bopper magazines so I could read up on Donny Osmond or Jack Wild (my second choice behind Donny) while the laundry was in the dryer. Jack Wild starred in a Saturday morning TV program called *H.R. Pufnstuf.* I couldn't decide between Donny or Jack but felt my chances were better with Jack because Donny was so perfect. At least Jack had played the Artful Dodger in the movie *Oliver* and could be sneaky and dirty like me. I went through a whole pack of Wrigley's Doublemint and several Eve cigarettes while reading about Donny through my smoke rings. No . . . Donny probably never smoked or said "shit" or "fuck," two words I'd recently learned from Penelope.

The more I looked around at the people in Laguna Beach, the more I felt convinced I needed to change my entire persona. I told Penelope that we needed hippie clothes so we would fit in. Penelope said she already was a hippie and that she'd invented the look. "People are finally catching up to me," she said, fingering her hair, which was growing back quickly and was already almost to her shoulders. She already wore bell-bottoms with wide belts. I just looked like a dork with my knee socks, stupid-looking girly shorts, and foo-foo midriff shirts.

We went to a store that smelled like incense and played Led Zeppelin on the stereo. Penelope strode to the counter and said in her crisp Boston accent that we'd like to try on some bell-bottom pants in men's waist size 26 and length 30, and she would like to try some of the thick leather watch bands "like all the hippies are wearing these days." I hid behind the racks of Madras shirts hoping she'd stop talking soon. The hippie guy behind the counter smiled at her and eagerly showed her the racks of low-slung bell-bottoms and thick belts. She emerged from the dressing room with several pairs of striped bell-bottoms, to which she added a thick watchband and a leather belt. I got some bell-bottoms, some hippie-girl skirts, and a loose peasant blouse that I thought gave the illusion of breasts.

I went to Cost Less Imports and bought Indian-print bedspreads, incense, posters of peace signs, and big throw cushions so my room wouldn't look like a dork's room anymore and would look more like a hippie girl's room. I used at least one "man" or "baby" or "far out" in every sentence. Penelope and I began to fight, usually about me becoming an adolescent and how I shouldn't be one. She always won.

But on the beach, in my aloneness, I indulged my inner teenybopper by reading *16 Magazine*, *Tiger Beat*, and *Fave* magazines to my heart's content and dreaming of the day when I would happen to bump into Jack Wild on the beach, where he would fall instantly in love with me. Summer was in full swing, and there were other teenyboppers on the beach who noticed my magazine collections, which served as instant best-friend-bonding material. The girls I met had moved with their families to Laguna Beach for the summer and lived in beachfront apartments, but their dads were there too. Their LA teenybopper mannerisms were so contagious that I couldn't conceal them completely when I went home. I tried to act like Penelope and speak eloquently and intelligently, but my inner teenybopper was pushing its way out as aggressively as the blackheads peppering my chin. The colloquialisms leaped from my lips before I could stop them, causing Penelope to groan and leave the room shaking her head, asking in God's name where she had gone wrong.

Penelope's righteous indignation alternated with downward spirals of tears and rage after a few glasses of Wente Brothers, when she'd tell me she didn't think she could manage life on her own. She'd look at me through swollen purple eyelids and hiss about how that horrible prick of a father of mine had ruined our lives. Somehow, he became *my* father again when Penelope was in one of her moods. She aligned me with the enemy, leaving me begging her not to be unjustly accused of treason. But with each successive glass of wine, her rage roiled and built momentum like a Wagner opera.

Gardiner came to Laguna Beach with a moving truck full of our belongings. Penelope avoided him as much as possible as he unloaded furniture and duck decoys from Abercrombie & Fitch, her shotguns, cowboy hats, and what seemed like thousands of books. I trotted to and fro after him as he made trips between the truck and apartment. He ignored me as if I didn't belong to him anymore. I thought he might be angry at me for taking sides with Penelope, but I didn't ask. I just tried harder to be his daughter, hugging him when Penelope wasn't looking. He didn't hug back.

The rent on beachfront places went up in the summer months, so we were going to be moving to a house away from the beach, which Penelope blamed on Gardiner. I wanted to say something to soothe her and make everything okay, but instead of something wise and poetic, all that came out was, "Hey, man, it's cool, baby. You're gonna make it." The instant I said it, I knew it was a big mistake, possibly unforgiveable.

Penelope looked up at me, squinting through her swollen red eyes, and growled. I slunk to my room and closed the door, lit an Eve, opened my blue diary with the flowers on it, and wrote of my love for Donny Osmond, how I was going to take a bus to Hollywood and look for him at the television studio. But then I looked at his impossibly unblemished face and the row of glowing white teeth through the curls of smoke coming from my cigarette held loosely in my lips as I wrote. He would probably want a girl that didn't smoke, a girl who had nice perky titties like Marcia Brady; long, perfect, blond hair; perfect teeth . . . and a mother who wasn't crazy. I gave up on the bus-to-Hollywood idea and went back to hoping he would find me on the beach.

26

JUNIOR HIGH

I WAS BEGINNING TO WONDER ABOUT SEX. Gardiner's *Gray's Anatomy* lesson back when I was seven seemed to be missing a few elements. I saw the book *Everything You Always Wanted to Know About Sex *But were afraid to ask* on the paperback-book rack at Gene's Market. At the checkout counter, I told the pimply guy ringing up my stuff that it was for my mother. He looked at me with a creepy grin and put the book in a brown paper sack, licking his lips as he handed it to me. "Up yours, weirdo," I muttered under my breath and hurried out of the store to the safety of the laundromat. I hid it behind *Fave* magazine while the clothes were drying. I read that book cover to cover, only stopping to eat and sleep, and hid it under the mattress when I slept or took a shower. I cringed with embarrassment reading certain sections, after which I had to stop and close my eyes to erase the images in my mind. How did people put light bulbs up their assholes? I felt kind of dirty and slutty. The best thing to erase the guilt was to do clean things, like scrubbing the bathroom or vacuuming. I was sure Penelope could read my thoughts, and I went overboard trying to show my good-daughter side. I wasn't going to turn into a bad girl who thought about penises, boobs, and finger fucking day and night.

"Oh, please, don't let me turn into a pervert," I wrote in my diary and then scratched it out in case Penelope found it. I read one story about a guy who got erections by wearing women's underpants, and one about women who put vegetables and other objects into their vaginas because it felt good. Although I longed for womanhood, it was the idea of womanhood I'd created in my mind, not the stuff in this book about sex and orgasms, putting produce in your vagina, and foot fetishes.

When the beachfront apartment got too expensive, we moved into a different house away from the beach. The woman who owned it had a thing for white—white carpet, white walls, white bricks on the fireplace. It was not the place for a dog who occasionally peed indoors, the seven cage-free parakeets I'd acquired from the local pet store, and the cat who still had his testicles. The house was on a hillside nestled amid palms and eucalyptus trees. Penelope's room had a huge bathroom with a big, rectangular, sunken bathtub that reminded me of movie stars' bathtubs. On hot days, we took cool baths in it with expensive bath gel that Penelope said she couldn't afford but for which she intended to send the bill to that horrible prick of a father of mine, who, all of a sudden, could afford to support that stupid tart and all her illegitimate children.

I had never really been conscious of money before, except when Gardiner had been paying bills at his desk and said we were going to the poorhouse whenever I lost mittens or a jacket. As far as I had known, we'd always had enough of everything. Penelope had driven a Porsche and bought most of her own clothes, and all of Gardiner's, at Brooks Brothers; we'd had horses and a nice house. Penelope had worked from time to time as a private photographer but only when she'd felt like it. Now we lived on the money Gardiner gave us, which, according to Penelope, was never enough, and we were poverty stricken.

I was about to start junior high school and needed school clothes. I was afraid to ask, but Penelope enthusiastically agreed, saying she too could use some new clothes, and she dialed the number for I. Magnin in San Francisco to speak to her personal shopper. "Eileen? This is Penny Converse (she'd gone back to her maiden name, even though it wasn't legal). Yes, I'm fine, thank you. I wonder if you could help me with a large order? Oh, wonderful! You can just send the bill to my husband. Let's begin with school clothes for my daughter." Gardiner became her husband again when she was using his credit cards.

When the boxes arrived, I untied the satiny ribbons and found my two new dresses tucked in tissue paper with matching knee socks, new underwear, and my most cherished new pieces of lingerie—three brand new training bras, each with a pretty preteen on the box looking lovingly down at her budding breasts held inside the lacy pink satin and nylon. They had enough room in the tiny cups in which to stuff some tissue. I wore them all the time, often allowing the bra strap to show outside my sleeveless shirts so people would notice I was wearing a bra.

I could hardly wait for school to start when I would be in the seventh grade, which I imagined to be more mature than, and not as childish as, elementary school. No more playing tetherball or swinging on the monkey bars. Now I would sit around the outdoor lunch area with the other girls and talk about boys. I entered Thurston Middle School's cool-looking campus with its octagonal buildings surrounding the grassy area where kids ate lunch outside in the sun.

At elementary school in Tahoe City, all the classrooms were all in one building. And at lunchtime, you got your brown plastic compartmentalized plate and walked by Mrs. Hoff's little table, where she punched your lunch card. My card was chronically out of punches because Penelope never paid attention to the notices I'd brought home. "Kimball, your card has no more punches. Please tell your mother she needs to give you money for next month, honey. We'll just charge it today, okay?"

At Thurston Middle School, the cool thing was to buy french fries only. Nobody dished up your food for you, and there were no menus to warn you of food you didn't like or build your excitement, like fish-stick Friday. The girls ate daintily, dipping one fry at a time in a shared dish of ketchup. None of the girls wore knee-length dresses with matching knee socks, so I skipped lunch and went to the bathroom, where I lit an Eve and removed my knee socks. I wanted to make my dress shorter, but there was no way to do that until I got home.

I hemmed them to an inch above my knees, which was the rule at Tahoe Lake School. I only had red thread that showed on the purple dress fabric, and I didn't know how to hem a dress, but it looked easy enough after looking at the tiny stitches on the existing hems. Soon it started feeling like I'd been sewing for hours, though I'd only made it about a quarter of the way around the hem. I began to take huge impatient stitches that looked horrible, so I cut the dress off as evenly as I could. Then I threw away all my knee socks and decided to switch cigarette brands. Maybe Virginia Slims. I liked the TV ad slogan telling me I'd come a long way, baby.

When Penelope's rent check bounced twice, we had to move again. Returned checks seemed to come in the mail a lot, and Penelope would send me to the electric company or the bank or the phone company to give them the standard sob story. "They won't turn down a child," she said.

I could never tell what might set her off—maybe I hadn't done the laundry or been agreeable to doing what she'd asked. Once she got started, there was no stopping her, and it would escalate, especially if I challenged her. I never looked right. I felt like being rude a lot. I felt uncomfortable in my skin, and my face was breaking out.

One day, we got into it about something, probably me exhibiting offensive adolescent behavior, and she got so mad that she packed her suitcase, got in the car with Patience, and drove off, leaving me screaming in the driveway. She said she was going to leave me, and I believed her. With each episode of rage, I wondered if any forgiveness was possible. I would cower outside Penelope's locked bedroom door and gather my courage to ask if she still loved me. Penelope would say she wasn't sure.

The reward for hours of suffering and crying was the sweet forgiveness that Penelope eventually gave me, along with strong warnings about my selfishness, my rudeness, and my mean streak, which she said would be with me forever because I'd inherited these traits from Gardiner and they meant nobody would ever love me. I could deal with being rude and selfish, but I was willing to do just about anything to get rid of the mean streak.

At Christmas time, we went to see the movie *Scrooge*, and I was so terrified by Scrooge's experiences of having the three ghosts visit him to show him what a horrible, wretched man he was that I had to sleep with the lights on. I suspected that Scrooge and I were exactly alike. That must have been what Penelope had meant about a mean streak. He was alone and nobody liked him, which also was true for me. I put two and two together. I gathered my courage and decided to check in with Penelope on that. "Am I like him . . . Scrooge, I mean?"

"Well, yes, I would say that you share similar traits," Penelope said.

I was leveled with fear and vowed from that moment on to be perfect and good in every way. Maybe then Penelope would not give up on me.

27
WAITING ROOM

IT WAS AFTER CHRISTMAS ON A dreary day. The fog was thick, and it gave me a headache. I was busy picking my blackheads in the bathroom when Penelope called to me. "Could you listen to my stomach and see if you hear a sort of high, whining sound?"

"What will that mean?" I asked, wondering if she was kidding.

"Well, I may have an intestinal block. I haven't crapped in days . . . not even so much as a bean . . . or a fart." I tried not to laugh, but Penelope was laughing. She joked about her intestines all the time. She'd had five surgeries, and some of her intestines were gone. I listened and didn't hear anything; it was just silent in there. "Lower," said Penelope.

Then I heard it, a faint sort of high hissing sound. "I hear it," I said, suddenly feeling really scared.

Penelope called Gardiner, who called her doctor at UCLA Medical Center. Within minutes, we were on the freeway heading toward Los Angeles. It took four hours to make the two-hour trip. Penelope was unable to navigate on-ramps, off-ramps, and merging traffic, even though we had a Porsche. It was old, but it went really fast when Penelope wanted it to. Somewhere in Oxnard, she broke down in tears and pulled into a gas station where someone was able to draw her a legible map. I was helpless, and Penelope was sick again.

When we finally reached the UCLA Medical Center, I was happy to find my place in the waiting room and do what I did best: wait. When Penelope emerged from the exam room with the doctor, he explained that a colostomy was necessary due to an intestinal blockage, but that she could have it done in the hospital at Laguna Beach. We drove south and got pulled over for speeding, which happened from time to time in the Porsche.

The next morning, we took a cab to the hospital in Laguna. After Penelope was checked in, I stayed as long as the nurses would let me, but eventually I went home. In daylight, I had all the confidence in the world that I could stay by myself in the apartment and take care of the dog and the birds. We'd given the cat away because he'd shit in the fireplace. But as night began to fall, the fear was overwhelming. It used to be the Big Bad Wolf from "Little Red Riding Hood" that I'd imagined. Now it was the three ghosts from *Scrooge* who would visit me, even if I slept with the lights on. I tried to be brave, but it was no use. I called Penelope. "Can I stay at the Surf and Sand Resort? It's closer to the hospital, and there are people around so I won't be scared there," I said. Penelope called the hotel and charged a room on Gardiner's credit card. I took a taxi to the hotel using the money we kept in a sock in Penelope's bureau drawer. She liked to keep money in socks, as if somehow socks were off limits to thieves.

Once settled in the hotel room, I turned on the television and tried to sleep, but even with the lights on it was no use. It was midnight, and I called the hospital and spoke to the nurse on her floor and begged, "Can I just stay there with her tonight and tomorrow morning, so I can be there when she wakes up from surgery?" The nurse told me I couldn't sleep in the room with her, but I could sleep on one of the sofas in the waiting room just for tonight. I got ready and walked to the hospital.

The waiting room was empty except for a Mexican woman who rocked back and forth on a pea-green, fake-leather sofa. All the sofas except one had green vinyl cushions and smelled of dirty hair and antiseptic. One sofa was forest green, just like my favorite chair on the KT-22 chairlift back home. It was new looking and sat in a corner underneath the window, and it would be all mine tonight. I settled in and tried to read a magazine. One of the nurses came out of the emergency room with a doctor, and the woman got up. They told her they were sorry, that they'd done everything they could but her husband was dead. She began to scream and wail, clutching the doctor's white coat when her legs couldn't hold her up. I wanted to be the source of her comfort, but I was only twelve. When they disappeared into the emergency department, I wondered how she would make it through life without her husband.

Maybe it was the memories of sleeping in the back of Gardiner's blue VW Beetle when he had to tote me back and forth between our house and the emergency room during his on-call nights that gave me comfort. I slept peacefully on and off on the green waiting-room sofa, awakening occasionally to the murmurs of the nurses as they went about their business, or to a door swinging open, but my wakefulness was a drowsy, comfortable interlude between sleep and consciousness, not the tense, anxious jolts of wakefulness I felt when I was alone.

In the morning, I went into Penelope's room, but they'd taken her into surgery at six a.m. The bed was empty and turned down, waiting for her return. I found her pocketbook in the closet, and luckily there was a twenty-dollar bill, enough for cab fare to our apartment, where Patience was probably frantic, starving and peeing all over the carpet.

Our landlords, the Wilsons, lived downstairs. They knew I was alone. I went to school with their dorky son Steve, but since I too was a member of the dorkdom, we got along pretty well. Mrs. Wilson asked me if I would like to stay with them. At the time, I was listening to records with Steve in his room. Mrs. Wilson must have sensed I was guarded and didn't push too hard for me to stay. I felt like I wore a suit of armor around most adults, especially because they were always wondering about me and Penelope and why sometimes I wasn't in school for days at a time, or why I was the one who went to the utility companies to explain why the check had bounced again. When anyone attempted to pierce me with questions or concern, I slammed down my faceplate and peered through the cracks at potential intruders. I knew how to maintain an innocent face with bill collectors and utility companies, smiling appreciatively when they granted me a stay of execution on shutting off our power or the phone. But I couldn't wait to get out from underneath their questions.

Mrs. Wilson looked at me with her eyebrows knitted and a crinkled-up smile, with her head tilted to one side. I knew what was next. "I have some nice milk and cookies, fresh baked. I think Steven would like it if you would come over. Maybe you could stay at our house while your mommy is in the hospital. Would you like that, dear?"

I felt an overwhelming urge to be rude but swallowed it down and mustered up some politeness instead. "No, thank you. I need to go home and feed the animals." But she curled down onto her knees and looked up at me as if she were about to burst into prayer. "I'm sure you must be very frightened about all this."

"I'm fine," I said, feeling the seepage of her sweetness creeping too close and taking a step backward toward the door.

"Of course you are, dear. Won't you stay just one night with us and see how you like it?" I thought about how afraid I was of the dark. And about being alone. I would not want to cry in front of Mrs. Wilson, and if Penelope died, I would not want to be at Mrs. Wilson's house. Yet, they had a television with all the channels and a whole library full of books to read if I couldn't sleep. And I did go to school with Steven, who was kind of fun. I accepted Mrs. Wilson's invitation with the caveat that I would only stay at night, starting at bedtime. It wasn't like Mrs. Chisholm's house, and I cried with longing for Mrs. Chisholm as I crawled into the strange bed in their study. I went to school with Steven in the morning, and then Mrs. Wilson took me to the hospital to see Penelope. She invited me to attend church on Sunday. I resisted until she told me we would be going out to lunch afterward. The Wilsons' house smelled like cookies all the time, and I began to like sleeping on the little sofa bed in their library with all the books.

When Penelope came home, I learned how to take care of a colostomy. It looked like there was a pinkish slug all curled up on her stomach, covered by a bag that stuck to her skin. The bag was her toilet for the next six weeks, and every time it filled, she had to change it. Penelope said she could ward off bill collectors by exposing her bag to them if they came to the door.

I was clinging to hope that the colostomy would be a single incident of sickness and hospitals, but about a month after the surgery, something went horribly wrong. She noticed that the wound and the intestine itself smelled funny, and the color wasn't good. It also looked as though it was telescoping instead of being the tight little knot it had been, so we went to the doctor, who immediately admitted her to the hospital, saying the colostomy was gangrenous.

This meant another major surgery, but at least she would come out of this one with her intestine back where it belonged instead of hanging out of her stomach. I stayed with the Wilsons again, where I politely took a few bites of dinner. I pushed the food around on my plate and waited until I thought I could ask to be excused without too many questions. Then I went to the room full of books and lay down, pulling the soft, crocheted blanket up around my head so nobody could hear me cry.

I woke up with my heart pounding. Mrs. Wilson let me have Patience in the room with me, but she said I couldn't let her sleep in bed. I just had to have her near me, so I woke her up and invited her up under the covers. I thought for sure I was going to throw up and tried to take deep breaths. My breath was ragged, and my teeth chattered. I was shivering violently, yet I was drenched in sweat. I held Patience close and tried to soothe myself somehow by going back to my old way of inventing games and songs and stories about things I loved, like Christmas and horses and the meadow back home in Squaw Valley, bright with purple lupines and red Indian paintbrushes.

Religion had never been a big part of my life. The Wilsons practiced Christian Science, which I'd never heard of. Their oldest son was eighteen and had been brain damaged by a terrible surfing accident two years earlier. He'd been knocked unconscious and had been underwater for a very long time. Everyone had thought he was dead, but they somehow brought him back to life, although he was in a coma for weeks afterward. When he awoke, he was unable to do to anything, and he had to learn even the simplest things all over again, but it was a miracle that he was even alive. The doctors had pronounced him in a vegetative state and had told his parents there was no hope for anything more than occasional eye contact, if that.

Now he talked, walked, and was able to enjoy television and companionship, and the Wilsons attributed all of it to their faith. They went to church every Sunday and did a lot of reading and talking about faith and Christian Science in between. In Squaw Valley, there were two churches—the little church with the stained-glass windows that looked out onto the mountains, nestled in the trees right next to Squaw Creek, smelling of Pine-Sol and cookies, and the Queen of the Snows Catholic Church, where everyone dressed up and the kids had to go to catechism. I had liked to go to the little church with the Chisholms for Sunday school. It had been an excellent opportunity to wear my red, velvet party dress and my black, patent-leather party shoes with the straps and black bows on the toes. I had liked to sing songs about Jesus and listen to the stories in Sunday school, and I had liked Reverend Evans. His wife had been our Brownie Troop leader. Going to the little church and dabbling in prayers and songs about Jesus had been my only exposure to religion, and as far as I was concerned, I was in church for exactly the right reasons—to sing and wear my best shoes to Sunday school, and then to celebrate Jesus with graham crackers and juice.

One night, Mrs. Wilson must have heard me sobbing into my pillow. She knocked softly and then came in. I was grieving my father and wishing he just could come and save us from all this, and wondering why this whole sickness stuff had to be happening again. She sat on the bed and took my hand and talked to me about how Jesus could comfort me if I asked Him to. She smelled good, and the room smelled good, and I wanted to feel better, I really did, but the concept of prayer as a means of comfort was a very difficult concept for me to grasp. I just wanted my daddy. She pointed out some sections in the Bible where Jesus gives comfort and hope to people who suffer. I clung to verses I could make sense of in the Book of Psalms and the Book of Matthew and tried to pray.

28
THE NEW LIFE II

IT WAS APRIL AND THE WATER was getting warmer in Laguna Beach, and I looked forward to another summer of boy watching and hanging out at the beach, hoping that my breast buds would be noticeable. Penelope and I were walking on the beach where the boys were surfing without wetsuits on. Penelope announced that she wanted to body surf. Her scar had healed and the waves were not too big, and I demonstrated the technique in the medium-sized waves so as not to scare her. "I can do *that*," she said removing her shirt and unashamedly revealing her white stomach with its multiple railroad-like scars and her black bra. I stared. "Are you ashamed of being seen with me?" she challenged. The sight was pretty horrifying, but I shook my head and took her out to where the waves were breaking.

"Now," I instructed, "just wait until the wave is just starting to crest, and then ride it until it breaks. When it breaks, dive through it so you don't get rolled on the bottom."

"Remember, I turtle-turned in Acapulco . . . I can handle this," she said, taking off her sunglasses and handing them to me. She barely weighed ninety pounds, and when the wave crested, she got whacked and came tumbling to shore in the foamy surf. She was all in one piece except she'd lost her teeth. "Thank God it wasn't my uppers," she said as we searched along the beach for her teeth, but to no avail. "They'll wash up on someone's private beach in La Jolla," she said, laughing and out of breath. "Imagine their expressions when they see a set of grinning teeth coming in with the waves. They'll choke on their martinis!"

When we got home, we showered the sea water away and were drinking iced tea on the porch when there was a knock on the door. "Probably a bill collector," I thought out loud. I answered the door prepared to give a spiel about the check getting lost in the mail. But was not a bill collector; it was a police officer, who asked for Penelope. "What have I done?" she asked, a little startled. He took his hat off and said he had attempted a call, but our phone was disconnected, and that he was very sorry to inform her that her mother had passed away. Penelope turned gray. We went with the officer to call Grandpa Converse from the police station, and then he drove us home again.

I didn't feel sad, even though I thought I should. I couldn't squeeze out even one tear. I sat there while she cried and tried to comfort her. We needed the phone turned on, and the only way to get money was to ask Gardiner. I went to Mrs. Wilson's and called him.

"I just sent money, for God's sake!" he said. "What are you doing with all of it?"

"I don't know, Dad, I just know that we don't have any, and Grandma just died, and Mom's crying."

"Oh, Jesus," he said. "Let me talk to her."

I ran upstairs to get Penelope. She started crying again and told him what had happened. She said Grandma had been sick with something and had been on the mend, but then she'd fallen in the bathroom and hit her head. After that, she may have had some kind of stroke or blood clot or something. Then she told him we were going to move back East to be with Grandpa.

Gardiner sent money, and I went to the phone company to give it to them. So we had a phone again. Penelope called Fishballs, who was in Beverly Hills, and she invited us up to spend some time with her at her hotel. We needed money to move back East, and we engaged in a well-traveled discussion about how we could get money. "What about asking Fishballs?" I suggested. Penelope said the price would be too high. "I'd probably have to agree to go to Davos and stay there for months as compensation," she said ruefully. But after several hours of worrying, she called anyway.

"We'll have to hire a mover to move all this stuff. Call Bekins. They advertise 'moving without tears,' and I want to move without tears."

She decided to sell the Porsche. With her thick, Converse eyebrows raised, she said, "That car will bring a fortune."

"Mother," I said, looking at her with disdain, "that car is old and crappy! It's so loud that it's embarrassing." It had been a very nice car until the muffler had either gotten a huge hole in it or had fallen off completely. Otherwise, its only flaw was that it smelled like dog drool.

"I'll have you know that this car is a collector's item. They don't make these anymore, and I assure you, I will have no trouble selling it at a very good price."

"Right," I snarled under my adolescent breath, rolling my eyeballs. She mixed herself a Canadian Club whiskey with honey and milk. "A complete meal in itself," she said.

29

DUXBURY

EVER SINCE MY FIRST EXPERIENCE OF flying in 1966, I'd been in love
with the whole experience and decided that I would be a stewardess for
United Airlines. I was in awe of their fitted blue suits, matching hats, and
perfect makeup as they walked up and down the aisles with little baskets
full of slippers, chewing gum, and cigarettes in tiny little packs. I drew
airplanes on every piece of paper I could find, and if I couldn't find any
paper, I drew them on the walls of my bedroom. I drew DC-8s and colored
them blue.

As she always had done for airline travel, Penelope wore her "airplane
suit," a black, cashmere Chanel skirt and cropped jacket, and her black velvet
heels to match, the ones I'd always used to dress as a teacher when I'd played
school. I always wore my best dress with my shiny black party shoes, and
Gardiner would wear his gray, flannel Brooks Brothers trousers with a tweed
jacket, Oxford cloth shirt, and a bow tie.

I'd been keeping track of the different types of jetliners, and I knew that
the new Boeing 747s were the newest type of jet, with an upstairs in first class.
When I'd spoken to the travel agent to arrange the trip to Massachusetts,
I had been insistent that we had to fly on a 747 to Boston and that it had to
be TWA or United, and it had to be first class. Penelope reminded me that

she would not fly in the coach section with the riffraff. We couldn't afford to pay the phone bill, but she had to fly first class.

When Bekins came with their trucks and men in white coveralls, we let them do the packing and moving while we packed our necessities in our suitcases.

I now had twelve parakeets and Mr. Peabody the cockatiel. I'd decided to give all the parakeets back to the pet store and keep Mr. Peabody, who was tame and rode on my shoulder almost everywhere. Patience was a wreck and sat on the suitcases shivering and drooling. The Porsche was packed with our suitcases, camera bags, and carpetbags loaded with my mother's medication, which rattled with every bump on the freeway. Patience sat hunched between the bags, drool cascading in slimy rivers down the back of the Porsche's leather seats as she strained to see out the window. I wanted to slow down as we approached L.A. International Airport so I could watch the planes fly over the freeway right above us as they landed or took off. "The 747s look like penises," I said, gazing at the underside of the huge aircraft taking off.

"Doesn't everything look like a penis to you these days?" she teased.

Penelope had coached me on crotch-gazing when we'd lived in Laguna Beach. She'd caught me staring at all the surfer boys whenever we'd walked on the beach. She told me I was too obvious and gave me a pair of sunglasses. "You can look now," she said. "But don't be riveted. They'll know you're looking. Just steal a few glances and then look away." Most of the boys wore loose surfer shorts, and it was hard to tell what was in there unless the shorts were wet. The men who wore tight bathing trunks or, worse, the bikini briefs were usually ugly and fat. "Men with decent-sized peckers don't need to show them off," she explained. "It's like money and breeding; when you've got it, you don't need to advertise. Same with peckers." And we donned our dark glasses for some spectating.

Fishballs always stayed at the Beverly Hillcrest Hotel. Whenever we stayed with her at her hotel, she got us a room right next to hers with a connecting door. While they went off to sell the Porsche, I dressed up in my most *Vogue*-model-like outfit—a pair of knickers and knee-high, lace-up boots with a matching vest, and my hair in a shag haircut like Mrs. Brady on *The Brady Bunch* TV show, where everything was perfect and her home-baked cookies were always fresh out of the oven. I put on my huge, dark glasses and rode the elevator up and down, hoping to run into Jack Wild or someone else who was famous, so I could pretend I was one of them. After a few dozen rides and no luck, I had to switch hotels and walked to the Beverly Wilshire to try that elevator. By late afternoon, I needed a rest and went back to the Hillcrest to watch *I Love Lucy*. It had been hours since Penelope and Fishballs had left, but I finally heard the key turn in the door. Penelope looked serious. "I told you it was a piece of crap. You didn't sell it, did you?" I said in a surly tone.

"Well . . . you were right. I only got . . ." Penelope reached into her leviathan-sized leather purse that looked like a saddle bag, a gift from Fishballs, who shopped at Abercrombie's for pretty much everything except Scotch. She pulled out a wad of cash and threw it on the bed. "Thirty-five hundred dollars!" she announced gleefully. It was enough to fly first class and then some.

We stayed our last night in Southern California at the Bel Air Hotel. Fishballs flew to New York on a business trip involving the filming of safaris and the slaying of wild animals in Africa. On the taxi ride, Penelope told me about the Bel Air Hotel and how difficult it was to stay there unless one is the sort of person they approve of. "And they do not just *allow* dogs, they *welcome* dogs, but only well-bred dogs," she said with a snobbish sniff. "The best of the best movie stars will stay *only* at the Bel Air," she went on, her Boston accent becoming crisper. I wondered where the rest stayed. "Oh, they go to the more bourgeois places like the Beverly Wilshire to be seen."

"Do they have room service, a pool, and television?" I asked before I gave my approval.

"Of course! I would never stay in a hotel that had no room service!" she exclaimed. "And wait until you see the ponds with the swans and flamingos." She'd sleep in a tent, with coonhounds smelling of horse shit, and eat beans from a can, but she wouldn't stay in a hotel unless it had a five-star rating in the *Mobil Travel Guide*.

Our bungalow was like a little cottage in a fairy tale, and there really were swans and beautiful little gardens. Our dinner was brought to us on a table lit by candles with a special plate prepared for Patience. Penelope sipped one of several Canadian Clubs with milk and honey that she would have that night. She looked beyond the swans and the weeping willows at a sliver of sunset, and I sensed that she didn't want to go east. To me, everything seemed perfect here—the sounds of crickets and the birds in the trees outside, the smell of fresh bed linens and soap mixed with lilacs and lavender from the garden cooling in the dusk. I asked her if anything was wrong, hoping she wasn't feeling sick or in pain, as she so often seemed to be.

"Oh . . . I don't know," she said, blowing her nose. How often I had cried in the night fearing Penelope would die. And yet, somehow, I could not connect my own feelings with how she might have felt losing her own mother.

The flight to Boston was not on a 747. I was disappointed and argued with the TWA ticket clerk that there must be some mistake. He said they'd had to change the plane to a Boeing 707 at the last minute, so I had to be satisfied with first class and no stairway. Penelope's cousin Peter was to meet us at Logan Airport in Boston and take us to Duxbury. I'd never met him, but when I saw him, Penelope pointed out the Converse eyebrows. She hugged him and they both cried. "Do you see the Converse eyebrows?" she asked. "And his hands shake, and he cries at the drop of a hat . . . like all Converses do." I tried to see the resemblance in his eyebrows and checked to see if my hands were shaking. I was afraid of not being a Converse, whatever that meant. On the hour drive down to Duxbury from Boston, Peter said that Grandpa was not the same.

"He's lost a lot of weight," he said. "He only goes out to get the small amount of groceries he needs, and he goes down to Weymouth to get whiskey from the Navy outlet . . . he buys it by the case. All he does is sit in the dining room and stare out the window, smoking Pall Mall after Pall Mall. He really misses his Hellie." They were both crying again.

I wanted Grandpa's house to be nice, like the houses that lined the streets of old Duxbury, grand women standing on old foundations of handmade brick and stone, rising up and insisting that age only deepens one's aristocratic position. The colonial design, the shingles curled and warped from hundreds of wicked New England storms and stifling summer days, the twenty-four-pane windows and widow's walks made me wish I had grown up here just like Penelope. She spoke of the Cape Cod house where she had grown up, on Friendship Lane, at the very edge of the marsh overlooking Duxbury Sound. The house was built in 1657 and stood on old stone foundations, its roofline bowed and warped with age. She took me to see it, and we asked the owners if we could come inside so Penelope could show me her bedroom. The steep stairs were divided, as most had been in those days, to accommodate huge chimneys and fireplaces large enough to hold iron kettles and a bread oven embedded in the brick off to the side of the main fireplace. Her bedroom was tucked into the south corner with a dormer window looking out onto the water. As a child, she'd loved to sail and had pasted old ship charts all over her walls, imagining that she would be a sailor one day. The old wood floors were worn smooth from hundreds of years of pacing, wondering, and holding families safe, a mothering sort of house that heard everything and loved you more for your struggles.

I wanted to become Penelope, to live her childhood and be a perfect replica of her. If I could be her, maybe she would love me more and never be angry enough to tell me I was just like Gardiner. I never wanted to be like him. I wanted to be everything she wanted me to be.

She thought of herself as a mistake, and I wanted to fix it. She told me that her mother would get angry and tell her she wished Penelope had never been born. Penelope said Grandma had tried to commit suicide right after Penelope was born by slashing her wrists and her throat. Penelope had to know that I idolized her, but just in case, I would show her every day how precious she was to me. I wanted to wear sailor suits and learn to sail just like she had; I wanted have a Boston accent instead of my California girl non-accent. I tried, but I think I just sounded like a California girl with a speech impediment.

Grandpa's house wasn't an old house; it was what Penelope called a reproduction—a salt box built in the 1950s, painted gray with red shutters adorning the twenty-four-pane windows. It stood on a shady corner in a nice neighborhood on Captain's Hill Road near the monument to Myles Standish, one of New England's most skillful colonizers and eliminators of indigenous people. My mother spoke of our ancestry as noble and distinguished, our lineage tracing back to William Bradford, a passenger on the Mayflower and a separatist leader. She spoke of our breeding so much that I began to think I was somebody special, that I belonged to an enviable echelon of society. "Breeding speaks for itself," she said. "If one has it, one does not need to talk about it." So much for not talking about it.

The lawn looked lush, and the trees gave shade and protection all the way around it, but the shrubs and flowers hadn't been tended. The hedges had disobedient fronds, and the flowers had fallen over in resignation to the death of their mistress. We knocked at the kitchen door and heard a dog barking. Grandpa shuffled to the door telling Bonnie to shut up. He was wizened and unshaven, and he began to cry when Penelope put her arms around him and said, "Hi Dad." The memorial services had taken place two weeks earlier, attended by Peter and their other two cousins as well as Penelope's only sister, Ann, who lived in Plymouth and had been basically banished from the family for drinking and being a tramp.

Grandpa's house stank of cigarettes and old-man-who-never-bathed, especially in his sitting room, where he sat for hour after hour drinking whiskey and smoking filterless Pall Malls. I remembered Grandpa as a good-sized man, comfortable and easy to laugh with. Seeing him now, I could see why Penelope was stunned. His unwashed shirt hung loosely off his bones, and he hadn't shaved in several days, and the house looked gloomy and dark. He said he hadn't touched any of Grandma's things and hadn't wanted to take Bonnie out for a walk. He apologized for our having to step over the puddles of pee and dried-up dog turd piles in the breezeway. He just hadn't felt like cleaning up.

I had only seen my grandparents twice, once when I was six and once when I was about nine. All I remembered was that Grandma had gotten mad at Penelope and me for dropping by unexpectedly when her teeth were still soaking in Efferdent. She was never awake before noon.

Penelope's voice was shaking as she reassured him that the mess was perfectly understandable. *Two of the skinniest people on the planet*, I thought. Grandpa brought us inside.

"You remember Bonnie?" he asked, pointing to the very dirty, overweight terrier baring her teeth from under his table. My cockatiel, Mr. Peabody, began squawking from his travel cage, and Patience was barking at Bonnie under the table, trying to coax her to come out and introduce herself. "Where should I bring the suitcases?" I asked, wanting to take charge of the situation.

"Upstairs to Hellie's room, Kimmy girl," he said trying to be cheerful. "There are two beds—one for you and one for your mother." He managed a weak smile.

I went quietly upstairs to Grandma's room, feeling afraid to disturb anything and feeling like an intruder in a room that wasn't mine, and that

I shouldn't push Grandma out yet. There were two four-poster beds high off the floor, made with white bedspreads and big, fluffy pillows with white shams. The dresser was old, made of dark wood and smelling like an old dresser should, a little musty and imbued with perfume frequently sprayed on a slender neck before bedtime. A Boston rocker sat in the corner on its little rag rug, welcoming time with a book in the lingering quiet of autumn afternoons; a mirror hung on its stand in another corner, having reflected hundreds of moments of checking a bustle, tucking in a stray hair, or placing a lace collar, a witness to confession, self-doubt, and thoughts of suicide. Grandma's ivory-handled hairbrush sat on its silver tray on her night table. The wallpaper, faded by years of mornings when light found its way through the lace curtains, was light green with little red roses, and the curtains were delicate cotton with eyelet trim held back by sashes.

Penelope had to have her privacy, and Grandpa was more than willing to sleep downstairs in his sitting room so that Penelope could have his room. That way, he wouldn't have to climb up and down the stairs, sparing his Pall-Mall-saturated lungs the effort. He didn't like being upstairs anyway; it reminded him of Grandma. They'd married in 1918 right after Grandpa had gotten out of the Navy, and now it was 1971. I added it up to fifty-three years of marriage. I looked at the photo of them on Grandma's dresser, taken right after they were engaged. I had a moment of wishing my parents loved each other that much and had to lie down for a minute.

30

NOT FITTING IN

WE WERE IN DUXBURY ONLY A couple of days before Penelope mentioned school. There, wasn't much time left in the school year, and I'd hoped Penelope might just forget about it, but she said finishing the seventh grade was important. "Just look at it as an exciting adventure," she said, not very convincingly. As I considered the prospect, I couldn't sleep, and the adrenaline pumped as I wondered what to wear and whether anyone else would be wearing knickers with a matching vest and knee-high, lace-up boots. Maybe it would be too much, and I should try to look more like Marcia Brady and wear a minidress and my platform shoes. Where would I smoke? It seemed like the neighbor girls all had long hair, and mine was still in a Mrs. Brady short shag cut. I glued the wisps of hair to my face with hairspray and put on my mascara and lip gloss. I had my Marcia Brady purse containing my makeup, Virginia Slims Menthols, and a lighter. I had lunch money and tampons, so in case anyone asked me for one I would have one to offer. I had not started my period, but there was always the chance it would start. I carried a pad in a little gold, plastic case, too, because I was afraid to use a tampon. Penelope told me I wouldn't be a virgin anymore if I used tampons. But having them in my purse made me feel more grown up. Tampons and cigarettes were clear evidence that I wasn't a dork.

At thirteen, I danced between little-girlhood and womanhood and often was not sure which I wanted to be the most. I could be womanly when the mood struck and childlike when being womanly wore me out. Penelope was moodier and more bitter toward Gardiner as time passed. I felt her need for me to be her best friend, to agree with her on everything she felt about him. I tried to be more grown up when she wanted me to listen to how much she resented him. I put my teenage self away during those times, knowing that she didn't like that part of me. She hated my adolescence more now that I was showing some signs of breasts and a slight curve marking the place where my waist opened into hips. Sometimes, it was exhausting trying to be more like her, looking for multisyllable words and being careful not to use words she considered to be markers of bad breeding. It wasn't a couch, it was a sofa; it wasn't raaather, it was rawhhther; and, "Do not call me 'mom.' You may call me 'mother' or 'mum,' but please refrain from calling me 'mom.' It's so ghastly. Only ill-bred children call their mothers 'mom.'"

I wore loose shirts and baggy shorts for hiding beneath when I felt child-like, and indulged my womanly mood behind closed doors in Grandma's room. I floated in front of Grandma's mirror, glancing as I passed, hoping to see a glimpse of a woman reflected back at me. If I only looked for a second, I could see the shadow of woman out of the corner of my eye. I wanted the mirror to grant my wish for angular facial features instead of roundness. I ran my hand over the place where I longed for sensual hipbones and felt only a boyish straight line. I raised my shirt and tried to see breasts but saw only little buds, like little roses not ready to open. Impatient and frustrated with Mother Nature's pace, I dropped my shirt. Wearing tight shirts would make my slow progress visible, so I chose loose dresses and large shirts under which my feminine evolution could occur privately.

In Grandma's room, I found my roots, following a thread of Grandma's spirit into her closet and deeper still behind another door and into the attic, where I found an old sewing table long abandoned. In it, I discovered ancient spools of thread and patches of material sewn together, perhaps once intended to be a quilt, a story of something. In an old dusty dresser with many little drawers, I found another hairbrush made of silver so tarnished I could barely make out the engraving *HKC*, for Helen Knight Converse. In another drawer, I found old letters bound carefully with satin ribbon, all from Grandpa and all beginning with the greeting, "Dearest Darling Hellie girl . . ." Opening more drawers, I saw a large envelope and reached in to pull it out. The tiny skeleton of a mouse was underneath, and I felt a wave of terror, suddenly wishing for more light in the dimly lit attic. But I could not resist looking inside the big envelope and gently opened its ancient flap. Inside was Grandma's diploma from Smith College, all made out in Latin, granting her the honor of graduating summa cum laude in philosophy. The shelves full of her books became more precious, and I wanted to be connected to her too, a part of a family of women who did extraordinary things.

I felt welcome now in this room with its hardwood floors and twenty-four-pane windows looking out onto the tall trees. I slept in the four-poster bed with the horse-hair mattress while the spring breeze blew through the lace curtains and the moon shone on the faded rose wallpaper. I loved the smell of musty clothes packed away in trunks and ventured into each closet and cranny, opening drawers of old chests to discover my family's history in the yellowed pages of photograph albums. I kept Grandma's carefully bundled love letters in my bedside table drawer and pulled them out to read the carefully written journals of Grandpa's days at sea, the accounts of the things he saw and how he wondered what was happening back home, how he missed her and his friends and the dinners at his parents' house, where his mother would sing and play the piano after supper. I felt I needed Grandma's permission to read such private letters and asked her when I said my prayers at night: "The Lord is my shepherd; I shall not want . . . He maketh me to lie down . . . Grandma, is it okay if I read your letters?"

I rode my bike to the Mayflower Cemetery to visit Grandma's grave. The sod pieces were still easy to see over the grave. Death was everywhere in Duxbury, where nothing seemed to want to change, and Duxbury and old people lived in old houses, and the ghosts of all the families long dead lingered in the walls and cellars. I went to the other old graveyards, where the gray slate headstones, some more than three hundred years old, were so worn from icy gray New England winters and suffocating summers that the inscriptions were barely visible. It made me scared to think about all the death in the ground beneath me, and I had to run away from the graveyard, looking behind to see if any of the ghosts were chasing me. It seemed so lonely in Duxbury. Suddenly, I found myself missing Lana, and a huge lump caught in my throat. I hoped I would find friends, but there would never be anyone like Lana.

31
FRIENDS

THERE WAS A GROUP OF FOUR or five girls who always were gathered at the neighbor girl's house across the street from Grandpa's. I got up the courage to be outside one day when they were sitting in a circle on her lawn listening to the radio, and they waved me over. "Hey, you new here? Where did you come from?"

"California," I said.

The girls were amazed. I'd come from the land of blond boys and surfing. It turned out that all of them were in seventh grade, same as me. The problem was, all but one went to private school in Boston, and I never saw them except on weekends. My first week at the new school was enough to cause morning nausea and dry mouth, my morning toast rising to my throat throughout the bus ride. I couldn't stop worrying about how I was dressed and whether everyone thought I looked dumb in my *Vogue* clothes and my Mrs. Brady haircut. Nobody else had a shag haircut or *Vogue* clothes.

Only one girl made an effort to introduce herself. She had long, bright-red hair down to her butt, sprays of freckles, and braces. She was a little on the pudgy side as well, but nonetheless she seemed very popular. She said her name was Kate and whipped out a pack of Marlboros. "Wanna come over later? A bunch of us are hangin' out on the beach at the end of our street."

"Ummm . . . okay," I said, doubtful that I would be able to figure out how to get there. She lived far enough away that I couldn't go there unless I had a bike. Grandpa's solution to this problem was to take me down to the junk store and buy me a blue Schwinn that had a dirty white basket with plastic flowers on it for five dollars. It looked exactly like the one Gardiner had bought me when I was seven. In fact, maybe it *was* that same one; the rust and dents were a dead ringer. I acted as though I were overcome with gratitude for Grandpa's contribution to my independence, but I was embarrassed to ride it. It rattled and had a squeaky wheel, and the pink basket had to go. But, nonetheless, I rode it down to the end of the road and met up with Kate and some other kids. I took a Marlboro when it was offered, knowing that my Eve cigarettes weren't cool. I blew my usual perfect smoke rings and everyone stared. "You don't know how to inhale, do you?" Kate giggled.

"No," I said defensively. "But I can do it." So after inhaling several times, I felt nauseated and told Kate I had to go home. Penelope saw me weaving along the driveway, my face the color of Grandpa's hedge. "Did those girls teach you how to smoke?" she asked with a smirk.

"Yes. Am I going to throw up?" Tears filled my eyes as I burped and swallowed, trying to keep from throwing up all over the driveway. "No, you won't throw up. You just need to have some ice water and lie down. Now, go upstairs and I will bring you ice water," she said, chuckling. I felt as though I'd slept in the tailpipe of a Greyhound bus for several hours, and I could only eat saltines with 7UP for dinner.

I wished Grandpa would cheer up. It seemed he was just waiting to die, expediting the process by smoking at least two packs of Pall Malls a day and drinking whiskey from noon until he tottered to bed at about nine p.m. He would sit in his underclothes every morning, coughing and hacking in between huffs on his inhaler. His lungs sounded like a toilet trying to flush and it made me sick, so I tried to be gone when he went through this morning ritual. After he stopped wheezing and coughing up his tar-sodden lung tissue, he went to his dining room and drank instant Folgers and smoked the first of his many Pall Malls of the day. There he sat until eleven-thirty, when he said one of his five or six sentences for the day, "I think I'll make a sandwich," and rose from his chair to make a liverwurst sandwich, the only nourishment he'd taken in since suppertime the night before. He watched the clock, and when it struck one o'clock, he rose once again to retrieve his whiskey glass, which was shaped like a thimble and was inscribed, "Only a Thimble Full" in gold letters on the side. It actually held about six ounces, and he filled it to the top with the cheapest whiskey he could get at the Navy outlet in Weymouth.

Penelope, never one to nurse or do any kind of hands-on care for anyone, tried to take charge of dinner and ensure that he ate before he passed out for the night. The bathroom he used was off the kitchen and contained only a sink and a toilet, which Penelope and I both refused to enter. Penelope whispered that he probably hadn't bathed since Christmas and that she couldn't bear to touch his laundry, so she called a service to come and get it. He would perk up occasionally during dinner, especially when I let Mr. Peabody wander around on the table, where he climbed onto the plates and nibbled at the mashed potatoes. I could tell he couldn't wait to have another whiskey so the numbness would overtake him until he couldn't stay awake. And Penelope was drinking more Canadian Clubs than usual, too, but she didn't seem to be getting drunk. She just got weepy and cried over memories or kept me awake with stories of Grandma and the family.

I was determined to bring Grandpa out of his gloom, and having no understanding of alcoholism, grief, and depression, I thought I could easily accomplish this by doing things for him. I took Bonnie out for walks, which the dirty little dog resisted by sitting down on her fat butt with balls of poop hanging off it and growling at me when I attempted to coax her by tugging her collar. She showed her yellowed teeth, and I looked at her square in her eyes and told her it was time for a bath and a comb-out, and that now we knew each other well enough and it was time to get over herself. Her coat was so greasy and smelly that it was hard to tell what color she actually was. Bonnie's considerable weight made it impossible for her to climb the stairs, so I picked her up like a growling bag of wet flour and heaved her into the bathtub, closing the door behind me. Bonnie knew she was trapped in the bathroom and finally surrendered, lying down on her back, exposing her very dirty tummy.

After several applications of watermelon-scented shampoo and cucumber-scented conditioner, the rinse water was finally clear and not black with pebbles of poop swirling amongst dead fleas and Bonnie's hair, which I was hoping would return to its wheaten color instead of greasy brown.

Poor Bonnie, she missed Grandma, who would at least take her for a short walk now and then, but after Grandma had died, Grandpa would only let her out on the breezeway. She sat under his table all day except to be let out onto the concrete breezeway, which, being porous, graciously accepted all of Bonnie's offerings for months on end, and which now brought tears to my eyes each time I had to pass through, hopping over the piles as quickly as possible in order to avoid breathing.

On one particularly hot and humid day, I decided something really had to be done. I rode the Schwinn down to Sweetser's Market and bought some rubber gloves and scrub brushes, as well as some Lysol and other powerful cleaning products that advertised "no stain too tough, no smell too strong" on the labels, and put it all on Penelope's already-overspent charge account. The supplies fit nicely into the pink basket that I had painted with peace signs to make it look a little cooler. Then I rode to the hardware store and bought some bright red paint and a roller. The breezeway had used to be a reddish color, but the paint had chipped and peeled away so much that only patches could be seen through the dirt and poop. The man at the counter smiled at me and asked me if I was going to paint something. *Well, duh,* I thought and took out my list. "I'm going to paint the breezeway at my grandpa's," I said, just wanting to hurry up and get it done.

"Don't you need some sandpaper?" he asked.

"What for?"

"Well, you've gotta get all the old paint off before puttin' new paint on," he said in his broad New England accent, in a tone suggesting I lacked the basic knowledge for undertaking a home improvement project.

"No, thanks, I got it."

Why did he have to take a perfectly simple idea and complicate it so that it would take weeks to finish? I rode home feeling pissed off. I was planning on taking no more than a day for this project. I parked the Schwinn outside the garage and went inside quietly to avoid any questions that might deter me from my mission. I scanned the cluttered garage for other supplies I might need to protect me from all the turds and pee, and lucked out. I found a pair of hip waders and Grandpa's oilcloth raincoat, which was the color of martini olives, and his rain hat that smelled like old man scalp but would protect my head from the spray of the hose. My plan was to turn it on full blast with the idea that the force of water would pulverize a lot of the turds. After I donned my gear, I spotted a pair of clear goggles. "Perfect!" I said aloud, now feeling invincible against any foul matter or smell.

When I faced the breezeway with the hose in my hand, I was disappointed to discover that the force of the water was insufficient, and my pulverizing idea would probably not work as well as I'd imagined. I then got the idea that I could shovel them up and put them in a bag for the garbage man. But then what if the garbage man discovered that the bag actually had turds in it and not garbage? Maybe I could sneak the bag of turds into the neighbor's garbage at night, and the garbage man would think it was theirs? I settled on that plan and retrieved a shovel from the tool shed, then began shoveling turds like a snowplow, holding my breath as I leaned down to open the bag.

After the final turd was removed, I was ready to scrub the concrete floor so it wouldn't smell anymore. I found a bucket and filled it with hot water and half a jug of Clorox, feeling a huge sense of satisfaction when I flung the hot, bleachy water onto that nasty surface until it was thoroughly soaked. Then, taking a push broom, I commenced scrubbing with all the ferocity I had inside me, washing away all the layers and layers of filth until I felt certain that no trace could possibly survive.

My eyes watered from the bleach. Or were they tears? I couldn't tell. I was sweating and panting, and it sounded a little like crying. I stood up holding my broom like a warrior and marveling at what the breezeway looked like now. I could still smell pee but was not discouraged, certain that several coats of red paint would fix that problem.

It was dark and the concrete needed to be dry before I painted it. I went to bed, hardly able to sleep, and arose first thing in the morning to begin the final phase of the project. I felt giddy with a sense of purpose. I'd never felt this way, not even when I'd gotten a hundred percent on a spelling test. Right in that moment of brilliance, bathing in that glow of accomplishment, the ultimate achievement would be cleaning Grandpa's bathroom. I spent the morning painting the breezeway and, when I was finished, I was so pleased with myself that I could barely contain my rapture. I looked at the lumps where the old paint was and realized that sanding it first would have made a smoother surface.

Cleaning Grandpa's bathroom had to be the ultimate act of love. It was a small, foul little room Grandpa called "the head," because that's what you call a toilet on a boat. He called the kitchen "the galley," and said he was "listing to port" when he felt unsteady on his feet after the nine hundredth whiskey of the day. The head hadn't seen the business end of a toilet brush in years. Penelope looked at me with a worried expression as I stood poised in the doorway with my bucket of cleaning supplies. "Are you sure you want to do this?" she asked.

I lowered my goggles over my face and said, "Yup." Then, like a firefighter going into a burning building, I disappeared into the head, only instead of a fire hose, I held a toilet brush and Lysol lemon fresh bathroom cleaner.

I couldn't hold my breath long enough to get anything done. I really needed one of those surgical masks and remembered that Grandma had kept a bunch of them in the kitchen drawer. She'd worn them when she'd had a cold so Grandpa wouldn't catch it. I loved the mask. I could do anything as long as I had a mask.

32

MISSING GARDINER

GARDINER SAID HE WAS COMING EAST to visit Daddy Roy and Grannie at their farm in Williamstown and would spend a day in Duxbury. I'd been to the farm to see my grandparents only once when I was nine, and now I felt like I wasn't anybody's granddaughter, least of all in the branches of Gardiner's family tree. I felt the familiar panic welling up in my stomach again, waiting for him to call. Maybe he would change his mind and not come at all. It was easy for him to erase me from his life like a mistake on a blackboard. He was angry at me for choosing Penelope.

She'd told me her story of how someone had sneaked into the house one day while she was in her bed, too weak to get up, and how Gardiner had hung a wooden dowel from the ceiling so she could pull herself up to a sitting position. I remembered her telling me how she'd listened and held her breath as she heard footsteps on the stairs. The Demerol and morphine vials had been in the bathroom along with all the syringes, and she had known that's what they were after, she told me. "So I reached down into my bedside table drawer and got my gun. I was so weak, I couldn't hold it in one hand, but I was strong enough to raise the gun with both hands, and I fired a shot into the ceiling to scare the burglar away. But they made off with all my pain medicine." I believed Penelope's story, not connecting it with what

I'd found down by my swing set not too long afterward. And I knew what Gardiner said about the Demerol was true, that she'd been injecting more than she should have and had had to find a way to get more. So she'd tried to burn the bottles and syringes and told Gardiner someone had come into the house and stolen it all. He should have stuck up for her; he should have just let me believe Penelope.

My choices had been to be a traitor and leave her, or to live with her and give up being with Gardiner. I had wanted to fly out of Sammie's house that day and never come back. Maybe I could live with Mrs. Chisholm and pretend my life was normal, I had thought.

The memory of finding the Demerol bottles intruded on my fantasy that Penelope was all well now and that we were going to have a perfect life. Gardiner was angry that I had defied him. He told me that I could just live with her and see for myself, and I told him I was going to.

Then I got really scared that he wouldn't love me anymore because I'd chosen Penelope. While we were driving home after the scene at Sammie's, I wanted him to reassure me that I was still his favorite girl, like I'd used to be before Penelope had gotten sick and everything had fallen apart. He told me that his oldest daughter, Susie, had always been his favorite. I had been just an accident, he said. An accident wasn't so bad, I thought. Accidents can be good sometimes. I wanted to ask Gardiner whether he thought I was a good accident, but I looked out the window instead and swallowed back my tears.

Maybe that explained why he had never called me or written to me after Penelope and I had started our new life. But I'd waited for him anyway. Maybe he would change his mind if I could show him I wasn't difficult.

Gardiner visited, but he only stayed a day, and he seemed irritated that he had to be there at all. He was only passing through on his way to Williamstown to Daddy Roy and Grannie's farm. "Can I come with you, Daddy?" I begged, trying to stop him from leaving so soon.

"No," he said. "You have to go to school." He patted me on my skinny shoulder as if that should be enough. And then he was gone.

Penelope wanted to get out of Grandpa's house.

"It smells, and he's so depressed. He's either sitting at that goddamn table in that horrible little dining room of his getting shitfaced, or he's sleeping. Occasionally, he watches the ballgames, but other than that, he might as well be dead," she said. "So we're going to buy a house. At least I have inheritance from my mother . . . not much, but enough for a down payment."

So we bought a house with a big front lawn by a creek. The real estate agent, Dot, showed Penelope and me many houses, but none were old enough for Penelope's taste. She didn't think houses or any furniture less than three hundred years old reflected her good breeding.

"It's not an old house as I would prefer," she said when Dot showed her the one she would eventually buy, "but it's a nice reproduction of a Cape Cod house."

Finally, we could get our stuff out of storage. We didn't have any furniture from when we had lived in Laguna Beach, though, and I hoped Penelope would buy a nice soft sofa and a matching easy chair.

"I refuse to have boorish furniture," she said. "I've found some antique places where we can find some lovely old furniture."

I knew it would all be uncomfortable, and it was. Penelope unpacked her duck decoys and her pewter tea set, which looked perfect with all the uncomfortable chairs and old trestle tables. We had old cranberry scoops to hold magazines. After my begging Penelope for many days, she allowed me to buy some lacy curtains for my bedroom window and a girly comforter for my bed.

33

DOG GIRL

I DREADED SCHOOL EVERY DAY. MY MRS. Brady shag haircut and *Vogue* magazine outfits gave everyone plenty of ammunition to bark at me. "Get outta here, you ugly *dog*," the boys spat as I passed their seats on the bus. I tripped on someone's foot and went sprawling, my makeup and hair goop rolling under the seats. Everyone howled and barked as I struggled to my feet. The bus driver looked at me through the rearview mirror and yelled at me to "siddown!"

I had to swallow back the vomit each time I entered a classroom, preparing for the inevitable howling and barking, and I avoided the lunchroom, trying to choke down my lunch of Triscuits and peanut butter in the bathroom or behind the school. I had a few friends, but they didn't stand up for me. "Just ignore them," they encouraged. But it's hard to ignore a room full of kids shouting at you. The teachers sat at their desks and waited for the bell to ring, at which point the noise would die down to giggles and whispers.

One day, I made my way to science class, creeping along the walls and hoping to blend in with the crowd without being noticed. But I was late . . . again, after spending time in the bathroom, having another of many attacks of sweating, shaking, and fighting nausea. I was surprised when one of the gang leaders greeted me at the classroom door with a wrapped gift in his hand. He told me that everyone felt really bad about all the teasing, and that he and a bunch of the other kids wanted to show me how sorry they were for everything. And he handed me the gift. I was hesitant to accept it, wondering if it could really be true that suddenly they were going to be my friends, but he encouraged me. "No, we really mean it. Go on . . . open it," he said, smiling even more broadly. And so I took the gift, untied the ribbon, and opened a corner of the wrapping paper. It wasn't until I peeled away the first layer of wrapping that I saw the words "Milk Bones for Large Dogs" on the box. By then, the entire class was barking and howling like dogs and laughing so hard they couldn't remain in their seats.

I left school and ran all the way home, the tears making my mascara run in black rivulets down my face and sting my eyes. I begged Penelope, "Please don't make me go back."

She told the school psychologist to go screw himself when he came to the door one morning threatening to file a truancy petition after I hadn't shown up for a week. "If you can't even run a school where this sort of behavior is not tolerated, I'm certainly not going to send my daughter there. Now get off my property." And she slammed the door in his face.

"We're going to Provincetown," she announced one morning after purchasing a new metallic green Mustang from Herrick's Ford. "The owner used to love me," she'd said before she'd bought it. "Maybe he'll give me a good price."

"Why are we going to Provincetown?" I asked, unsure of this sudden decision to stay in another beachfront motel with a kitchenette and an ocean view. There was nobody to get away from except Grandpa and maybe the truant officers. "Well, it's a lovely little artsy-fartsy place, and there are some cabins on the beach with kitchens. Your father is coming to visit."

It had only been a few months since his earlier visit to Duxbury, so this was really surprising. He hadn't even sent us any Christmas presents. Maybe he was coming to rescue us, and we would all go back to Squaw Valley and live happily ever after. Penelope's swings into rage and depression were getting worse. At night, she stayed awake and drank wine until her words were slurred, and during the day she took Percodan, which kept her in a fairly euphoric mood, in addition to the Ritalin and Valium.

She hated that I was thirteen, she hated my desire to be like other girls my age, and she criticized the few friends I had, especially Kate, because she was a chubby Irish girl with red hair and freckles. But my friends didn't like coming over anyway, and I was always afraid of what Penelope's mood would be. There were days when she was downright strange. Kate said she was batty.

When Gardiner came to visit again a few months later, he was not as hurried and stayed for two days. I took a walk with him on the beach in Provincetown. I wanted Penelope to forgive him so he would take us back, but she wouldn't. She hung onto her anger at him and refused to surrender. She *liked* being the woman with the deadly disease who'd survived despite her horrible husband who had left her while she had been on her deathbed.

I wanted him to take me away and be definite about it, not load me down with the decision. I wanted him to take me and tell Penelope that he was making the decision. I would not have to decide to leave her; he would do it for me and all the guilt would be his. But he didn't want me, I could tell. He was fully woven in with Sammie's kids now.

"Your mother needs you," he said. And a thousand pounds of stone landed on my shoulders, crushing the voice inside that wanted to dare to ask to be taken care of. I wanted to tell him that Penelope thought he and I were just the same, to see what he thought—how much the same we were in our selfishness, the mean streak, and how I was going to end up with a big wide ass like Grannie's.

I was worried about that mean streak, but I was more worried that I would never start my period. Or grow decent-sized breasts. I tried harder to be the daughter Penelope wouldn't want to get rid of. I swallowed myself back down when my teenage identity bubbled up, knowing she would hate it. I daydreamed about belonging, being sought after as a friend, but I must have had a visible aura of desperation. They could sense it, as if they were lions and I were covered with meat juice. All I could do was watch other girls and try to be more like them. The cool girls that lived in my neighborhood wore crew neck sweaters, dungarees, and shoulder-length hair. They never read *Fave* magazine, and they thought Donny Osmond was a freak. They were into James Taylor and Carole King, not David Cassidy and *The Partridge Family*, so I had to make a few changes in that department.

"And it isn't cool to love your mom," said Drew, one of the rich girls who went to private school in Boston. Her dad was a psychiatrist who had his office on the bottom floor of their house, which was right on Duxbury Sound.

Drew could drive a power boat and invited all the girls in the neighborhood to go water skiing, but I was embarrassed to be seen in my bathing suit. I told them I listened to opera and symphonies by Mozart and Brahms, and they rolled their eyes and giggled, passing the Marlboro around. They laughed even harder when I said I didn't smoke cigarettes with brown filters. "Omigod . . . she calls them 'cigarettes,'" they teased.

"Call them butts," said MaryJane. "You kind of sound like your *mom*." They were so comfortable with themselves, and I thought they were all beautiful—how they wore their hair, how they wore their dungarees low on their beautifully widening hips with the cuffs dragging on the ground, with tight bodysuits hugging their breasts and wasp-like waists, giving their bodies a violin shape. I looked at every girl's breasts as if I were contemplating a sculpture. Some were round like little apricots or slightly cone shaped, newly developed, tender like rosebuds. Some had uneven breasts, one bigger than the other, and some girls had big breasts whose nipples showed, even through their bras. I would have taken any pair but my own.

My body was betraying me. I had no control over what it might do. It might develop my Grannie's ass or it might not develop an ass at all. Maybe I would have no waist and small, raisin-like breasts, or maybe they would be huge and saggy like Grannie's and Penelope would hate me. Each layer of my tender, new, feminine skin was scared into being unfeminine the moment Penelope noticed it. She loved that I was staying straight, skinny, and narrow-hipped, that my grape-like breast buds refused to grow. I tried to eat more to gain weight, but my nerves got the better of me, and I couldn't eat breakfast before school, and lunch was out of the question. It only took one incident to make me sick, when everyone in the entire cafeteria barked when I entered, and I ate lunch in the corners of the hallway or outside.

The school dance was coming up. Kate asked me if I was going, and I said I would if she would. "Pissa . . . we'll have a great time. It'll be soooo pissa, trust me."

"Does pissa mean it's cool or something?" I asked Kate.

She just rolled her eyes at me. "Uhhh . . . yah," she said.

I begged Penelope to take me shopping to buy a dress. I got a long granny dress with puffy sleeves, a low neckline, elastic right under where breasts were supposed to be, and a ruffle around the bottom. I had seen hippie girls wearing them in magazine pictures. The front made me look flatter so I wore it backwards. The back side was puffier and made me look like I had breasts. I waited against the wall to be asked to dance, but nobody asked. I never went to another school dance.

34
NEW YORK

It was August, hot and sticky in Duxbury. Penelope got a call from an old friend who lived in New York. She'd known him since childhood, and their families had spent a lot of time drinking martinis and hanging out on the family's yacht outside of Hyannis Port. Ed worked for *Newsweek* and lived in a hotel near the office.

"Ed has invited us to come to New York and visit," she said. "He's gotten us a suite at The Berkshire, which is a nice hotel, but not as nice as The Pierre or the Sherry-Netherland, but he is paying for it, therefore, I will lower my standards. He lives at the Berkshire because it's only a block or two from the *Newsweek* building where he works. He really doesn't need to work, but he likes his job," said Penelope, explaining to me why he lived in a hotel and how he could afford it. "He could probably afford to live in a nicer hotel. His family was loaded, and Ed was the only one of the three kids who worked. He was born with some sort of disability and has always needed to use crutches to walk. He walks to work every day on his crutches unless it's snowing."

Penelope knew which hotels were considered "dumps," which ones were for tourists and the *nouveau riche*, and which ones were where people who have decent taste and good breeding stayed. I looked at the *Mobil Travel Guide* to see how many stars the Berkshire had.

"It only has three stars," I told her. "Don't we only stay at four or five-star hotels?"

"Yes, but we're being polite and accepting the invitation to stay at The Berkshire, which he is also paying for," she said with her Converse eyebrows raised.

Penelope had a history in New York and began to educate me about New York and how to behave. "Well-bred girls don't ride buses or take the subway," she began. "And don't go over to the West Side; always stay on the east side of Fifth Avenue, but never go above 85th Street or below 42nd Street."

It was a five-hour drive from Duxbury, but somehow Penelope turned it into an eight-hour drive by getting confused on the off-ramps and ending up on the New Jersey turnpike. And the fact that Penelope had to stop every hour to take a pill, let the dogs pee, or stretch her shoulders made it even longer. I was always reaching in the back for something—her water, a cracker, more pills. She kept tiny bottles of Canadian Club whiskey and Tanqueray gin in the glove box. The bottles looked so cute and perfect, I wanted to try some. "Go ahead," said Penelope.

I took a sip of gin, which made my throat and mouth burn. "That's disgusting!" I reached for the water and gulped to wash away the sting.

"That's why you mix it with tonic and lime. And you mix Canadian Club with milk and honey. It's a complete meal in itself." She loved to say this every time she drank that particular meal.

"Ed's family estate was right next to the Kennedy estate," she said. "Those Kennedys are just a bunch of nouveau riche Irish people pretending to be Bostonians. Ill-bred and crooked, all of them."

I remembered when Robert Kennedy was assassinated and how sad I'd felt that day. And when I'd seen a film about his life at school in Duxbury, I had been enraptured and told Penelope and Grandpa all about how wonderful he was. "A bunch of pretentious crooks," Grandpa had muttered.

Ed's room at The Berkshire was a big corner room on the fifteenth floor. I had never seen anything like Manhattan and fell in love with its towering buildings, theaters, parks, and, best of all, Fifth Avenue, where all the stores I'd seen in *Vogue* lined the street between 50th and 57th Streets, where the Plaza Hotel was. Ed rented a long black limousine and took us all around the city. I saw the World Trade Center almost completely built, its two towers the tallest buildings in the world. I was awestruck and got out of the car just to see if I could look up and see the tops. They were the most beautiful buildings, so perfect and gleaming in the sun. I spent the days walking, filling myself with the excitement of the streets and going into the stores. Each store smelled of perfume, cashmere, and silk, a magical fragrance blending in with the *ding* of the elevators as their doors opened. The women who operated the elevators wore little uniforms and called, "Going up!" from the mezzanine, and then called out each floor and what you could find there. "Third floor—women's lingerie and sleepwear." And women would get out and women would come in, holding their shopping bags with the crisscross pattern of brown stripes and "Saks Fifth Avenue" written across in big letters so everyone would know you shopped at Saks.

I loved the atmosphere and explored every corner of Saks Fifth Avenue, which was only two blocks from the Berkshire. Penelope told me to go only to Saks, I.Magnin, Bergdorf's, and Elizabeth Arden's salon, but to avoid Bloomingdale's because it was on Third Avenue, which had a lot of riffraff. And never go to Gimbels or Macy's because they were way downtown, and things got crummy when you went lower than 42nd Street. She didn't go with me on my daily expeditions down Fifth Avenue; she never felt well enough. She was always tired and spent the days talking to Fishballs on the phone, writing letters, or sleeping. She called Gardiner and got a connection to a doctor in New York who could see her, so we took a taxi to the Upper East Side to his office. "He's on the east side of Central Park," she said, putting on her lipstick in the taxi, "which means his office isn't some dump. I would never go to a doctor on the West Side . . . well, at least not below 57th or above 85th."

She was in his examination room for a long time, and I was bored stiff. The waiting room had no interesting magazines, not even *Vogue*. Penelope's medical history was enough to fill a medical textbook, and she was probably illuminating every sordid detail to impress him with her remarkable strength. I'd heard her tell it over and over to all the doctors we'd gone to, wherever we had gone. She always said, "my disease," as if polymyositis were a rare breed of dog and a beloved pet, every wound and scar displayed as a soldier wears badges of honor, especially the wound left by my father's departure to the fleshier side of the pasture. "And then . . . *then*, he came to my bedside while I was on my *deathbed* and announced he was leaving me for another woman," she would say, raising her black Converse eyebrows. Her audience was always appropriately astonished at her strength in overcoming the relentlessness of the disease in addition to being left for another woman.

Our lives were all about Penelope's triumph over adversity, and I was her co-warrior. But when she was with me, all she did was cry about how horrible it was to live in poverty, always struggling to make ends meet, what a difficult child I was, how evil Gardiner was and how she was going to take him to the cleaners and sue him for every cent, so that he and Sammie would be eating cornflakes for the rest of their lives.

Ever since Penelope and I had started the first of several new lives, I had been Penelope's co-star in all her dramas. I would overhear Penelope on the phone or talking to herself late at night when she'd had a lot to drink and taken a few Percodans. She would tell stories and cry as her movements became more and more unsteady and her speech became deliberate as she fought to enunciate. I waited for her to say goodbye or just go to bed and stop talking. The combination of narcotics, sleeping pills, wine, and prednisone made her dopey and unable to think straight. I was afraid to go to sleep, worried that the cigarettes she'd lit and forgotten about would burn the place down. I rescued dozens of bedsheets and nightstands from burning cigarettes dropped as she nodded off in a stupor.

I only had time to myself late at night when she was in bed. Our suite had a separate living room, and I could watch old movies and order pots of coffee from room service. The adorable Asian waiter worked the late shift, and I made sure to dress in my most alluring nightie set, a light blue one made of chiffon and satin that showed off my tiny breasts and a little robe with lace around the collar. Ed had been giving me twenty dollars a day so I could get around by taxi and go to a movie or buy myself something, so I'd bought the nightie set at Saks Fifth Avenue's lingerie department. I tried to save it up to buy the more expensive clothes I saw in *Vogue*, but I never seemed to be able to.

The waiter knew I was flirting. He looked so cute in his tight, black waiter pants and the little red jackets all the waiters wore. He was very polite, but I didn't want him to be. I asked him his name and he said it was Sakul. "What kind of a name is *that?*" I asked, moving in a little closer so he could smell the perfume I was wearing.

"I am from Thailand," he said, smiling and showing perfect, white teeth.

"It's nice to meet you, Sakul," I said, handing him back his pen, having signed the check with a tip more generous than Penelope had taught me was appropriate. Sakul began to linger a little longer at the door when I ordered my evening beverage. One evening, the potency of the flirtation reached its zenith, and he asked in his broken English, "I like kiss you. Okay?"

"Okay," I whispered, my heart pounding through the satin ribbon of my nightie's bodice. The kiss astonished parts of my body Penelope had admonished me not to mess with, but I did it anyway. The next night, Sakul put his hand to my breast, and I backed away, fearful that I'd gone too far. "You'd better go," I said. "My mother might know you're here."

Sakul slipped me a piece of paper with his phone number on it. "You call me?"

"Yes, okay," I said. Penelope had told me never to call a man. "Always let the man be the chaser," she had said. "Don't be one of those needy, clingy women. Men are not attracted to those types."

But Sakul had asked me to call him, so I thought it might be okay this time. I checked with Ed, not wanting to tell Penelope about my secret affair with a Thai waiter. First of all, she would never approve of me kissing a waiter, and she would be even more disapproving that he was Asian. But . . . I couldn't keep anything from Penelope. There was some kind of force inside me that compelled me to tell her things I knew she would disapprove of.

"You cannot see a man who is a *waiter*, for God's sake. It is in very poor taste, and even worse that he's *Or-ee-ental*."

Before Gardiner, and during Fishballs, she had been living in Ketchum, Idaho, and had ended up marrying a French-Canadian ski instructor named Bert. "He drank like a fish, but he was very funny, and he had a huge pecker," she had once told me. "Almost down to his knees."

We had both laughed so hard we could barely breathe by this point. "What happened?" I asked.

"His drinking got worse, and I divorced him, which in Idaho only takes a week. But he promised to stop, and we got married again, which in Idaho only takes an hour."

"What about his breeding? Don't you only pick men with good breeding?"

"Well, as I said, he *was* terribly funny, and he was a *great* artist," she'd sniffed defensively. "And being well-hung compensates for mediocre breeding."

Penelope's standards would allow for well-hung, French-Canadian ski instructors, but not Thai waiters whose genitals she must have determined could never pass the test.

I visited Ed in his room on weekends and watched *Love American Style*, his favorite show, on television. Ed loved his Sunday limousine drives when traffic was light, and we drove all the way to Connecticut one Sunday, chatting the whole way about our dreams for the future. Ed wanted to move to San Francisco and work for the *Newsweek* office there. I wanted a Saks Fifth Avenue charge card so I could dress like a *Vogue* model. And I wanted to become a big star like Liza Minnelli.

I went to Elizabeth Arden's to get my hair done one day when Penelope was in a generous mood and gave me enough money to go. I was given a pink bathrobe and some ice water with lemon in it while I waited in the pink waiting room on a pink chair reading an article in *Vogue* on Liza Minnelli, until Roberto appeared and asked me to follow him. I asked him to get rid of the Mrs. Brady shag and give me the Liza Minnelli look. I showed him the page in *Vogue*. "Ju wan' I make the point in front like she wear in *Cabaret*?" he asked in his Spanish accent.

I'd seen *Cabaret* twelve times and wanted everything Liza had, including green fingernails. I bit mine until they were bleeding, but apparently Liza had the same problem, so she'd gotten some fake nails. "Can you give me some fake nails, too?"

Roberto looked at me and cocked his head. "I get ju Sylvia from de nails deparmen'. She help you, okay?" And he proceeded to snip and hum, waving his scissors every now and then and checking his work. "Hmmm . . . jes, I think so look very good on ju." I was thrilled. We were calling each other "dahling" by the end of the appointment. "Ju come and see me again, jes?"

"Oh I *will*, dahling!" I called out gaily and walked back to the pink waiting room in my pink bathrobe.

Ed slipped a Saks charge card under the door one morning with a note saying, "Make your dreams come true." I was afraid to use it as much as I wanted to, ashamed that I'd been so unsubtle at hinting about it. My longing was endless and bottomless for anything and everything, but nothing I ate, bought, or did seemed to make the emptiness go away for long. I wanted to look like the women in *Vogue*, imagining their lives were perfect and glamorous, but I would have to spend hundreds of dollars to buy the clothes the models wore. Penelope pointed out that my thighs were getting flabby anyway, and if I wanted to look like a *Vogue* model, I could begin by refraining from eating french fries.

"You have to have cheekbones to be a model, and you can't have jiggly thighs," she said. I was frantic to do something about the jiggly parts of my upper inner thighs and went to Doubleday's Bookstore on Fifth and 55th to see if I could locate an exercise book. I flipped through a Jack LaLanne book, memorized a few key points, and resolved to stop eating french fries and to eat only salads from then on, and to do fifty jumping jacks before eating each meal. I sucked in my cheeks and held the flesh between my teeth to look like I had cheekbones like Katherine Hepburn's.

I felt guilty about buying things for myself. Penelope told me how selfish I was at least once a day, and I wanted her to think I was the most generous, unselfish daughter, worth keeping. I went to the perfume counter at Saks and began to smell all the perfume. After coming close to fainting, I decided upon perfume in a beautiful frosted bottle with a top shaped like a bird in flight, called L'air du Temps.

After I got the perfume wrapped, I went to the sixth floor to try on more clothes in order to avoid going outside in the hot, muggy Manhattan afternoon. I was on a first-name basis with all the elevator operators now. The carpets were soft and the dressing rooms were huge, with big mirrors and velvet chairs. I tried on all kinds of suits and trousers, imagining myself modeling at the John Robert Powers Agency as soon as I got rid of the baby fat around my cheeks. The saleslady kept running back and forth to bring me more, exclaiming to the other sales lady in her nasally Bronx accent, "Oh look at huuuuh . . . Isn't that a figya just to die for?!" She waved a hand, fingers gnarled with arthritis but with perfect oval, orange-painted fingernails. "Aw, go ahead. It looks divine. It would be such a crime not to," she said, cocking one eyebrow and wrinkling her little nose. I was floating on the compliment about my figure and bought the outfit, unaware of how many times per day the sales lady said the same thing to customers, even when they were fat and trying to squeeze into skirts several sizes too small.

I was excited to give my mother the perfume and exited the store into the sweltering Manhattan afternoon. I heard the dogs barking as I unlocked the door. I was so excited to give her the perfume that my voice was quaking in my throat. "Ma? Oh Maaaa . . . Maaaa, I got you somethiiiinnng!" I set down the Saks bags and fished out the pretty box of perfume. Penelope was on the bed, not moving. Her face was gray. There was no response when I shook her.

In New York, when you called for an ambulance, the NYPD responded. When the police arrived, they put her on a narrow gurney and told me they were taking her to the nearest district hospital, St. Clare's on the West Side. They let me ride in the ambulance, but I had to ride in the front. There was no room for me in the back, where two medics were trying to keep her alive, I guessed. Nobody was telling me anything, but when they got her on the stretcher, they weren't moving slowly, and they put an oxygen mask on her face. They disappeared into the emergency room. The halls were lined with people sitting on the floor, spilling out of a waiting room where people were puking into buckets or lying on stained chairs, not reading, just staring. My body shook and rumbled with old circuits rebooting, and then all my muscles and nerves remembered. Waiting rooms and waiting, wondering, hoping, the fear so big that it made my body feel hot and cold. My mouth was dry and my fingers wouldn't stop shaking as I dialed the phone to call Ed. I barely held back tears when the receptionist answered, "*Newsweek* magazine, how may I direct your call?"

"Senior editorial department, please." I hoped Ed would answer.

"This is Ed speaking," he said cheerily.

"It's me. Can you please . . . come to St. Clare's Hospital," I sobbed into the phone. "I think my mother might die." He said he would be there as soon as he could get a cab. The waiting room smelled of urine and vomit only slightly masked by disinfectant. The hallway leading to the emergency room was lined with barely padded gurneys, each with a body suspended in the numen of the tiny bulbs barely able to give light, almost suggesting that death would be better. Abandoned humans were curled under rumpled gray blankets, feet hanging off the edges, some without shoes, their scarred, dirty feet trying to curl around something warm, their hands clasped together in prayers under dirty cheeks, eyes squeezed shut around the mania of the emergency room. Nobody really saw them lying there, it seemed. I had never seen a hospital like this one. I didn't want Penelope to be here.

Someone had thrown up in the waiting room, and the smell made me want to cry and run, run, run to a safe place. I needed Gardiner to just sweep me up and take me home. But I had to stay for Penelope. I leaned against a wall and found a breath of air that smelled good and waited. I argued with my fear. If Penelope was dead, they would have told me sooner, wouldn't they? Maybe the endless wait meant she was alive. Or maybe if she was dead, they were telling Gardiner first. Maybe they didn't even know I was here waiting, and I should tell someone. No, they knew. They told me to wait outside as always. Wait outside, just wait outside, as if I were a stray dog. Finally, a doctor in rumpled, blood-spattered scrubs burst through those dirty swinging doors and held out his hand to me. "Are you her only family?" I withdrew my hand. *I'm not going to shake the hand of someone who might tell me my mother is dead.*

"Well . . . yeah . . . I mean . . . well . . . I'm her daughter and . . . but my dad, he's not here, but Ed is." I needed to be careful. I had to appear as though I had people who cared.

"We have her stabilized for now, but she is very, very ill. Is there another doctor she sees here in New York?"

"Yes, he's up on 85th," I said, the adrenaline of fear and relief flooding my body. "I know his name." I gave him the name, and the doctor disappeared through the swinging doors saying he'd be out shortly. I couldn't hear very much in the din of the emergency room activity. After a few minutes, he leaned out of the doors and motioned for me to come to the phone. I listened to instructions and did not speak, other than to acknowledge I'd heard the instructions. A private ambulance would arrive soon to transport Penelope to Mount Sinai Hospital's emergency department, where her doctor would be waiting. I was told to ride along with her in the ambulance.

I hung up and told Ed, who was leaning against the wall outside the hospital on his crutches, with his hat and raincoat on. It had begun to rain, the steamy smell of garbage and dog shit rising up from the hot sidewalks. When the ambulance came, the men moved quickly and wordlessly, unfolding a stretcher with white sheets and gray wool blankets. I saw that it had a thicker mattress and white sheets, not just a hard wooden slab with a thin pad on it like the police ambulance's. The doors swung open, and men wheeled Penelope out to the waiting ambulance crew. They quickly lifted her on the count of three onto the stretcher and strapped her in with the IV bottle on a hook dangling above her head. Her eyes were closed. I watched her chest for signs of breathing.

I felt nothing coming from her face or her body. She was not awake, and she was not asleep; she was in some kind of in-between space. Her skin was the color of a dawn unsure of its own coming—grayish yellow, smoky and veiled. I knelt down beside her in the ambulance and took her hand. It was cold and wouldn't wrap around mine. The attendant riding along in the back kept talking to her in his New York accent really loudly. "Penelope! Stay wid' us! Don't go ta sleep, Penny, okay?" He told me to try talking to her to see if she'd open her eyes.

"Mummy, please don't go to sleep," I begged. "Just look at me one time, please?" But there was nothing. I was keeping her from dying with my own breath as I'd done so many times before. With my eyes closed, I put my hand on my mother's heart. As I breathed out, I imagined that I filled her lungs with life.

The sirens were going, and they were making different sounds. The worst was the siren that sounded like the ambulances in the movies about World War II when the Nazis were invading Poland. Chirping, wailing, screaming, the ambulance sped through Central Park, swerving around corners and barely slowing down at intersections. When it pulled into Mount Sinai's emergency entrance, the doctor was there with a lot of other doctors. I stood aside as they swooped in on her. And then she was gone.

I was left outside of the swinging doors, standing for a few moments uncertainly, like the stray dog who gets the door slammed in her face. I wanted to run in after them and demand to be included. If she was dying, I wanted to be there. I knocked on the swinging doors, but nobody came. I peeked inside but saw only an empty hallway with floors that shone and no bodies stacked along walls. I stepped back feeling it was a forbidden place and found the sign pointing to the waiting room. This waiting room was big and spacious with comfortable blue chairs, matching sofas, and magazines and plants. There were Kleenex and a snack machine and even a television. I could wait in this waiting room maybe for days if I had to. Several hours passed and I wavered between fear and faith, like blood between heart and limbs, finding a strange calm place in the seconds between.

When the doctor emerged from the elevator, I knew instantly that she wasn't dead. He said something about a perforated duodenal ulcer and bleeding, and that they'd had to pump her stomach, too. They were going to take her to surgery in the morning to repair the problem if she was strong enough. "She's very weak because of the bleeding."

He led me down the hall to the room. I felt the surge of fear wash over me when I walked in and saw Penelope's tiny body surrounded by beeping machines and tubes, one up her nose filled with a brownish-colored liquid. There were IVs and a catheter and transfusion tubes and a beeping heart monitor. Her face was gray, and I bent to kiss her on the forehead. Penelope's eyes opened slightly and tried to focus. Then they closed. I didn't want to leave her. She would die if I weren't right there to keep her alive, I was sure.

I had no money for a cab. Eight hours had passed since leaving the hotel, and darkness began to hover in the summer sky. I called Ed, who had gone back to the Berkshire after the St. Clare episode was over, and he said he'd pay the driver when I got there. I thought about walking the fifty blocks down Fifth Avenue back to the hotel. There was life in the streets, and it was warm outside. But I was only fourteen, so I took a cab.

I went up the elevator to the hotel room. The dogs were hysterical and very glad to see me, clearly not at all worried about being punished for peeing and shitting on the carpet. I was grateful for their comfort and spent the next several hours scrubbing the carpets and watching old movies on television. Upon refilling the metal wastebasket with water and soap for the umpteenth time, I looked at the small indentation in the bedspread where Penelope had lain so many hours earlier, and I felt very alone. Right next to the bed was the wastebasket that she'd vomited in and the crumpled Kleenexes with dark blood on them. There wasn't much in there, but the job of emptying it unleashed tears I'd restrained for so many hours.

I knew how Penelope hated throwing up, but nausea and vomiting were just part of life now. "Cortisone has rotted my insides," she had told me. In the past five years, she'd had two intestinal obstructions that had required colostomies. And being dependent on Percodan and other narcotics didn't help. She always got a strained expression on her face as if she was worried, and then she'd start to swallow a lot and breathe heavily, and I knew to get the wastebasket. She'd lie down and ask me to leave the room. Sometimes, she'd lose the battle, but sometimes she'd win and not throw up.

Once I had cleaned up the dog shit and tried to scrub the pee out of the carpet with hotel soap and all the hotel towels we had, I called room service for food for myself and the dogs. "This is room 2103. I need four hamburgers. No buns. And a chef's salad with Roquefort dressing on the side. And some bread, and a large pot of coffee. Please." A crisis did not change my mission to avoid flabby inner thighs. The waiter arrived, and I wouldn't let him into the room because of the dog pee and poop smell. I did not to go to sleep at all that night, in order to keep her alive. Sleeping was giving up. Sleeping was not caring. I stayed on the sofa with the television on and dozed on and off between old Bowery Boys movies and reruns of *The Honeymooners*. New York really is the city that never sleeps, even at four a.m. There was always something on television besides evangelists telling me I was going to go to hell if I didn't accept Jesus Christ as my personal savior, and to dial 1-800-Jesus-Saves right now and get a free Bible.

As the sun rose, I felt the fear fade. Daylight meant I wasn't alone, and it meant that she'd made it through the night without dying. She wouldn't die during the daylight hours. I went to find Ed to see if he wanted to go to the hospital with me. He shifted uneasily in his chair when I told him Penelope would be in the hospital for at least three weeks, maybe a month. "Well honey . . . you know, it's time for my vacation to Hyannis Port in a couple of days, and I'll be gone for a month."

"That's fine. Go ahead and go, Ed. I will be just fine here on my own."

"Well, honey . . . when I leave," he began, beginning to shift and sweat, "You'll have to leave, too." In the space of several seconds, I felt fear, shock, and shame. I'd assumed I could just stay in the hotel. I flipped through my mental file looking for occasions upon which I'd earned demerits for bad behavior. I'd been a little whiny about wanting to have clothes that looked like the model's clothes in *Vogue*, and I knew I'd been just a tiny bit manipulative about the Saks charge card. Maybe that was it. If he just erased me from his life, I wouldn't ask him for anything more.

Then I remembered. This wasn't a new experience; this was familiar. I knew how to be amputated. Once I recognized I was being cut off, I assumed the role and became a warrior with a shining suit of armor. I did not protest or cry or beg. "Okay, I'll move," I said without emotion, yet not having the first clue as to where I'd move, or how. I saw through the slits of the armor that he was relieved. He could have his tidy life back, and that was that.

"I'm sure you'll be just fine, honey," he said, wiping the sweat from his brow with his crisply folded handkerchief.

"Yes. I'll be fine."

I left the hotel for the long fifty-block walk to Mount Sinai Hospital in the warmth of the summer morning and arrived on the sixth floor of the Klingenstein Pavilion just as they were wheeling Penelope into the operating room. The surgery would take a long time. I went to the nice waiting room with the blue chairs, and I read every magazine while the sun eased its way across the windows looking out onto Central Park. Then I went to the newsstand and read all the movie magazines. I was tired from my sleepless night and went to Penelope's room to sit in that chair and wait for her to come out of surgery. I turned the chair toward the window and sat back, letting the sun warm my face and drifted in and out of a poor-quality nap. A knock on the door jarred me to consciousness, and a woman appeared who introduced herself as a social worker from the New York City Department of Social Services. She wanted to know how I was doing. I quickly pulled on the suit of armor, which I now wore everywhere and without which I would never leave home from this point forward until I was nearly through menopause. "Fine. I'm fine. Thank you," I said.

"Tell me," she said, sitting herself on the edge of the bed, "who is taking care of you while your mother is in the hospital? Are you being taken care of?"

I viewed her through the slits in the faceplate. *Not safe. Too smiley. Hair is too perfect.* "Oh yes," I said, trying to appear well-fed and well-slept. "I'm staying in a hotel, and my . . . uhhm . . . godfather lives there." I hoped the social worker would be satisfied with that information and leave me alone.

"Is your mother going to stay there after she gets out of the hospital?" she persisted.

"Well . . . no. We'll probably just go back to our house in Duxbury, Massachusetts," I replied. The social worker began to write on her clipboard. "She'll be too weak to travel for quite some time. Is there a place you can stay in New York? If not, we'll probably need to put her in a convalescent hospital, and we would place you in a temporary foster home so you can go to school and have people look after you."

She may as well have pointed a gun at my head. "Yes, we have a wonderful place to stay. We have it all planned." My voice was solid.

"All right, but I'll need to come and inspect it to make sure it's suitable," she said.

"That's fine." I would have to manifest a place to live in New York.

The social worker tried to hand me a card, but I didn't accept it. The social worker smiled and put it on the table. "Now, you call if you need anything, okay, honey? We'll be in touch."

As soon as the door eased shut, I turned back to the window, letting the tears fall. My throat began to ache, strangled by its need to cry out for Gardiner. I called him, but Sammie always answered the phone at his office. She said he was busy, that he'd call me back. She hung up before I could tell her that Penelope might be dying. My brain did its usual magical trick of shoving all the fear in the back of its closet and began to work on this new problem of finding a place to live.

Penelope didn't come back to the room after the surgery. Dr. Mercer came in wearing his scrubs and told me she would be in the intensive care unit for a few days. She had lost a lot of blood, and it would be a long night. He said she might not make it. "A lot of it is up to her," he said. "She has to have the will to live and not give up."

I couldn't be next to her to keep her alive. I couldn't stay there all night. I had to give up my vigil.

I had four more nights in the hotel before I had to be out. Any less would be a disaster. I was thankful for the sounds and lights of New York that kept me company as I waited through another night hoping the phone would not ring.

The faithful sun rose, and the light began to filter through the tall buildings. I stayed awake, believing that sleep would allow death to sneak in. I ordered coffee, hoping it would make the heaviness in my eyes go away and give me strength to walk the fifty blocks back to the hospital. I should have been spending time looking at *The New York Times* classified ads for apartments for rent, but I needed to see Penelope just to make sure she was really alive. And I really wanted to tell her about the social worker, but I would have to wait until she was out of the intensive care unit. I also needed money, and Gardiner knew that. Which explained why he was ignoring my phone calls.

35

LIKE LIZA

I LEFT THE HOSPITAL BY MIDDAY AND worked intently all afternoon on apartment hunting. I looked under "Apartments for Rent – Manhattan," in *The New York Times* classifieds and saw a lot of places available, but most were rented through management companies, so I circled one near the hotel. Then I went to Saks Fifth Avenue to shop for clothes that made me look older than fourteen. I bought skirts, pumps, and blouses, and blazers and hats to match the shoes, so I'd look like Liza Minnelli when she had done the spread in *Vogue* wearing Halston originals. I couldn't get the Halston stuff, but Saks had good knock-offs, according to the saleslady. When I got dressed to go to the management company, I thought I could easily pass for twenty, especially since I'd stuffed my bra with socks. And I was wearing bright red lipstick and spiky false eyelashes, which Liza Minnelli also had worn in the *Vogue* spread.

When I reached the management company office, an agent came out to greet me. I was business-like. "I need to rent an apartment as soon as possible on the Upper East Side, in either this building or that one," I said, pointing my gloved finger at the drawings of two of the newest apartment buildings offering apartments available immediately.

The man introduced himself as Barry Weinstein and smiled. "You certainly know what you want," he said.

"Yes," I said, lowering the faceplate on my armor. "I do."

We got into a cab and drove to the high-rise buildings on York Avenue and 72nd Street. I couldn't believe my eyes. I looked at the brand new building thirty-five stories high and thought for sure we could never afford to live there. Barry must have sensed my shock. "Actually, the apartment you're seeing is not as expensive as you might think. The apartments get more expensive the higher you go." There was a big fountain in front of it, and there was a doorman standing at a little podium inside the lobby, which had a polished stone floor that echoed as I walked in my spiked heels. "Mornin', Joe," said Barry when the doorman came out to open the car door. "I'm takin' this young lady here up to see 2245."

When we got out on the twenty-second floor, everything smelled brand new. The apartment had a balcony with a view of the East River. "You'll see that this one-bedroom has a parquet floor, lots of closet space, and all the modern appliances in the kitchen, includin' a garbage disposal," he said, turning it on. "And this is your security system here," he said, pointing to a speaker with a button on the wall. "Anyone wants to come up, they gotta go through Joe first, and he'll buzz up here and tell you who it is." He took me out in the hallway and showed me the garbage chute and the mail chute. "Laundry room is on the basement level. So you use this here." Barry showed me a pullout door with a sign above it saying, "Laundry Chute."

"You got soap and bleach down in the laundry room for ten cents a pack, and you can use the carts to bring it back up. Oh, and you can go up to the roof anytime you want and use the pool. It's an indoor pool, but there's a rooftop garden to walk around in when the weather's good."

"How much?" I asked, afraid to hear. "Four-fifty a month, and if you take it today, I can waive the security deposit for ya."

"Okay," I said. "But I can't take it today. My mother is in the ICU." I worried he would tell someone. "The apartment is for her, and she has to sign the check." I extended my spine for courage.

"Oh . . . geez, I'm sorry," he said. "How 'bout I wait 'til tomorra'?. Can ya do it then?"

I told him I could and hoped Penelope would be conscious enough to sign a check. If not, I would just have to forge her signature. Then I could tell the social worker I had a place and not be lying, as I'd been doing every time she peered around the corner of the hospital room and asked how things were going with the new place. As we drove back to his office, I calculated whether we could afford it, given the amount of money Gardiner sent each month. "Eight hundred fifty dollars per month. So if we spent four-fifty on rent, we'd still have four hundred left for phone and food and stuff," I thought. We could sell the house in Duxbury. And the Ford Mustang . . . it was parked somewhere around the hotel, and we could sell that. I needed to find a way to get money fast. As soon as I got back to the hotel, I changed out of the hot clothes I wore and wondered why women wore ridiculous clothing like pantyhose and high heels when it was ninety million degrees. I looked in the closet and found Penelope's pocketbook and rummaged for the checkbook. The pocketbook was another gift from Fishballs, a huge, shiny, leather, saddlebag-looking thing that could hold a lot of crap. I decided I'd better bring the whole thing to the hospital. I put on my shorts and tennis shoes for the long walk back to Mount Sinai. I walked fast up Fifth Avenue chanting, "Please make her be awake, please make her be awake." Each landmark, now so familiar, encouraged me on. "Phase one complete," I said when I passed the Sherry-Netherland Hotel, then The Pierre. I always hoped I might run into Cher coming out of The Pierre, where she had a penthouse. If I ran into her, my plan was to tell her that I loved every single Bob Mackie gown she wore and that she had the best belly button on the planet. Then I passed Jackie Onassis's house. "Phase two complete," I said. After the final phase, the Metropolitan Museum of Art and then the Guggenheim Museum, my journey would end under the blue canopy of the Klingenstein Pavilion. "Four, please," I told the elevator man, who recognized me and tipped his hat.

Penelope had been moved out of ICU that afternoon, but the nasogastric tube wasn't out yet. She was awake, and she could listen, and she could write even with the IV needle in the top of her right hand.

"Ma . . . I found an apartment. We have to stay in New York 'cuz the social worker said you'd need to stay for a while, maybe a few months." I was talking so fast that she put her hand up for me to slow down. "Okay, so I found this apartment . . ."

Penelope wrote, "Hotel?"

"Ed said I have to move out, and tonight is my last night," I said, swallowing.

Penelope's face looked startled. She wrote, "Why?"

I shrugged. "He said he had to go to Hyannis Port, and he didn't want me there anymore."

"Oh shit," she rasped through the tube. Tears welled in her eyes.

"Mom . . . Mummy, it's okay, but I need to have money. Do we have any money? We need four hundred fifty dollars."

She rolled her eyes and wrote, "Pocketbook in closet at hotel."

"No, I brought it. I have the checkbook."

Penelope smiled and wrote, "Good girl. Call Gardy. Tell him to wire $$. I will give you blank check for rent. Hope does not bounce. Ha ha."

"He hasn't returned my phone calls when I've called him from here using the credit card," I told her. "Why would he talk to me now, especially if I'm asking him for money?"

Penelope wrote, "When that fucking bitch Sammie answers his phone, don't tell her it's you. Change your voice and do a nasally accent. Tell her you're a social worker."

When I called, Sammie answered the phone, and I lost my nerve and couldn't fake a voice. I was next to Penelope's bed. Just the thought of calling Gardiner caused a rush of fear. Sammie had answered the phone at his office in Squaw Valley. I felt her hatred when I asked to speak with my father. Sammie always told me I ought to know better than to call him at work; he was so busy and it was disruptive. I knew that he worked at his other office on certain days and tried to call him on those days. He was always nicer to me when Sammie wasn't around to eavesdrop. But this couldn't wait until another day.

"Hello, Sammie? It's me, Kimball," I hiccupped. "May I please speak with my dad? It's really important."

I had been taught good telephone manners, and I tried to use extra good manners with Sammie so she would let me talk to him.

"I'll see if he's busy." Long sigh. "I'm going to put you on hold, okay, hon?" she said curtly.

I squeezed my eyes shut and prayed, "Please, please God, let him talk to me, pleeeeease!"

Penelope rolled her eyes and wrote, "Should have faked nasally accent."

I was on hold for a long time, probably because Sammie was yelling at him, but he finally picked up and was not pleased that I was calling with yet another Penelope emergency, which always included asking him for money. I swallowed my humiliation and the familiar feeling of being the wart that kept growing on the face of his new life, but we needed the money. His irritation eased into kindness, but he was rushed. I breathed a sigh a relief when he agreed to send extra money by wire. He said he had been talking to the doctors attending to Penelope, and he knew the seriousness of the situation. Still, I knew that he wished Penelope and I would just go away. I wished he would drop everything and rescue me. I wouldn't beg; begging made him angry. I could tell that when he did call me, and he always cut the calls short when he sensed there was room for me to beg. I could sound fine. Sensible and stoic. If it was just money and not his time, he would be okay. If I wanted more, the thread would be severed, and he would be unreachable. I was business-like and told him to send the wire to the hospital cashier. I brought Penelope the checkbook, and she signed a check. I filled in the rest, glad I didn't have to forge the signature. I told Penelope I had to get going so I could get to Barry's before five o'clock. I would bring the lease back tomorrow for Penelope to sign.

When I got to the management company and delivered the check to Barry, I felt as if I'd captured the moon. We had a home. Now my trips back and forth that day to Mount Sinai seemed to fly as I became thoroughly engaged in the project of securing the apartment. I spent every step along Fifth Avenue planning how we could get money by selling our house in Duxbury and then selling the car. I remembered the real estate agent, Dot, in Duxbury who had sold us our house, where we'd only lived for a few months before getting marooned in New York. Penelope and Dot had gotten to be good friends, talking about good pewter and duck decoys whenever she came over to the house. I knew Dot wouldn't give me the brush-off just because I was only fourteen.

After another trip back to the hospital with the lease and then back to Barry's office, my legs ached. I only had one more night in the hotel, which meant one last opportunity to make phone calls. I called Dot and told her the story. "My mother says we have to sell the house in Duxbury or we can't afford to live here."

"What do you want to do with all the furniture?" Dot asked. I thought we would do what we had done when we'd lived in Laguna Beach and had to move east. "Call Bekins, I guess."

"It'll be really expensive if they have to come and pack everything," Dot said. "Tell your mother I'll work on a plan. Don't you worry."

I was relieved to hear someone tell me not to worry. I knew Penelope would insist on having all those ancient pieces of uncomfortable furniture shipped to New York from Duxbury. She loved colonial antiques. The colonial people must have enjoyed being uncomfortable. I thought about telling Penelope it would be impossible and that we'd have to buy all new furniture. Comfortable furniture.

I needed to get a phone put in and called New York Telephone. In my most sophisticated, grown-up voice, I gave instructions and insisted it had to be installed immediately, but my persuasiveness wasn't enough. It would be two days, which meant I would be all alone in an unfurnished apartment with no phone and no television. And I thought about beds and all the stuff we would need for cooking. I called Barry for advice about getting a bed. The social worker wouldn't be satisfied unless I could at least show her a place with a bed.

As it turned out, Barry had a friend in the mattress business who could get me a king-sized bed delivered for two hundred fifty bucks. "I need to get another check from my mother," I told him.

"You'd better get cash," he said. "He ain't gonna take an out-of-state check. Come back to my office, and we can go to my bank."

Another trip from Mount Sinai to Barry's office. I was beginning to wear a path in the concrete. After I'd completed my transaction with Barry at the bank, he called his friend about the mattress. "Yeah, I got it, Lou. So can you deliver the beds to 1345 York in, say . . . three days?" He looked at me and I nodded. The phone would be in by then, and I would only have to sleep there two nights without a bed or a phone. The television seemed more important than either of them.

After Barry dropped me off at the hotel, I went up to the room to spend my final night. I surveyed the room while the dogs looked worried. Two dogs now, not just Patience, the nervous Viszla. When we had bought the house in Duxbury, Penelope had decided she needed another dog and that it would be a miniature dachshund just like Pretzel, her first dachshund. Penelope called the breeder and got a female. She named her Buttercup after another Gilbert and Sullivan opera character from *H.M.S. Pinafore*.

"How am I going to get all this crap to the apartment?" I asked the dogs.

They wagged their tails looking hopeful and enthusiastic. There was no way I could walk, and a cab would cost at least five bucks, which I couldn't spare. Ed was leaving the next day, and I couldn't ask him for money. I decided to go back to Mount Sinai and see about cashing a check there where everyone knew me. Then, feeling the ache in my legs, I changed my mind and began packing instead.

The dogs hated the packing ritual; it always meant a terrifying wait to see if they would be going to go to the kennel or included in the journey. I was feeling excited and energized with my new plan and felt renewed determination to make it all work out. I had the television on to keep me company while I packed. The dogs climbed up on the bed and attempted to sit on the suitcases to make sure they weren't going to be left behind.

Early the next morning, I went to the hospital and hoped I could cash a check for enough money to get a taxi and some food. I was ecstatic when I went to Penelope's room, and she showed me a check from Gardiner. She wrote a note telling me to go to the cashier's office and cash it. We had no bank account in New York yet, which meant I would be carrying cash to Barry for the rent. I could use the rest for taxi fare and food.

"I don't know why your father is so cheap . . . bastard," she wrote.

I took the check to the hospital cashier, who eyed me suspiciously and demanded to know my mother's room number before she would cash it. "Four twenty-three," I said, praying she wouldn't ask me any more questions.

Back at the Berkshire, Mel the bellman loaded the bags on his cart. I looked at the room where I'd spent the past three weeks, and it seemed like a lifetime had passed. I hoped I'd cleaned the dog pee stains enough so they wouldn't be able to tell, but it was so pungent, especially on hot days. I was so used to everything we owned smelling like dog pee. In fact, the whole city of New York smelled like dog pee on hot, humid summer days. Mel loaded the bags into the trunk of the taxi, and I climbed into the back with the dogs, who were still worried about the kennel.

"Goodbye, miss. Best of luck to you and your mother," said Mel comfortingly. Penelope had always stopped to chat with Joe when she had taken the dogs out for walks, and he liked her.

"Thanks a lot, Mel. For everything," I said, feeling a lump in my throat. This whole thing was feeling really scary all of a sudden.

In the new apartment, with nothing but suitcases and dogs, the space looked huge. It echoed without any furniture or carpeting or anything on the bone-white walls. At least there was air conditioning, and it was cool. My clothes stuck to me after two trips up the elevator with all the bags. I wished I had television. I had a long way to go before the place would be habitable. There was a little grocery store across 72nd. Maybe it would seem homier if I had food.

The Food Mart was family owned. Every aisle was packed to the ceiling with almost everything I could think of. And like almost every store in New York, they delivered. I indulged in some of my favorite magazines, now preferring *Vogue* and *Harper's Bazaar* to the teenybopper magazines I used to obsess over.

Once I'd carried my groceries up to the apartment, fed the dogs, and put the food away, I would have to walk them, and then it would be time to go back to the hospital, which would require planning a new route. It was a straight shot up Fifth Avenue from the Berkshire hotel, exactly fifty blocks. And they were short blocks between the numbered streets, but the apartment building was five long blocks east of Fifth Avenue, so even though I was almost twenty blocks closer, it took almost as long to walk. I would have to cross all the nasty streets Penelope had told me to stay away from: First Avenue, Second Avenue, Third Avenue, Lexington; then the luxurious townhouses of Park Avenue, Madison Avenue, and, finally, Fifth Avenue. From there, it would only be thirty blocks to the hospital.

Then, later, I didn't want to leave Penelope's hospital room, knowing I would be going back to an empty apartment with no phone, no bed, and no television, but I had to get back before dark. If I could just make it two nights, then the phone would be hooked up and the bed would get there. I hurried down the sidewalks, stopping only once to buy a hot pretzel as the light faded. The dogs were hysterical when I got there and in need of a pee break. I noticed that some New Yorkers brought pooper scoopers along on their walks, but most just let their dogs pee and crap on sidewalks or on the curb. The signs said, "Please curb your dog," which meant people should let them poop off the curb on the street so the street cleaners could clean it up. The whole city still stunk like dog crap.

The night went on and on. I strained for the light. This was almost as bad as the night after Penelope's surgery, but at least then I'd had television to keep me company. That night might have been worse because Penelope had been so close to dying. It was hard to say; there had been so many nights of keeping her alive by staying awake. Television kept death away, and as long the television was on, I didn't feel so alone. She wasn't in danger of dying right now, but still, I was enveloped and almost crushed by the silence in the empty apartment. I made a bed out of Penelope's overcoat and all the soft clothing I could gather. There was no other voice but the one inside that kept telling me not to go to sleep. I held the dogs close to me and buried my face in the wool of Penelope's overcoat that smelled so much of her perfume. Patience licked the tears on my face as I tried to think of ways to feel less afraid. It was such a long wait until dawn. Even if Penelope wasn't teetering on the edge of death anymore, she could still die. I panicked thinking of what might happen if I got sick in the night. There was no phone and I didn't know anybody, and nobody cared anyway.

I sobbed out loud while the thoughts whirled faster and faster. What had I done? Why wouldn't Gardiner come and rescue me or talk to me? I let myself feel it, all the stinging, burning pain of missing my father. Once, he had been all mine, and I hadn't been afraid to ask for anything. Once, I'd had him on demand, and he never would say no to me when I asked to go along with him, or asked him to sing with me, listen to me read out loud, or play hide and seek with me. And then he was gone.

The heat of grief rushed through my chest and into my stomach; the heavy ache of longing soaked into every cell and carved out a nest. I cried big sobs until I drifted, exhausted, into sleep. When I awoke, I saw the pink light of dawn in the window and felt elation that I'd slept the night away into daylight again. I felt a surge of power. Today was a new day, and the sun was out. Today, I would make another plan. Only one more night, and then I would have a bed and a telephone.

I looked around at the empty room and thought about how to resolve the problem of getting towels and blankets, pillows and sheets, cooking utensils and dishes and a television, a survival tool I could not do without, especially on the long nights when I couldn't get Penelope to go to sleep. I knew every old MGM movie ever made and knew the words to every Judy Garland song. Television was my company, the guardian that kept death away in the darkness of night. I was so desperate I thought about spending what little food money I had on a television. It would be another month until the next support check. The furniture from the Duxbury house wouldn't come until the house sold and we had money to pay the movers.

I had my Saks Fifth Avenue card. Saks had a linen and bath shop and a kitchen shop. Maybe it would work to buy what I needed for the apartment, but I worried that Saks would try to call Ed and verify the charges. It was worth a try. I put on my Liza Minnelli outfit, a sure way of convincing anyone I was older than fourteen.

36

MAKING A HOME

A TINY SALESWOMAN WITH PINKISH RED HAIR and black spectacles hanging on a chain around her neck wasted no time when I walked in the door of the linen and bath shop. "I need to buy household items for my new apartment," I said in my most authoritative voice. "I need sheets, towels, blankets, pillows, and dishes."

The saleslady looked at me suspiciously and put on her spectacles. "And how will you be taking care of the bill, dear?" she asked.

I became the warrior again in full armor. "I have my card," I said, looking the little pink-haired lady straight in her suspicious eyes. I fingered some pillowcases with eyelet trim.

"My name is Flo. Will you be taking or sending?" she asked, brightening up and adjusting her facial expression from suspicion to delight. "If you have it sent, you don't pay tax," she said, rubbing her arthritic hands together.

"Okay, I'll have it sent," I said, feeling relieved that I could at least avoid that cost. The only problem was that the delivery address on the card was Ed's hotel. "Actually, I guess I'll just take it with me," I said.

I had to come up with a plan for hauling the stuff home on foot in the heat in high heels. I told Flo I would be making a few trips by taxi. I would take all the stuff I could carry in one trip and then wait a few hours and come back for the rest.

I lost myself in selecting the beautiful bedclothes, blankets, pillows, and towels, forgetting about how much it would all cost. I hadn't even started on the kitchen yet. What if they called Ed and he told them to take my card away? Maybe I would be banished from the store forever for being a devious little thief, or maybe even arrested. Worse, the social worker would find out, and I'd be placed in some foster home.

I excused myself and went to the ladies' room to calm down. *So far so good*, I reminded myself. I would tell Ed and make it up to him somehow. I thought about how I would open the doors of the bedroom to show the social worker the beautifully decorated the bedroom and how the social worker would say I was amazing. That thought kept me buzzing to and from Saks in the sweltering heat, loaded down with bedding, with my feet on fire.

On my final trip, I stopped to look inside of St. Patrick's Cathedral across the street from Saks. It was so beautiful and sacred-looking; I wanted to go inside even if I wasn't Catholic. Maybe nobody would check. I followed people wandering in and tried to look as if I belonged. The inside was breathtaking with its vaulted ceilings and pipes for the pipe organ soaring upward. And it was so peaceful and cool. I looked at the rows of beautiful, dark, wooden pews and the candles lit on little tables. If there was a God, I thought, surely he would be here. People were kneeling in prayer at the pews, but I wasn't sure if I should kneel. I sat on the edge of a pew in the very back, poised to flee in case someone came up and asked me if I was Catholic. I would have to say no and admit I wasn't anything. If I *thought* a prayer instead of saying it out loud, maybe it would still count, and God would hear me. I just thought really hard and mouthed the words of the only prayer I knew: "The Lord is my shepherd; I shall not want. He maketh me to lie down in green pastures . . ." Then I added, "God, please let the social worker be happy about the apartment and not take my mother away, and please let Ed forgive me for all the money I'm spending."

I knew little about the Catholic Church, only that my friends across the street in Squaw Valley seemed to have to go to Our Lady of the Snows almost every day. Their mother would interrupt a really good game of gas station or playing rodeo to tell them it was time for catechism. On Sundays, they were at church the whole morning in their best dresses, suits, and ties, and enough Brylcreem to paste a house together.

I had only gone to church when the Chisholms had, to our little church in the trees. I had gone so I could go visit Teacher Elenita from our old nursery school. She'd taught Sunday school, and we had sung songs, colored, and eaten graham crackers and juice. I went to church once with Grannie when we visited the farm in Williamstown. Grannie said we were Episcopalian, which seemed exactly like being Catholic with all the standing up, sitting down, and saying things that I couldn't understand. Grannie told me just to watch her and not say a word. I watched her out of the corner of my eye, not daring even to turn my head to look at anyone or anything, and matched her movements, kneeling when she knelt, standing when she stood, and trying to mouth the words to hymns I didn't know.

After spending what I thought might be enough time praying to God, I went across the street to the Saks Fifth Avenue kitchen shop to commence sinning again. I needed pots, pans, dishes, and eating utensils. I searched for price labels on the plates. One plate cost as much as the entire set of Corelle Livingware I had bought at the Duxbury hardware store. Flo led me through displays of beautiful dishes complete with soup tureens, salad bowls, and serving platters, all in sets to serve eight. My terror escalated again as Flo began writing up the sales ticket. I bought two sets of Limoges china, which was insane. I tried to rationalize and escape guilt by telling myself that I was justified in abusing the credit card when Ed had deserted me. If Ed hated me forever, I'd just have to deal with it, but right now, I had to buy pots and pans, and the only kind they had were copper. There were only two pots and two pans in the set, but we never seemed to cook much other than canned soup, so it wouldn't matter.

Then I saw it. A tiny little television set with a radio. I pounced on it, not even looking at the price. "Can you add this, too, Flo?"

She smiled, her glasses sliding down her nose. She was breaking a sweat writing up all my stuff. "Okey-dokey, dawling," she said, sticking her pencil behind her ear. "Will that be all today?"

I thought. *Can opener? Nope, have to get that at the Food Mart. Spatula? Nope. Food Mart for that too. Sharp knives. Yup.* Flo grabbed a set of knives, which was probably a million dollars, and wrapped it up. *Coffee pot? Yup.*

Flo put a weird-looking one on the counter that had no plug-in thing. "It's a filter pot," explained Flo, getting the filters. "Much better than percolating." I shrugged.

Finally, I was finished for the day, breathless and all lit up inside as if I'd just pulled off a bank heist and was looking for the getaway car. There was no getaway car, and I faced at least three trips on foot from Fifth and 50th Street all the way to York and 72nd. Forty-four blocks round trip, not including the really long blocks.

I wanted to make my trips with all the bags and boxes look easy, as if I were having a good time, but I wished Penelope hadn't drummed it into my head that well-bred people don't take buses and subways. There were plenty of well-bred-looking people getting on buses and going down the stairs to the subway, and their feet probably weren't on fire from wearing the high heels. Adrenaline had gotten me this far, but my body was protesting.

I made it home with the last of my household items and then couldn't stop unwrapping, organizing, and putting everything together.

The next day, I went back to Saks for a final sweep to make sure I had everything. The social worker had asked if I had a blender at our house. "Due to your mother's dietary restrictions, she will need to be eating bland foods for a while—no meat, no cheese, no raw vegetables," she said.

I thought of Penelope's usual diet, which was mostly soup, turkey sandwiches, Sara Lee cheesecake, yogurt, and warm milk and honey with whiskey. "I can't eat anything that isn't the consistency of snot," she said one morning when she was trying to eat hospital Cream of Wheat.

"Maybe we can put Sara Lee in the blender," I suggested.

Penelope stifled a laugh. "Don't make me laugh," she said. "I'll tear the stitches open and my intestines will be on the floor."

Flo was on me like a magnet when I walked into Saks for a blender and eating utensils. "Hi, Flo," I said, remembering one item I'd overlooked last time. "I need utensils for eating and a blender."

"I happen to have a blendah with five different settings," she said. "And would you prefer sterling or stainless for the utensils?" She rubbed those gnarled hands together and peered at me over her spectacles.

"Stainless will be fine, I'm sure," I said, knowing that even the stainless would likely cost enough to pay a month's rent. I was already so scared about how much I'd spent that I wondered if it would be easier never to call Ed again and just be his enemy for life. He wouldn't know where we lived or how to call us. The guilt would be pretty heavy. And what if he found me anyway? Would he be so mad that he'd put me in jail for using his credit card? I was caught up in my horrible fantasies until Flo's nasal Queens accent interrupted. "Dawling . . . would you like this on your account? And is this a take or a send?"

"Oh . . . I'll take it with me, and yes, it's on the same account, and I'll take that blender, too," I heard myself say, so crushed by my guilt that it hardly even mattered anymore. There was a loud, canary-yellow dinette set on sale. We didn't have a dinette set or any kind of table to eat on, not even in Duxbury. We always ate on the bed or on the floor. "Can I have that delivered to a different address? It's a . . . gift . . . for . . . a, um . . . a friend."

"Sure, sure. Yeah, but there's a charge, and it will take a few days," said Flo.

"That's all right," I said, calculating when the nosey social worker would be coming to inspect. "Will the delivery address show up on the bill?" I asked, hoping I wouldn't arouse suspicion.

"No, just on the delivery man's paperwork," Flo said, shoving the sales slip into the tube that got sucked down to the bowels of the store where they processed all sales. There were no cash registers anywhere in the store. Every transaction was done using a tube that got sucked by a central vacuum system to some other place, and then sent back with a receipt and your change if you paid cash.

After that final trip, I vowed I would never go to Saks again, not even for a pair of underpants. "I had to do this," I repeated to myself. I couldn't make it up to Ed other than to bake cookies for him every day.

37

Orphan Lies

W HEN IT WAS DELIVERED, I MADE up the bed with the comforter Flo had said was hand-embroidered in Switzerland, with tiny flowers in different colors. The dogs were watching, waiting for the opportunity to jump up on the bed and try out the new comforter and mountains of down pillows. "You are not allowed on *this* bed," I told them, knowing that as soon as Penelope got home, they *would* be allowed on the bed. Penelope always said dogs weren't selfish and rude like humans, particularly adolescents. Finally, I took a taxi to Mount Sinai and brought her home. The social worker had come to the apartment and given her approval in the days before Penelope was discharged, and I'd had everything in order in the nick of time. When Penelope came in the door of the new apartment, the dogs went insane. She looked at the bedroom and then at me. "I used Ed's Saks card." I swallowed and began to shake inside.

"Oh . . . dear. Ohhh, dear, dear me," she said, trying to stifle a laugh. "Dearie, dearie me . . . Well . . . I guess we'll have to find a way to tell him when he comes back. But it is beautiful. What a great job you've done!" I wallowed in every word of her praise, so thirsty for her approval.

Penelope had been in the hospital almost a month, and she still couldn't eat anything but hot cereal and soup. The scar looked like a jagged railroad track running east to west across her upper abdomen, and the wire stitches underneath the surface scar looked like a barbed wire fencing. "Don't they poke you and hurt every time you breathe?" I asked, rubbing vitamin E cream gently over the scar.

"It's all numb around the scar. I don't feel anything," she said, easing into the brand new bed. She was exhausted just from walking from the lobby to the elevator. She weighed ninety pounds and her skin looked transparent.

It was September, and we had the inevitable discussion about school. I should have been going into my freshman year of high school, but I had no inkling of how to go or where to go in this huge city that had hundreds of schools. I didn't want to go anyway, and Penelope didn't want me to go. "You'll learn more here with me anyway," she said, lighting up a Benson & Hedges. "You're my reason for living. In fact, you're my *only* reason, and I like having you with me." She offered me the pack and I took one. I'd been smoking her cigarettes, having given up Marlboros when I'd gotten away from the peer pressure to take up the brown filters. Being her only reason for living didn't seem so difficult when we had fun and smoked our cigarettes with the tortoise-shell cigarette holders I'd bought for us at Saks along with the dishes.

Ed was due back any day, and I felt like hiding under the bed and plugging my ears every time the phone rang. Penelope said it was time I came clean. "Just be honest. After all, he did just leave you when he went to Hyannis Port. And he can certainly afford it," she said. She seemed so comfortable just taking things she felt entitled to; I never felt entitled to anything. I'd taken only what I'd needed, and still I could barely live with myself. When the guilt reached critical mass, I called him. I launched into a confession and finished it by telling him I would visit him every day and bake cookies as often as he wanted. And then, silence.

"Well, honey, don't you think that was a little bit taking advantage?" His voice was kind.

"Yes." I closed my eyes tightly, trying not to cry and grit my teeth as I waited for the ax to fall and cut me off forever. "We'll talk about it some more after I look at the bill," he said, "but I'm going to ask you not to use the card anymore for now."

I couldn't believe he was so polite. "Oh no! I won't, I won't, I promise not to use it ever again," I said. "Are you still going to be my friend?"

"Well, sure, honey." He laughed uneasily.

I didn't feel reassured. I felt like an ugly stray dog he'd fed out of generosity. He had only wanted to feed me a little food maybe one time, but instead, I'd kept showing up wanting more. A real pain in the ass, that's what I was. He tried to shoo me away, but I wouldn't leave him alone and became a nuisance. I felt doomed to be that forever, entering people's lives, pooping all over their carpets, bringing fleas and worms into their pristine lives. I caused mayhem and drama they didn't want. Ed's life had been so simple before we came along. What was meant to be a brief visit had turned into a life and death ordeal. I felt his need to escape it all; I wanted to escape, too, but there was no way out for me.

As the days passed in the apartment above York Avenue, Penelope's polymyositis returned and perched like a raven over her body. Steroid craziness liked to come out at night in unpredictable explosions, which included rage at almost anything at any time, crying jags, and sleeplessness. The narcotics and sleeping pills took her into fugues of letter writing, mostly to Gardiner—pages and pages of scrawl, burning cigarette after cigarette. She sometimes dropped off for a few minutes, forgetting it between her fingers. The Swiss, flowered quilt and the matching sheets had burn marks. I learned to watch and predict her weather patterns like a human barometer. I stayed awake watching old movies almost until dawn to make sure Penelope would stay asleep. She staggered out of the bedroom, weaving her way to the kitchen, where I sat by the window watching movies. It was time for her to eat, but letting her make her own food would mean cleaning up mayonnaise and mustard smeared on the counters and the refrigerator handle and spilled soup all over the floor. I steered her back to bed and told her to stay there. And then I would make the soup or the tea or thaw the Sara Lee cheesecake, sticking it in the oven for a few minutes. I plucked lit cigarettes from her hand when she nodded off.

Written in her narcotic stupors, her long, wandering letters to Gardiner began with the greeting, "Dear L. P. Cat," an abbreviated form of his old nickname, Lonesome Polecat. She filled pages upon page with nonsensical, run-on sentences, endearments, veiled insults, and criticisms, and she insisted upon reading the letters out loud to me. She slurred and cried as she read, making me irritable and impatient.

"Don't you think it's time to go back to bed now?" I'd ask, and her rage would be unleashed.

"Don't you tell me what to do!" she'd scold, slurring and slobbering as I tried to lead her back to bed. "You're just a fucking adolescent, don't forget."

"I know, I know," I soothed and tried to cover her tiny little body with something other than just her undershirt.

Once I put her back to bed, I prayed that she'd stay there, but once she got started, it usually went on for hours. She'd weave back out to the kitchen where I was watching television. "You know," she slurred, "you're so selfish . . . you're just like your father, who, by the way, was one of the most selfish men I ever met. You two should live together. I think you'd make a *grand* couple."

"Ma, please just go back to bed," I pleaded.

"And you're evil, too," she said, coming toward me wearing only her stained undershirt. I rolled my eyes, and Penelope caught it. "Well, aren't you just the little queen!" She did a little dance step and nearly fell. "I am so sorry to *bother* you, your *highness*."

I crouched against the wall and looked away. "Yes, you are bothering me. Now *go* to bed," I said, my irritation scratching at my lungs, wanting to fly out. I got up and took her arm to lead her back to bed.

She began to cry and wailed, "Please don't treat me like a child!" as her tears mixed with drool. "I can't help it, I'm *sick*!" Then she reached for yet another cigarette, which would be lit and then left to burn another hole in the stool she used for a bedside table.

"Oh, *God*, I hate this," I muttered to myself, hoping Penelope wouldn't hear as I left the room, wishing I could just tie her up to make her stay in bed. It wasn't until four or five a.m. when she finally fell asleep, and I could finally relax. I didn't want to be her reason to live. For a tiny second, I wished she had died at Mount Sinai. I would be home with Gardiner, and he would choose me over Sammie. Then I took it back and hoped God wouldn't punish my evilness by killing Penelope. I coveted my time alone in the kitchen nook by the window, where I could look out onto the East River or lose myself in MGM musicals and old movies until I felt safe enough to go to sleep, usually not until after five in the morning. On one of my outings, I spotted a huge book called *The New York Times Guide to the Best 1,000 Movies Ever Made*, an anthology containing the names of every movie and every actor since the beginning of the industry, along with the critics' reviews. I chose a time when Penelope was in a good mood to beg her for the money to buy it.

Penelope was always in a good mood when she had to go see Dr. Mercer. It was her opportunity to shine, like Gloria Swanson in *Sunset Boulevard* when she said, "I'm ready for my close-up now, Mr. DeMille." I never thought to tell Dr. Mercer about Penelope's bizarre behavior, or that she played around with her medication like a kid sorting through M&M's, taking more of a certain color or eating all the peanut ones first. I associated addiction with derelicts who slept behind garbage cans in their own vomit, or hippies who shot heroin—young people, not older women, and certainly not mothers. I would wait for hours in the waiting room, and then we always went to the drugstore. Which, after Dr. Mercer's office, was my mother's second favorite place to go.

I wondered if perhaps Dr. Mercer was married and whether he was listed in the Manhattan phone directory. I thought that even if he was married, his wife might be ugly, and he might be willing to leave her and marry me. I scheduled an appointment with him, telling his nurse that I was suffering from insomnia and headaches. I wanted to make it difficult for him not to fall madly in love with me and take me away with him to Connecticut or the beach. I dressed up in my best Liza Minnelli outfit and spent an hour on my makeup, which included spiky false eyelashes; fake, red-painted fingernails; and bright red lipstick. "That ought to do it," I said, modeling for Penelope.

"He'll dump her for you, no question about it," she said.

I looked at Dr. Mercer seductively from the exam table, crossing my legs and dangling a high heel from my big toe. He looked at his clipboard and asked without any rapture or lust, "So, what seems to be the problem?"

My power as a seductress evaporated, and I stammered out something about not being able to sleep.

"How old are you?" he asked, scribbling in his chart and ignoring my crossed legs and the shoe on the end of my toe.

"Almost fifteen," I said, hoping he wouldn't pin me down on my exact age, which was fourteen and a half.

"When do you go to bed?" he asked.

"Well, ummm, I like to stay up late, so I sleep late."

"Any coffee or tea at night?" he asked, still scribbling.

"Maybe a little," I admitted, not telling him about the entire pot of coffee I would drink at night in order to maintain my vigil over Penelope. I hoped he wouldn't ask me about school. Penelope and I told anyone who asked that I had a private tutor, which of course was a huge lie.

I didn't tell him that I had to be awake when Penelope got up to pee, to pick her up when she passed out on the toilet and fell off. I didn't tell him that I was so afraid Penelope would die that I wished I didn't have to be alone with her. Or that Penelope got really angry when she was all fucked up and would inevitably threaten to kill herself or send me back to my father, who didn't even want me anyway. And I didn't tell him about the night I had really wanted to die and taken two or three of Penelope's Seconal sleeping pills. I hadn't had the courage to take any more than that, and I had been pretty sure I would just sleep for a long time and give Penelope a good scare. Teach her a lesson. She'd be sorry. Penelope often offered me Valium as if she were offering me a piece of Godiva chocolate. "Would you like a Valium? *I'm* going to take one," she'd say after completing a trip to the drugstore, as if it were a Himalayan expedition. I would take the Valium in a gesture of camaraderie, but they made me too sleepy, and I'd miss all the late-night movies, not to mention Penelope falling off the toilet or trying to make ham sandwiches. After I had taken the Seconal, I had been afraid I might die and told Penelope.

"Will I die?" I had hoped Penelope could behave like a mother just this once.

"No, you'll just feel like you want to die," Penelope had said reassuringly. I had wanted her to care about whether I would die. She had shaken me awake fifteen hours later, and the room had appeared barely in focus. She'd made me drink several glasses of water and then taken me outside to walk it off, as if I'd been a drunk. I'd felt carsick, like the time I had to ride in the back seat of Daddy Roy's Rambler with the heat on and all the windows shut on a winding road. I had made a mental note that if I wanted to kill myself in the future, I would not take Seconal.

Our furniture arrived from Duxbury after the house sold. I was not pleased to see Penelope's uncomfortable antiques. I wanted soft furniture and palm plants, not duck decoys, old rocking chairs, preacher's benches, and the cranberry scoops we used for magazine racks. But it was better than nothing, and it filled the empty living room. New York was getting colder as Christmas approached. I had no idea how or where to get a tree, and we had no money to spare for presents. Somehow, the money always ran out, and Penelope was always sending me off to the Bankers Trust to explain why all the checks were bouncing and plead for a grace period until the alimony check arrived. I knew every drugstore on the Upper East Side, and every pharmacist knew me. I was always running here or there with a bad check to pick up Penelope's medication. When I went with her, it was like a Broadway performance at the drugstore. "Oh my *God*, you have no *idea* how *horrible* life would be without your *exquisite* service, George. You've made life *so* much *easier*, and my pain is better already!" she would say to the pharmacist in her Katherine Hepburn Boston accent as he gazed lovingly at her beautiful blue eyes with their black eyelashes, and her perfect white dentures, and her tiny little body dressed perfectly in gray, flannel Brooks Brothers pants and cashmere sweaters, with a scarf tucked at the neck. Her black hair had threads of gray running through it, and it was thick and long. She was still beautiful despite being so bony. Even when she'd had butt cheeks, they had been small, but now there was nothing at all.

On her better days, we dressed up and went out, maybe to have lunch at the Sherry-Netherland or to Elizabeth Arden for a facial we couldn't afford. Penelope had a mustache from all the steroids, and Elizabeth Arden offered waxing. "I look like Clark Gable," she said, looking into her magnifying mirror. I savored those good days like a delicious hot fudge sundae.

"Let's go to Fifth Avenue to see the Christmas decorations," Penelope announced. "Lunch at the Sherry, then F.A.O. Schwartz to see the toys. It's what the very chic do for lunch," she explained, penciling her thick Converse eyebrows even blacker than they were already. We dressed up, took a taxi to the Sherry-Netherland, and had a chic lunch of spinach salad, consommé, and espresso with lemon zest. Afterward, Penelope was so exhausted from the outing that we never made it to F.A.O. Schwartz, and she fell asleep in the taxi on the way home.

I saw a Christmas tree lot near the apartment building and remembered the address. It was twenty blocks from the apartment, but if I got a small tree, I could manage to get it home. I asked Penelope for the money, knowing she would write a check to the Food Mart for cash and that it would probably bounce unless money from Gardiner came soon. I remembered the Christmases in Squaw Valley, the ritual with our toboggan, the wool sock hanging on the Franklin stove, and how I had trusted all of it to stay. My sadness transmuted into determination to recreate Christmas amid the gray concrete and horns honking and people who didn't know me and never would know me. I found the plant store where I'd seen the Christmas tree, and it was marked down to five dollars. I hauled the short, bushy tree home, alternating arms when one got tired and began to ache. I looked for ornaments at the drugstore, hoping to recover a feeling that would bring me back to the living room in Squaw Valley. Green and red glass balls and tinsel. And lights, I had to find colored lights. I loved tinsel and put big handfuls of it on the branches, filling all the empty spaces. Penelope got the support check just in the nick of time, two days before Christmas, which meant we could go Christmas shopping at the drugstore.

On Christmas morning, we shared a precious hour as the muted winter sun shone in the bedroom window. We were on the bed with the dogs, surrounded by presents wrapped in drugstore Santa Claus paper. Each little gift was wrapped separately to make it seem like more. Penelope opened gifts of shower caps in pastel green and pink with little bows, and a large bottle of Woolite so she'd stop using the dish soap to wash her underpants and then cursing about how it made her crotch itch, never remembering to put the fucking Woolite on the shopping list. And a five-pack of little footie socks with tassels on the ankles, which she loved wearing to bed to keep her feet warm. I unwrapped three large Snickers bars, my very favorite, second only to Hershey's with almonds, which I broke into squares, held on the tines of a dinner fork, and melted over the gas flame on the stove. And Vitabath shower gel, fake nails and nail polish, more Liza Minnelli false eyelashes, and Liza's newest record. We gave each other facials and pretended we were at Elizabeth Arden. "We really should pluck your eyebrows. You look like Walter Huston." I got the tweezers and the eyebrow brush.

"You certainly will not!" she said indignantly. "These are Converse eyebrows, our trademark, a sign of . . ."

"I know, I know . . . a sign of breeding," I grumbled, trying to trace Penelope's eyes with eyeliner that ran into tiny folds of swollen, papery skin.

"And I think my eyebrows are more Joan Crawford-ish than Walter Huston. He's so old. And his eyebrows are longer than his hair."

After the facials, we went walking with the dogs. The day was clear and bright with enough bite in the air to make it wintery, but not too cold to enjoy. Days like these were so rare, when Penelope seemed like the mother she had been long ago. I was too afraid to let joy in all the way. For dinner, I made pumpkin pie with homemade crust that was like cardboard. The directions said to chill it and then roll it out, but it kept sticking to my makeshift wine-bottle rolling pin. I got impatient with it and smashed it into the pie pan with my hands. We just ate the filling with vanilla ice cream in bed and watched a Christmas special, and then it was time for *Bonanza*. Penelope was in love with Lorne Green, and I was in love with Michael Landon. He wore tight pants, and everything showed.

38

STARTING NEW LIFE

III

W E'D BEEN IN NEW YORK FOR ten months, and Penelope decided city life was not for us. I was playing John Denver's hit record, "Rocky Mountain High," and missing springtime in the mountains, and Penelope decided we should move to the mountains again. She had a friend who lived near Aspen, where John Denver had bought a ranch, and I hoped to meet him and possibly marry him if he would leave his wife. Moving to Ashcroft, Colorado, which was close enough to Aspen, would be the solution to whatever was wrong with life in New York. It was time to start another new life. Penelope was lonely without her friends. Fishballs never visited New York, and Penelope didn't know anyone, except every pharmacist within a fifty-block radius and Dr. Mercer. One of Penelope's closest friends lived in Aspen, and they'd been talking on the phone about horrible husbands and starting new lives. It seemed that Penelope couldn't be in one place for longer than a few months before the need to start a new life struck her again. I loved change and adventure and went to Doubleday to purchase all the *Mobil Travel Guides* I would need to plan the route from New York to Colorado. I really liked starting new lives once every couple of years or so. That way of life had stuck with me, and it seemed like it was always around April. "Northern route or southern?" I asked Penelope through the haze of my new favorite cigarette, Virginia Slims Menthols.

"Let's go more south. The weather will be better. Just keep us out of Kansas and Nebraska if possible."

I plotted the route going south through Virginia and North Carolina, at which point we would turn west. I planned mileage according to what I anticipated Penelope's stamina would tolerate in a day and made sure that each stop had a motel or an inn with at least three stars and would allow dogs. The Holiday Inns were usually the safest. And they usually had room service and pools. Our first stop was Washington, DC, where I selected a hotel with four stars. It was expensive, but Penelope wouldn't take the risk of three stars in a big city.

"I will not stay in some dump on the wrong side of the tracks," she instructed.

After calling Bekins again and scheduling a pickup date, there was another problem to solve. Penelope had sold the Mustang that had gotten us to New York, and we had no car. After careful consideration as to thrift and practicality, Penelope decided to go back to German-made automobiles. However, this time it wasn't going to be a Porsche. "I'm going to buy a Volkswagen Super Beetle," she announced after looking at a color brochure advertising the roomier and more chic version of the old Beetles that had no dashboards, pitiful heating, and apparently no thought given to their drivers' comfort. The new ones had comfier seats with adjustable backs, air conditioning, dashboards, leather upholstery, and AM/FM radios. One could also order custom floor mats to match the interior, which Penelope did.

"Is Gardiner paying for all this?" I asked. We were always so broke. I worried about how Penelope was financing all this.

"Your *father*? Absolutely *not*. It's money from the sale of the house in Duxbury, that *my* father helped us buy. *Your* father had nothing to do with it, unfortunately. He has to support that tart and all her children."

"*Okay* . . . I was just asking, geez," I said, wishing I could claim a different father.

It never failed. Penelope missed road signs and exit ramps until we were lost on some narrow country road where there was no sign of civilization.

It was only a four-hour drive from New York to DC, but it was nine hours until we finally found our way back onto the right turnpike. It was midnight when Penelope made her way to the front desk of the hotel, barely coherent from taking too many Percodans and not having enough food. I was worried. I spent a sleepless night watching Penelope's irregular, labored breathing with long periods between breaths. I shook her awake a couple of times to make sure she wasn't dead. I cried silently for my father and felt sorry for wishing I had a different one, and longed for his comfort as the night wore on. I struggled to stay awake, watching old movies on television and drinking coffee from room service.

Penelope slept until almost noon the next day. The driving had been too much for her and she couldn't move very well, so we stayed another night and left the next morning for Virginia. The plan was to drive until five p.m. and then stop for the night, but we only made it as far as Dumfries before Penelope was in too much pain to drive any longer. She complained that her muscles ached, and the wire stitches beneath her skin from the surgery in New York were painful. It looked like they might actually be beginning to pierce through her flesh. We pulled the forest green VW Super Beetle into the driveway of the Holiday Inn in Dumfries and checked in.

39
NOT AGAIN

WE WERE AT THE DUMFRIES HOLIDAY Inn for about a week, during which time I forgot all about marrying Dr. Mercer and fell in love with Kevin, the front desk clerk, and spent practically every waking hour lingering at the desk. My only breaks were to go to the swimming pool and practice diving in a way that Kevin would notice. I prepared for Kevin's shift each day by spending at least an hour on my makeup and deciding on an outfit to wear. Now fifteen, I was finally filling out a small bra and could find the gentle curve between my waist and hips, if I didn't overindulge in french fries. My hips were boyish like Penelope's, and I fretted about how I looked in a bikini, but I was happy that I had finally started my period and had breasts. I made the most of what I had, using foam enhancements in my little bikini top and making sure to safety pin them inside, as each dive off the diving board could easily dislodge them (as I unfortunately had discovered one day). I had to feel around underwater to make sure they were still in place.

Kevin was my island in an endless, turbulent sea, where there seemed no rest from the constant lashing of waves and storms. I knew in my heart that we'd never make it to Colorado. Penelope was unable to drive even for a couple of hours. The stitches were poking through, oozing blood and pus from the holes in her skin. She found a doctor in a nearby town who put her in the hospital immediately. The polymyositis had come raging back, which meant high doses of steroids for at least a few months. The stitches would have to be removed surgically. I stayed by myself at the Holiday Inn, which was actually a relief. For a few days, I would not have to be on alert for constant mood swings, misunderstood emotions, angry outbursts, and long periods of wondering whether Penelope still loved me. I also knew we couldn't stay in Dumfries forever, but for the time being, I could hang around Kevin as much as I wanted; I could stay up late, eat what I wanted when I wanted, and watch *I Love Lucy* to my heart's content.

Yet, the moments when Penelope and I laughed and talked and enjoyed our little rituals made all the drama disappear. I couldn't stop my hope that one day she would be normal and fun, that all my adolescent flaws would vanish, leaving her no reason to hate me. Gardiner was irritated that I was costing him so much money by staying at the Holiday Inn. "Well, what do you want me to do, Dad?" I said. "Are you going to come back here and help us?"

"No. I can't come back there. There is nothing we can do. I guess you'll just have to stay there until she gets out. Then we'll see."

Fishballs was coming to town. Penelope had called her, and it happened that she had been in New York on business, so she rented a car and drove to Dumfries. I dreaded her arrival. She barely tolerated my existence and treated me like an intruder, an unsightly wart growing more obvious with age. Fishballs might have been helpful in some ways, but she was disagreeable and difficult to talk to, being Swiss, partially deaf, and partially inebriated most of the time. But she was rich, and her money would help. When she arrived, it was in a rented, red Ford Mustang, and she was wearing all her gold jewelry. She'd had all her red suitcases custom made, and she wore her silk scarves tucked into the collars of her men's silk shirts. She always brought her own scotch and, upon check-in, requested a bucket of ice be brought to her room immediately. I was treated in the usual fashion, just like a stray dog that kept showing up and getting underfoot. Fishballs wanted Penelope's undivided attention, to whisk her off to Davos, away from all her poor choices in men. Penelope finally told me that Fishballs had been in love with her ever since they'd met in Vermont back in 1942. Penelope had left Duxbury for Vermont before the ink was dry on her high school diploma. She'd had no intention of following her mother's plan for her, which had included a coming-out party at the Duxbury Yacht Club and meeting her future husband, who had to be a Harvard man. Penelope's sole mission had been to ski and wear pants as much as possible.

Fishballs stayed a week, which felt like a year, until Penelope was out of surgery and stabilized on more steroids to get the disease under control. I was happy to stay another two weeks until Penelope was recovered enough for the next move, which was uncertain at this point. I spent my time adding more layers to my fantasy about marrying Kevin, who had a girlfriend, but I was pretty sure he didn't like her that much. I overheard a conversation between him and Vena, the other desk clerk at the front desk. She rolled her eyes when Kevin was talking about the girlfriend . . . something about being a little slutty.

When I wasn't at the front desk, I passed the time at the swimming pool or in my room reciting scenes from Carson McCullers's play, *The Member of the Wedding*. I could relate to Frankie Adams, who never felt like she was a member of anything. I thought I could attach myself to someone and fix that problem. I wanted to be a part of Kevin's body more than anything. I obsessed over him, worried about every little nuance of our conversations, and without dependable motherly advice, I could only rely on my few shattered fragments in piecing together an understanding of what love seemed to be—frightening, treacherous, mysterious, and unreachable.

40
RETURNING

THE RED MESSAGE LIGHT ON THE wall was blinking when we came back from a trip to the drugstore in Dumfries. I had bought more Love's Fresh Lemon products, and Penelope had restocked her dozens of medications, which now required a whole separate purse. I wanted to have every single item in the Love's Fresh Lemon line. The smell of lemons made me feel beautiful and fresh just like the girl in the commercials.

The red message light changed everything. Penelope's sister Ann had called Gardiner to find out where we were. The message said to call Ann back right away, that it was an emergency. Penelope began to cry and called Ann. I figured it had to be Grandpa, whose emphysema had gotten so bad he'd had to be in a convalescent hospital for about two months. Penelope was sobbing and asking when he'd died and why nobody had called her to tell her he had been getting worse. He'd just died in his sleep. Penelope said that was some consolation, better than weeks and weeks of slow deterioration. It had been more than a year since Grandma died, and his life had withered away as his days became marked only by the hour hand on the old ship's clock as it crept toward noon, the hour when he could reasonably begin drinking his whiskey.

Our trip to Colorado to start New Life III aborted, we left for Duxbury as soon as Penelope was ready to travel and arrived there only after his memorial service, which Penelope said she could not bear to attend anyway. He was given a Navy burial, which was attended by a few old men wearing World War I and World War II uniforms. Ann and the cousins attended, and there were cocktails late into the evening. He was buried next to Grandma at the Mayflower Cemetery.

It wasn't so bad being back in Duxbury. We settled back into Grandpa's house and Penelope took his room, which needed to be aired out for several days and scrubbed down with Pine-Sol and wood cleaner, but Penelope seemed unable to feel settled in the house where the ghosts seemed to speak, even in daylight. There is something about the smell of old sheets and clothes, worn for many years and laundered too infrequently, that embeds itself into walls and floors. I felt as though I needed to take a sander to the wood or peel away the wallpaper and replace it in order to make the house smell new. Or at least make it smell like something other than Grandpa's decaying lungs and alcohol-saturated flesh.

Poor Bonnie had died earlier in the year, probably due to neglect more than old age. I had the stamina to go through the closets full of old clothes and chests full of decaying photos and half-written letters, shelves of books and piles of papers, and cabinet after cabinet of ancient canned food, faded boxes of rice, and bags of flour infested with weevils. Penelope needed frequent breaks from the culling, the memories filling the space around us, along with the dust and mold, inviting stories and gazes out the window, punctuated by unfinished sentences and tears.

My same group of friends was still intact, but I paired off with Penny, a friend from when we'd first came to Duxbury. Penelope said, "You know why she was named Penny?" I waited for the inevitable story. "It was because her father was mad about me once. He wanted to marry me."

"Everyone wanted to marry you," I said, rolling my eyes and flicking the ash off my Virginia Slims Menthol. "Could you, like . . . *not* tell Penny that story?" Penelope raised a Converse eyebrow and smiled.

Penny and I got really close that summer. I felt like I'd lived a hundred years, closed down the adolescent part of myself, and forgotten what it was like to be a teenager. Penny brought me back: the deliciousness of lying on the beach dangling a sandal off my toe; wearing cut-offs and listening to the American Top 40 with Kasey Kasem on the radio on Saturdays while we talked about boys; riding our bikes to the five-and-dime for more cigarettes; and hanging out with Kate and the old gang at Colleen's house, where we swam in the pool, drank Cokes, and smoked Marlboros. Penny had a real boyfriend; mine was in my imagination. I made my relationship with Kevin sound more real than it actually was. I imagined what it would be like to kiss him, and if I ever had the opportunity, I would give myself over to him completely. I knew I would. I wrote him letters and signed them, "love." He wrote me back and signed his, "Take care." I looked at each letter he wrote a thousand times, searching for unwritten meaning in each word, milking every drop I could within the boundaries of reality and fantasy. And what didn't meet my fantasies, I embellished. He alone would be the medicine of love and attention I craved, if only I could convince him that I was "the one." I wrote Kevin every day after we moved back to Duxbury and fantasized that he would drive up from Virginia in his blue Chevy Nova and take me away. I had this awful feeling that I was too much for anyone except for maybe a really old, patient dog. Why would an eighteen-year-old boy with a beautiful girlfriend want an emotionally unstable, fifteen-year-old weirdo? Still, the feelings I had for Kevin occupied every single cell in my body, and I ached for him. His attention and kindness released a river of longing, with a current so powerful that even I was overcome by its strength to pull me under. I had worked so hard to seem well-dammed, but my will crumbled, and I surrendered to the undertow.

In one of my letters, I invited him to come up to Duxbury to visit, and he wrote back saying he would think about it if he had time, which I took as a definite yes. I looked for his blue Chevy Nova on every bike ride, every blue car making my heart pound. It was the letter in which he mentioned his girlfriend that caused the rage hidden under the layers and layers of armor to sting me like a fist to my eyes. I responded to his letter, warning him that I didn't want her anywhere near him, thinking I was behaving within my right to determine him off-limits to anyone else.

I received a gentle reply. He did not appreciate my possessiveness and went on to define his love for me, which was not at all passionate, but caring and steadfast, like a friend, he wrote. He signed it, "Love _my kind_, Kevin." I hadn't been chosen, and that was all I heard in his words. I went into Grandma's closet and sobbed without restraint, hopeless and trapped forever inside my empty, stupid self. He would forever remember me as some weird girl who'd hung around like a stray dog, and I would always be a stray. Penelope found me exhausted and sweaty, curled up in the fetal position in the closet, eyes swollen, gulping for air between sobs.

She read his letter and poked her head in the closet. "Come out of there and look at me." I made my way out and sat on the floor, looking up at her sitting on my bed. "He loves you, and you should be thankful that he cared enough to write back and be honest with you. You've obviously chased him too hard, and he's telling you to back off. So don't be a fool and destroy this by being a cloying, overly emotional female. Be gracious and strong and write him back with an apology and acceptance of his friendship, because friends last much longer than lovers."

For all the times she was exasperating and scary, Penelope could make it all disappear with one brief lecture. These few seconds of mothering that nobody else could offer me were so golden that I almost believed it could last. Almost. I'd learned to catch myself before hope got the better of me. But I caught myself now. I felt better if I could pull myself out of the sticky grip of hope and yank my mind into something real. Disappointment was always on the other side of hope, waiting to slap me in the face and laugh at me. It was easier to expect the endless nights when she staggered and couldn't put together a sensible sentence. If there was one good night when I slept for a few hours, I spent a few seconds feeling happy, but that was all I could afford. It was far too costly to pull myself out of disappointment when I got too comfortable. "Comfortable" was like a foreign land I had once known but had been away from so long, I forgot the language. If ever I visited, I felt like I was trespassing and got back on the train to the familiar walls of scarcity. I hated hoping; it was so exhausting. Easier just to expect the worst.

When I'd recovered from my grief enough to write with clarity and maturity, I wrote Kevin, and he responded with loving kindness. I would not give up on marrying him, but I felt I could slow down, that his love for me would not die. And it didn't.

I was faced with the school question again when fall came. I registered as a sophomore and wondered if I would be questioned, having not attended my freshman year at all when we lived in New York, where it had been easy to be truant. Nobody had ever looked for me, and I hadn't made an effort to be found. But nobody questioned me, and I landed in a sophomore classroom, oblivious to the challenges I would face, having never completed eighth grade, let alone my freshman year.

I shook inside when I saw the same kids on the bus and in the hallways, my gleeful torturers from middle school, and my stomach lurched and tightened. I didn't trust their niceness toward me; my armor was on, and I could be pleasant but not trusting. I wanted to have friends and do things other kids were doing, like going to McDonald's, which I'd never done because Penelope wouldn't be caught dead in a fast food joint. My reality was that with Penelope at home, every minute that I wasn't in school, I needed to be in charge of shopping, cooking, laundry, housework, and trying to manage her increasing craziness.

41
WOMAN-ING

B Y MY FIFTEENTH YEAR, I'D LIVED in a big city, gone through crises greater than I'd thought my courage could stand, and learned to survive. I'd fallen in what seemed like love—all-consuming, dripping with the sweet honey of my imagination—and my fantasies were dashed upon the rocks of reality when I received his letters signed, "Your friend, Kevin." My beloved menstrual periods had settled me comfortably into the predictable cycles of womanhood with pride and relief that I had finally crossed that threshold. In New York, I'd been french kissed by a Thai waiter, walked hundreds of blocks to and from Mount Sinai Hospital, learned to manipulate bank tellers into redepositing Penelope's bounced checks, and faced the reality that my mother was a drug addict in addition to having an illness that would never go away completely.

I primped, I posed; in the privacy of my room, I shaped my eyebrows as carefully as I was shaping my inner self. I didn't want thick Converse eyebrows; I wanted my own. I wanted anything that would dissolve the glue that kept me so bonded with my mother that I couldn't see myself in a reflection. It was so hard to see myself as anything but a thing, an object made for doing and conforming and adapting in order to avoid crises, a human barometer that measured even the tiniest change in the emotional air pressure around me.

I wanted Kevin so badly that it ached in all my fingers and toes. I wanted him to appear one day and take me away to Virginia, where we would get married and live in a quaint subdivision with perfectly trimmed hedges. I imagined riding my bike around the corner and seeing him standing there in my driveway leaning on his blue Chevy Nova with his jeans slung low on his beautiful, slender hips. "I love you, and I have come to take you away with me," he would say, looking into my eyes the way Jesus looked into the eyes of Mary Magdalene in *Jesus Christ Superstar.*

People always asked me if I was mad about something. I became a watcher, a waiter, always looking out for intruders. Restraint and mistrust becomes a veil after a while. I drove my emotional vehicle with one foot on the gas and one foot on the brake. I could laugh and have a good time but always made sure I knew where the door was.

When school began, I had to get up at six a.m. in order to get ready and catch the bus. Getting up was as bad as getting into ice-cold water when you're already cold. I was chronically sleep deprived from keeping my vigil over Penelope until two or three in the morning. Over the summer, she hadn't seemed to have as many bouts of drug-induced depression and sleepless nights when she'd write nonsensical letters to me, or to my father, in illegible writing that wound around the edges of each page. Occasionally, I'd find her up, tinkering with her jewelry or attempting to redo her scrapbook while her brain was floating along in a river of Percodan, phenobarb, and wine. I was worried that she'd fall down the stairs or fall asleep holding a lit cigarette, which she'd done many times, though she was spared a fiery death in her bed by my vigilance and sense of smell.

Whenever I'd been up keeping watch, it was torture getting up after only a few hours' sleep. But school made me feel a little more normal. Once there, I let myself forget about Penelope for a few minutes at a time before anxiety poked a hole in my bubble. It seemed she'd deliberately gotten worse once I'd started school. She dropped little bombs to let me know I wasn't allowed to have a life more important than hers. "Don't you think it's a little selfish of you to ignore your responsibilities here so you can go play with those girly-girl friends of yours?"

I retreated to my room to avoid the inevitable fight. I longed for privacy and continued to fantasize about being rescued from my life and then felt terrified about my evilness in wishing I were away from Penelope. It took all my psychic strength to subdue my rage and pretend I wasn't evil and selfish, but, sometimes, I couldn't pull it off, and it exploded out of me like verbal projectile vomiting. "I wish I was *dead*!" I would cry.

"*Then* you'd be sorry!" Penelope would just chuckle and sneer. "You haven't got the *guts* to commit suicide." I wanted her to know how difficult life was for me living with her and all her craziness and sleepless nights. "Well, how do you think *I* feel?" she would swoon dramatically and storm off to her room, slam the door, and sob. I could never be important.

"Well, then, I'll just run away!" I would scream outside her locked door.

"*Good*, I'll help you pack," she would say, wrenching her door open and storming over to my closet to drag Brown Suitcase out. It was no use. Penelope would not allow me to steal her show.

42

VIGILS

A S THE AUTUMN DARKNESS STOLE THE daylight, Penelope began to wake me up in the middle of the night saying she was in terrible pain and needed Demerol. This meant I would have to drive her in the VW to Dr. Wiggin's house over by the school. He was so old he could barely walk or remember anything, but he had Demerol. He made house calls during the day, but at night when she called, he would be too woozy to get himself up and dressed to drive to our house. He had a tendency to fall back asleep once he'd hung up, so she had to keep calling him. I had to drive, which I didn't know how to do very well, and once we got to his house, Penelope would have to spend several minutes banging on his door because he'd fallen back asleep again. I settled in for the usual long wait at one or two in the morning, sometimes for over an hour. The good thing was I could get radio stations that came from as far away as Chicago, and I could listen to all my favorite songs while I waited. But I wondered why it took so long to get a shot of Demerol. The thought crossed my mind that she might have to have sex with him in order to get the drugs. I tried to scramble that image by turning up the radio.

After a few weeks of this, I was desperate, and then I remembered that my friend Drew's father was a psychiatrist. I wondered if he was still working out of their house by Grandpa's house, and I called him hoping he might be able to help. Maybe Penelope would feel better if she talked to someone, and maybe if it were a man who didn't want to have sex or dump her for a blackjack dealer from Reno, it would take some of the pressure off me.

I had to beg her to go because the idea of going to a shrink brought her back to the time she'd threatened suicide in Squaw Valley by standing in the bedroom in front of Gardiner with her .38 pointed at her head. "I'm not crazy," she said.

"I know, but he says he can help. There are medicines for depression, too, and you can't just keep taking Demerol in the middle of the night because it's killing me. I can't even make myself get up for school, and the principal is starting to get all over me about it."

"Okay. I'll go," she said.

Dr. Solomon had to be my savior; he just had to be. I couldn't take it anymore. When she emerged from his basement office after her first session, he had given her a prescription for Elavil, an antidepressant she had been on before. I wanted it to perform miracles. Penelope was convinced that being in Grandpa's house was causing the depression, so she did what she always did, which was to find a really old house with no carpeting to move into. "It's divine," she said when we went to look at it. An old Cape Cod house on the edge of a cranberry bog, built in about 1800, it satisfied her need to live out her New England-ness. She needed old. She needed floors that creaked with age and smelled of the moisture collected from many generations of humid summers, freezing winters, the sweat from bending over washtubs and butter churns and tears from losing babies too young. She needed the windows to slide up, allowing the wind to carry the curtains outside to flap in the evening ocean breeze; she needed old doorknobs made of brass that barely worked; she needed foundations made of stone or brick and shingles that had long since turned gray. When they flooded the cranberry bogs, she said, we could go ice skating. The Boston rocker, the Chippendale tables and chairs, the Windsor chairs, and Grandma's comfy sofa would replace the uncomfortable preacher's bench that Penelope had wanted in the living room. I had put my foot down. "No, I want something to actually sit on that doesn't make me want to scream," I'd said.

To make it even more like a house from an Edgar Allen Poe poem, the house was close to the Mayflower Cemetery, where Grandpa was now lying next to his beloved Hellie-girl. The new gravestones mingled with those so old that the epitaphs written in Old English were barely visible. The police department wasn't far away either. *Could be a good thing,* I thought. But maybe not, given my tendency to be absent from school, arousing the suspicion of the principal and that shit-heel Mr. Gagliardi who called himself the school counselor. It was too far to ride my bike to Sweetser's for groceries, and the road had no shoulder. "We'll use 'Call Paul' livery service," Penelope said. "And on my good days, we can go in the car." Usually, she didn't really want to go shopping and sent me in her place because our bill was so huge that she was embarrassed.

I knew she'd gotten money from Grandpa's estate; she and her sister had argued about who was going to get what. Ann was usually drunk when she came over to our house. One night, when we were packing up to get ready to move from Grandpa's, she had come over in a panic saying we had to hide her because the police were after her.

"Penelope, I'm telling you, it's no joke! That bastard hit me, so I shot him. I was aiming for his balls, but he turned around to run away, and I shot him in the ass instead! I called an ambulance and then left him there with his ass bleeding." Ann's voice was husky from years of unfiltered Camels and vodka. "Where's Dad's whiskey . . . I need a *drink!*" she'd said, pushing bottles aside in the cupboard. I had known the night would be endless as the packing had gotten more disorganized and the stories had come out in bursts of laughter interspersed with gulps of whiskey—old stories about the men they had been with. Ann was not arrested and thrown in jail that night as she'd feared, and the stories had continued as the crickets sang into the night. Penelope began to talk about Bert. "His pecker was down to his knees . . . he pole vaulted out of bed each morning." And Penelope thought *I* was obsessed with penises.

"You poor thing . . . I remember you begging me to drink with him so you could get some sleep! He wouldn't leave you alone!" And another page of the album turned. "My God . . . why did we ever go out with *him?*" Ann said, looking at a photo of a skinny, balding man on a sailboat. "He was stinking rich, well-bred, and at the top of his Harvard class, that's why," Penelope slurred after her third shot of whiskey.

We moved into our new house right after Penelope's birthday in November. "I'm going to live to see my fiftieth birthday," she said as we walked the dogs around the cranberry bog near our new house. "We're going to have a new start here. I know it . . . I can feel it. I'm going to stop taking the Percodan and sleeping pills as soon as the Elavil starts working." I maintained safety inside my armor. The promises were tempting, but the midnight trips to see Dr. Wiggin went on, and I rarely slept.

In December, Dr. Wiggin referred her for annual tests at the hospital in Boston, to see whether her polymyositis was out of remission. For Penelope, this was a perfect opportunity to stay at the Ritz-Carlton hotel. "I always stayed at the Ritz whenever I was in Paris, and, of course, the Ritz in Boston is where *everyone* who is *anyone* stays." I wondered how we would matter to anyone if we had no money. Penelope said it was breeding that mattered, not money, that Boston society was still intact, and that "old families" still garnered respect on Beacon Hill, and at the Ritz. Penelope strode into the lobby with Patience and Buttercup on their leashes as if she were royalty. "I'd like to be sure that our room is on one of the higher floors and that it will be quiet," she told the desk clerk.

"Yes, Miss Converse," he said and handed her the key to a room on the fifteenth floor. The window overlooked the park across the street, and the blue canopy of the hotel's main entrance was directly below. The first thing she did was order herself a Canadian Club, a tray of nice meaty bones for the dogs, and 7UP for me. The waiter brought the huge, silver tray inside, with bones piled high and covered with a white napkin. "Silver plate," said Penelope, looking at the tray. "But it's decent silver plate."

Penelope set about her usual routine of creating kitchens on windowsills. She never stayed at hotels where there was no room service, and there were always leftovers. The kitchen staffs always asked if they could keep her left-over food for her in the kitchen, but she refused, preferring instead to use windowsills as de facto refrigerators.

Penelope said the tray of bones needed to be properly chilled, as the dogs could only chew on one at a time, and bones sitting at room temperature would begin to smell. I set the tray down carefully since it teetered, danger-ously off balance, on the narrow ledge of the sill. Perhaps it was a gust of wind, or a shifting bone disturbing the delicate balance of the whole pile, but the tray slipped from its perch. I turned just in time to see the white napkin covering the tray sail gently off in the breeze and then watched in horror as the tray turned over and over, bones flying in all directions but ultimately headed directly for the blue canopy over the main entrance of the hotel. The tray bounced off the canopy and onto the shiny black hood of what appeared to be a very expensive car, and then clattered onto the sidewalk, while bones rained down on pedestrians and startled Ritz-Carlton doormen. I might have killed someone and feared the police would be called. Penelope went calmly to the window and peered down at the silver tray on the sidewalk and the people looking up to see where this mysterious object had come from. "Oh, dear, dearie me," she said, not the least bit aroused. She dialed the front desk and went into an explanation oozing with graciousness and proper Bostonian apologies, which somehow managed to sound sincere without contrition. In under ten minutes, a new tray of bones was brought to our room . . . on a table.

It was old and smelly, but the Peter Bent Brigham Hospital was where the doctors wanted her to go for tests. The results were not good. She was admitted immediately for more tests and quantities of cortisone administered intravenously to stop the polymyositis from progressing. I was glad I didn't have to take care of her for at least a few days. But I didn't want to stay in our old spooky house in Duxbury alone. I asked Penelope if I could go stay at the Holiday Inn in Dumfries, Virginia, to visit Kevin, something I knew she would approve of now that we had a little money from Grandpa's estate. I told her I'd gotten Ann to come up and take care of the dogs. "Well, there won't be a drop of booze left in the house by the time we get back, but go ahead."

My goal was to get out of Boston as quickly as possible, so I forged Penelope's name on a blank check and cashed it at the Ritz-Carlton front desk, having a strong suspicion that it would bounce. She always called people and made some excuse that sounded plausible enough that they would redeposit checks while she freaked out about how she would cover them. Then I bought a plane ticket, and Kevin picked me up at Washington National Airport in the Holiday Inn van.

I spent seven blissful days in Virginia flirting with Kevin and returned to Boston glowing from a kiss on the cheek when he'd said goodbye. Penelope was still in the hospital, and I went to stay at a bed and breakfast in Duxbury, not wanting to be alone in a house by the graveyard. Ann had gone home to Plymouth with Patience and Buttercup, her boyfriend's ass having healed and no threat of being jailed. And she couldn't be away from her cats. I felt so free without Penelope. Going to school was actually fun when I had sleep. I got annoyed when she called me. "Don't you want me to come home?" she asked.

"Yeah, it's just that . . . I just don't want you to come home too soon and still be sick," I said, trying to cover my dread of being with her again.

"Fine, I won't come home then," she said and slammed the phone down.

The next morning, she called and announced to me that she'd attempted suicide the night before by swallowing pills she'd been saving up, and that they'd pumped her stomach. I sat in the sunny sitting room of the guesthouse and didn't know what to say. "Are you there?" she asked.

"Yeah," I said. "Why did you?"

"Because you acted is if you didn't want me home, and I didn't want to be in your way anymore."

"That is *not* what I said and you know it." My rage was instantaneous, like a flash of lightning that lit up every nerve. This time, I let myself be enraged. I had neither the energy nor the fear that she would banish me from her life to bite the bait anymore. I held the phone limply in my hand until she'd finished telling me about how hurt she was and that she was fighting for her life, but how could I possibly know anything about that, since I existed in my own narrow little world.

This had been her second suicide attempt that I knew about. When I'd found her in the hotel room in New York, she'd swallowed a bunch of pills, but I hadn't known about it until Gardiner had told me months later. "That's why they pumped her stomach," he'd said.

When she came home, she gave me the cold shoulder, and I returned it. I wished she would die and get it over with. She hated the prednisone she had to take; it made her face bloated and hair grow on her chin. "I look like some old crone from the medieval days. I need a pair of hedge clippers to cut my chin hairs," she'd say. We still had our laughs and jokes, but I knew to put the brakes on any hope for our relationship to stay that way.

It was dark and cold in the early mornings now, and getting up was excruciating. I had to stay awake at night long enough to be sure she was sleeping soundly. The stairs were old and steep, and the worn wood was slippery and dangerous for her. On days when I could get up, I went to school, but I couldn't focus on anything while I was there except getting home. I begged the school to make it possible for me to go home early so I could care for her, and they allowed me that, but it was so hard for me to get out of bed in the mornings that I still missed many days.

I lived for her appointment days with Dr. Solomon, hoping that her mood would be brighter afterward and that she would stop taking so many different pills. The school was on my back, warning me that I couldn't miss any more days of school. Mr. Gagliardi was watching me, as he had in my middle school days when the bullying had gotten so bad I'd stayed home from school for days on end. He'd made up his mind about the kind of kid I was. "You can go to juvenile hall for truancy," he said through his narrow, cruel lips. He came to our house threatening to put me in juvenile detention for being truant, and he told Penelope she was not being a responsible parent. Penelope did what she'd always done when Mr. Gagliardi called or came to the house—she told him to go screw himself, or to leave her property this minute or she'd let the dogs loose on him.

I tried to get myself to school as regularly as possible, though I was sleep deprived and anxious about leaving Penelope even for a few hours. I didn't want to tell anyone at the school what was really going on; I just continued to make up lies about being sick or missing the bus in order to avoid Mr. Gagliardi's scrutiny.

One night in January, I was on my usual vigil downstairs in the kitchen, watching Johnny Carson until I was pretty sure she was asleep. Old houses creak and groan, so with every sound I listened closely to determine whether it was the wind or her footsteps on the creaky floorboards of her bedroom.

Her sleep time was my peace time, a time to be free of her, to loosen the stranglehold that her life had on me. When she was awake, the drug cocktails she made would take over, and her high drove her to wild jags of jewelry repair, flights of errant ideas, more plans to start a new life, and manic promises to begin writing again or restart her photography career, singing old songs, and talking to herself. She would insist that I participate in whatever drug-induced tangent she went on, even though her eyelids could hardly stay open and her balance was shot. And she would smoke a lot when she was loaded, forgetting she'd lit one and lighting another, eventually leaving it to burn on the edge of a dresser or her bedside table. I could predict when she was going to have a sleepless night, and I tried to keep her from sleeping all the next day to get her back on track. Her favorite pattern was to stay awake all night, sleep most of the day, then get loaded on wine and narcotics and be awake all night smoking and writing thirty-page letters to Gardiner.

On that January night, when I felt sure she was asleep, I turned off Johnny Carson and went up to my bedroom across the landing from hers to settle in for a few paltry hours of blissful sleep. I was in that wonderful place right before sleep takes over when I heard the creak. I startled and leapt from my bed but was not in time to catch her as she fell, crashing on the wooden stairs and, with a final thump, landing on the wood floor below, her tiny body crumpled and curled on its side, naked but for an undershirt she was wearing to bed. Her mouth and her nose were bleeding. Certain she was dead, I ran screaming to her side to see if she was alive. "Mommy! Mommy, *please!*" I cried, shaking her gently to try to get her to respond to me.

Slowly she opened her eyes and looked at me in a daze. "Is anything broken?" I asked, panting and trying to overcome my panic.

"I don't know," she mumbled in a whisper.

"Should I call an ambulance?" That seemed to get her attention.

"No, no . . . don't do that. I'll be all right; I just need to get cleaned up," she said, trying to get up, but she couldn't. I laid her back down and went to get a washcloth because she was bleeding from her mouth and nose. I was in the haze of panic, not knowing where the blood was coming from, just that I had to clean it off to see. It looked really bad, but while I was in the bathroom, I put the cool washcloth to my face and tried to regain my composure. Emergencies were not new to me, and once I had my bearings, I felt competent and powerful, as if the world could throw anything at me and I could handle it. I got her situated on the sofa downstairs with an ice pack and a blanket, and then I called Dr. Solomon to see if he could tell me what to do next. He sighed and said, "Your mother is being dramatic. She wants you to feel sorry for her and turn your life upside down as you always have. Go ahead and go to school. I will handle your mother."

I watched her all night while she dozed in and out of sleep on Grandma's sofa. I was sitting in the matching wing chair watching her breathing, hoping it wouldn't stop, feeling remorseful for all the mean thoughts I'd been having and all the times I'd wished she would just hurry up and die so I could stop worrying.

I went to school knowing that if I didn't go, they would come after me and take me away. I went to the office between each class to call her, having told her before I'd left that morning that if she didn't answer, I would call the cops. I arrived home after school, beyond exhausted, to find her fully dressed and ready to go see Dr. Solomon. She was wearing dark glasses to cover the darkening bruises under her eyes and a heavier-than-usual coat of red lipstick to hide the cut on her lip. Her tongue had been cut by her dentures and it hurt her to talk, so we tried not to. I slept in the car while she was in with him. I hoped maybe he would have some magical way of making her sane and easier to live with.

"I'm really going to do it this time," she said, getting in the car and giving me a kiss, telling me (again) that I was her reason for living. "You are my treasure, my life, and I want to make a new start . . . for *us*, for *you*." As she sat stroking my forehead, I wanted to slap her hand away. I was listening to Elton John singing a song that had become my all-time favorite, "Goodbye Yellow Brick Road," and she said, "Just like the song . . . I've finally decided my future lies beyond the yellow brick road. It's going to be my new inspirational song."

I felt sick. I wanted so badly to believe that life could change in one sweep of a magic wand or a pill from Dr. Solomon. "Don't say that to me anymore. Tell your*self* that this time, and do it," I said, then I turned my face away, so weary and angry.

A couple of days later, I came home from school, and she wasn't making sense. Sentences drifted off into space; words were tossed like salad ingredients into nonsense. I'd never seen this before, even in the worst of her drugged states. I called Dr. Solomon. He didn't tell me she was just being dramatic this time. "I will make immediate arrangements for her admission to Peter Bent Brigham's psychiatric unit."

When I told her, she answered coherently, "Oh, not the Bent Peter hospital again." Tears sprang into my eyes. She could be so much fun.

He told me to figure out a way to get her up there. Call Paul's Livery was busy, so I called Herrick's Taxi, which was operated by one of the many Herrick brothers in Duxbury, though Ralph was the only brother who actually drove the taxi. Ralph's conversations were only with himself and an imaginary audience, but he knew his way to Boston. On the drive up to

Boston, she was relatively quiet except for a sudden urge to get out of the car to get a cigarette while we were moving at sixty miles per hour.

I walked her to the admitting office down the old green-tiled hallways lit by dull overhead lights, which showed the grime of many years on the walls. I couldn't wait to leave, only slightly disturbed by guilt that I would be leaving her in this morbid place. When the nurse took her away, I blew Penelope a kiss and walked quickly out the swinging doors. I never wanted to do this again. Not ever.

Ralph was waiting in his taxi smoking one cigarette after another and having an animated conversation with himself, punctuating his words with hand gestures that left tendrils of smoke from his cigarette curling around his head. "Back to Duxbury please, Ralph," I said, settling into the back seat and feeling glad it was dark outside.

"Yes, Miss. And ya motha? She stayin'?" he asked in his broad New England accent.

"For a while," I said and settled back for the long ride back to Duxbury. I was glad it was dark outside. It offered a kind of insulation from dealing with all the questions and problems that would inevitably surface once the daylight came again.

When I got home, the dogs jumped all over me to tell me they were hungry. I fed them, sat down, and lit a cigarette. There was no sound at all from upstairs, where I knew every floorboard's creak. I called Dr. Solomon and his wife to tell them she was in the hospital. "Do you want to come and stay with us?" he asked.

"No, I'd just like to stay here tonight," I said.

"Okay, we'll have to talk tomorrow about all this. Call us if you need us."

"I will," I said, knowing I would be fine all alone. I could not talk, listen, or explain anymore.

I played Elton John's "Goodbye Yellow Brick Road" and "Candle in the Wind" over and over as I walked around and tidied everything up. I felt peaceful and powerful. I cleaned the bathroom. I cleaned closets and found pills stashed in different bottles in various hiding places. I stripped her bed and found more pills under the mattress. I found pills in her shoes and in her underwear drawer, and I flushed them all. I scrubbed and scrubbed in the kitchen. Just like the perfect old wood beneath the layers of filth on the old floor, I felt liberated of old dead skin and felt a shiny, resilient part of me emerging. I wanted order, and I could create it so easily after four years of making order out of chaos. I could make anything shine no matter how ugly it looked on the outside.

On that night, as I lay in my bed with the dogs at my feet, I made myself free, severing myself from this life, allowing the flood of relief to wash over me, bringing with it a serene sleep I'd not known for a long time. "Now, *I'm* going to start a new life," I thought to myself. I could do it easily now. I knew how to pack up and leave people and places behind, to cauterize and scab over where I'd severed relationships or where they'd severed me.

Dr. Solomon came by to get me the next morning for school and told me we were going to meet with the principal and his buddy, Mr. Gagliardi. They'd already made up their minds about who I was, and I had reason to be afraid. I shrank back against the upholstery of Dr. Solomon's front seat, my eyes filling with tears. Why couldn't they just leave me alone? The worst thing I'd ever done in school was smoke in the girl's bathroom or skip behind the school to avoid bullying. They'd treated me like the bad kid I now thought I was, with all their threats to put me in a juvenile detention facility. I went into the principal's office and sat down, but I didn't look at him. "We know your mother is in the hospital," he said.

"Yeah . . . *so?*"

He leaned forward and pressed his fat fingers together, tapping, tapping, tapping, as if clapping for himself. "Well . . . why didn't you tell us things were so bad at home?"

I bristled, the disgust rising in crimson from my throat to my cheeks. He leaned away from me in his chair, holding the lapels of his light blue polyester jacket like curtains he could close to avoid an uncomfortable confrontation. I leaned in toward him, unafraid now of what he could do to me. "Remember your most recent visit to my house when you threatened to take me to juvenile hall and told my mother she was not being a responsible parent?"

He gripped his lapels a little tighter and said, "Well, we want to help you now. The law has intervened on your behalf, and the police are here to take you to children's services so you can talk to a social worker. Because your mother is not competent to care for you, you have been placed into the custody of the State of Massachusetts, until we can contact a relative.

They will want to place you in foster care unless there is a relative. Where is your father?"

My head spun. Of course he pretended to be sympathetic. Of course there had to be a police car waiting for me right in front of the school. My friends watched as a social worker led me to the police car and helped me get in the back seat as if I were being hauled off to jail.

It sounded strange when the social workers asked me where my father was. He was in my psyche somewhere, not a villain, just someone who'd once seemed to adore me as I adored him. I'd done something to make him stop adoring me, maybe choosing Penelope. Penelope needed to see him as the cause for all her suffering, but over the past four years, I had begun to wonder if he had just run out of patience and stamina. I knew I was running on fumes but couldn't decide to leave her. If I could assure Gardiner that I wouldn't be a problem, maybe he would take me back. If I could make myself wonderfully small and insignificant, like a sparrow that sits under a bush. I knew this life so well now—of waiting and wanting, of hoping for rescue; of organizing comforting, perfect spaces inside closets and cupboards; of folding and refolding towels to find the paradise in completion; of turning things this way and that, moving a broom across the floor, making the bed so that all the corners matched, tying and retying curtain sashes until the bows were smiling evenly. It was impossible to imagine him being different from what he had been during my childhood—loving and lovable, funny, easy to play with, easy to feel comfortable with. Even though I hardly ever heard from him, I knew how to keep dying things alive by holding my breath and waiting. Penelope's illness had waited patiently for a moment when I had dared to breathe, thinking we would be free of it at last. Moments of comfort were its favorite time to strike, and I couldn't hold my breath anymore. I wanted to go home and leave Penelope.

43

GARDINER

IT WOULDN'T BE SO BAD GOING home to be with Gardiner, I thought. I had given up on the idea that he would rescue me. He'd never made the attempt, and I'd asked twice in the past three years. He said no each time, and I could not bear to hear it again.

Even when he'd left Penelope to shack up with the bulbous and vitriolic Sammie, who liked to pretend she was a nurse, his friends hadn't abandoned him. I'd watched people take pity on him because he had taken care of Penelope during her illness while also taking care of his patients and me and our dogs, and he'd managed to go running in the mornings or go out rowing on Lake Tahoe. I'd wanted to defend him when Penelope would launch into one of her tirades about him for having disappointed her in some way or for having lied to her about why he had come home late. He had just taken it and agreed with her character assassinations. She would tell him he was weak and selfish, a liar from ill-bred, stoop-shouldered, social-climbing boors who did not deserve to breathe the same air as she. He would just hang his head and ask for her forgiveness. I'd just wanted to comfort him, but in the steely tension between Penelope's need for my allegiance, I had kept silent.

I loved how he could smile even when he was worried. I loved that he would talk to me, not just ask me shallow, stupid questions and then pay no attention to my responses. He had engaged me in challenging conversations and rarely missed a teaching moment. If I wanted to sing in the car, he would sing with me, finding a way to harmonize. He hadn't minded singing Christmas carols in July or many rounds of "Frère Jacques" and "I've Been Working on the Railroad." It was impossible not to love him.

Gardiner loved dogs, but not as much as dogs loved him. He would curse and swear as he slid on frigid dog turds on his way to the living room in the early morning, but he never punished the guilty dog—usually our old dachshund, Felix, who couldn't bear to go outdoors in the wintertime because his testicles dragged in the snow. "That miserable hound," he would say, scooping the mess into the dustpan. "I ought to send him to reform school for stubborn dachshunds."

He met Penelope in 1956 at the Marin General Hospital emergency room. Suffering from relentless amoebic dysentery she'd picked up in Italy, she'd gone to the emergency room seeking relief. "And in walked your father with those rusting bedspring curls," she said lovingly, when she recalled first meeting my redheaded father. The love affair began, and he told himself his marriage to Emily, his first wife, was over. In his mind, he severed the connection. Emily doubted, but she did not act. Gardiner came home late. And then he just didn't come home. He left the marriage to bleed, without proper stitching to prevent hemorrhaging, and left the limbs of his life strewn about the living room of his Marin County home. There were jagged and messy attempts at being truthful, but being brutally honest would have resulted in an irreconcilable schism. He would no longer be able to say he was decent, a family man like his father.

Out of his three children, Joanie was the only one who wasn't deaf. His oldest daughter, Susie was deaf, and his only son, Mike was deaf and autistic. Joanie was the family lighthouse and barometer who saw, heard, and felt everything. Enlisted by her mother as the main helper and confidante, Joanie was the unmothered daughter, and her beloved father, once dependable and steadfast, was never home anymore.

He was captivated and intoxicated by Penelope, as most men were. A bewitching mixture of excitement, danger, and beauty, Penelope behaved as if she didn't need him, but underneath the gauzy cloak of aloofness, there was a swift and strong undertow, irresistible for Gardiner, whose favorite books were about the Knights of the Round Table. But those knights were heroes without humanity, men written into life by other men for whom humanity was something to be stuffed into a suit of armor.

He left gnarls of scar tissue in the heart of his only hearing child. He did not keep his promises, thinking that words alone would keep her from hating him. A new life began, almost as if the old one had never existed. He never intended it to be so cold; it was antithetical to his nature as a healer, but he told himself it was all Emily's fault, all those years of her blind, drunken episodes and blackouts, when she would disappear for several days. He swore that he had tried his best to be a devoted husband, but blamed Emily for his sudden need to be in Sausalito on Penelope's houseboat with his trousers unzipped. his sudden excused his she was hopeless. Gardiner had always replenished his dried-up emotional bank account by endearing himself to other women, and he had done the same in his marriage to Penelope. Women found his neediness irresistible and lovable because he wore it on his sleeve, like an armband that read, "Feed me, I'm hungry."

He had been a devoted husband to Penelope for as long as he could be, given his lifespan as a husband. Penelope was not welcoming to her stepchildren, nor was she able to understand the level of resentment and bitterness she felt from Joanie, who, as the caregiving child to her deaf siblings and her mother, had an exceptionally acute emotional radar. None of my father's placations satisfied Joanie. In fact, they made her more steadfast in her loyalty toward her mother and less conciliatory toward Penelope, who, sensing the heat of Joanie's knowing eyes, just wanted her to stay away. Joanie was the tiny sentry surrounding her fragile family, a lone soldier whose innocence became shadowed by contempt, laden with resentment. Penelope chose only to believe Gardiner's tragic story, and Joanie's coldness only fortified her need to believe him.

Gardiner used his ability to elicit compassion and empathy to shift the focus from his self-centeredness to his seemingly genuine self-deprecation. "I'm a shit," he would say, furrowing his brow and hanging his head. "I'm a lousy father and a shitty husband."

The predictable response from others was, of course, to soften his self-flagellating and excuse him, which was what he wanted. Had they done what Joanie had, which was to agree with him, he probably wouldn't have enjoyed as much warmth and acceptance as he did. It was easy for friends and colleagues to forgive and excuse; it makes relationships easier and more enjoyable. Besides, he was the kind of doctor you like to imagine, an embodied Rockwell painting, a faithful friend that you knew would not so much as raise an eyebrow in judgment. Nobody that I knew had anything bad to say about him. For them, it was easy to imagine that his escape from his former family had been necessary and prudent, that he had been a victim, caught in a relationship with a shrew from whom he'd had to escape or die.

But his children knew only this: Once they'd had a wonderful daddy, and suddenly he was gone. Gardiner had left them behind, thinking somehow that his absence would not matter much. Having done that once, maybe it was easier for him to leave, as if we were pairs of old shoes that had lost their shine.

44
Going Home

IT SEEMED GARDINER HAD REPLACED ME with Tammy Jo, Sammie's younger daughter—perhaps a better daughter than I had been, not so much trouble. He'd only spoken to me when I'd called him in a panic over one of Penelope's medical emergencies or when we were broke. When I heard the words "foster family" as I sat in the principal's office at Duxbury High School, I felt orphaned but tried to hide my shame. Dr. Solomon and his wife met me at the social services offices and sat down on the sofa next to me. I couldn't hold the armor to my body any longer when the social worker offered me some hot chocolate or coffee and stroked my back. I cried rivers and rivers, all my power carried away into a sea of surrender. "Honey, will your dad in California take you?" she asked gently.

"I don't know. I don't think so because he hardly ever talks to me," I sobbed. What if he didn't? That would mean I'd have to live with people I didn't even know.

"Can we take her until she finds out if her dad will take her?" Mrs. Solomon intervened.

"We'll have to issue temporary orders saying that you can have her for two weeks, but no more," said the social worker. "It's just the law."

The thing was, I had to *ask* Gardiner if I could live with him, which was basically asking someone I knew didn't like me or want me. But I didn't want to live in a stranger's house. And then the thought dawned on me that I might have to leave the dogs. Who would take care of them?

I spent the next several hours sitting in the Solomons' study staring at their black telephone. My heart filled my throat as I picked up the phone to call him. I dialed slowly, and I put the receiver down in its cradle before it began to ring. My mouth was dry. I swallowed and swallowed, trying to ease the panic, and picked up the receiver again. I squeezed my cheeks to stop my teeth from chattering. I finally made myself hold the phone to my ear. Gardiner answered his phone at the office, and my heart pounded a little more softly. At least I didn't have to get through Sammie first. "Dr. Pier," he answered brusquely.

"Daddy?"

"Hi, honey," he said. "How are you?" I felt a little better when he called me "honey."

"They say you have to take me or I have to go to a foster home." My heart pounded. A voice that felt like it came right from the back of my heart whispered, *Tell him it wasn't your idea to call him and ask this. Tell him! Or he'll think you're begging!* I stammered, "The social workers said I had to call you. If you decide not to take me, I'll have to go to a foster home." I then added, "And that would be okay, really . . . if you'd rather not."

"Of course you can come home!" Gardiner said with warmth that stunned me. I forgot about all the times he'd hung up on me. I could do that. I could ignore it all for just one tiny drop of love. I could make a single drop seem like a bucketful.

The next two weeks were spent in a frenzy of saying goodbye to friends at school and then getting sick for the first time in several years. There hadn't been room for me to be sick; Penelope's problems had kept me in a constant state of vigilance and my immune system had not allowed me to falter. I was already in my new life, happy to be going home to Squaw Valley, happy to be free, but Dr. Solomon insisted I go up to the hospital and say goodbye to my mother.

"No. I won't go," I said.

"You have to tell her you're going," he said gently.

"No! Why? Why do I have to?"

"Because you need to say goodbye," he urged.

"I can't. Why can't you do it for me?"

He was asking me to commit the ultimate act of betrayal. I'd told her so many times that I would never leave her, even when she had challenged my ability to be loyal or threatened to send me home to Gardiner, "that miserable prick of a father of yours," as she would put it. Suddenly, freedom was a sin. I was relieved to be free of taking care of her, but I hadn't imagined that I would have to tell her. Maybe I'd thought someone else would tell her, and I wouldn't have to face my sinfulness.

"Maybe I won't be gone very long," I said as we drove. "Just a little while maybe." I had not seen her now in two weeks, so I didn't know what to expect when I saw her. When I got to her room, she was dressed in her best gray, flannel pants from Brooks Brothers and her black cashmere sweater. The black and blue under her eyes and around her nose were almost gone and her long black-and-silvery hair was combed and parted on the side as she'd always worn it, and she had lipstick on. She hugged me tightly and said, "Oh, *baby*, I've missed you so!" I had to remain in my armor so guilt couldn't eat me alive, so I pushed myself away gently and looked down. "Mama . . . I have to leave. They told me I can't take care of you anymore, and they're going to put me in a foster home if I don't go back to Dad's. So . . . I'm . . . I'm going back." I was Gardiner in that moment, abandoning her just the way he had. I looked at the floor, and my legs felt tingly and rubbery. She was so brave. She sat down on her bed and looked at me. She had her dignity after all; it showed through the faint blue-green shadow of the bruises around her eyes.

"It's all right, sweetheart." She looked down at her hands folded in her tiny little lap.

Then Dr. Solomon asked her this question: "Penny, if you had another chance, what kind of mother would you be?"

Her eyes filled with tears, and she said, "Oh, I'd be the best mother in the world! I would change everything!"

I couldn't stand myself. I couldn't raise my head to look at her, and I wanted to die. Why did he have to ask her that? He was ruining everything by trying to make me forgive her, to give her another chance, and I didn't want to give her any more chances; there had been so many chances.

I left the house so perfect—all sheets and towels clean, food in the cupboards, soap in her soap dish, clothes washed, floors polished. As I swept, dusted, and polished, I crafted a lie to cover my shame. I was offering her a chance for freedom from the encumbrance of me. Yes, that is what I would tell anyone that asked me. At last she could return to the life she'd had before I had taken it away. She could go to Europe and resume her career as a photographer. She could live with Fishballs in Davos again without worrying who might be missing her. Fishballs had given Penelope her chance for a brilliant career, and she could provide her with everything I couldn't, traveling to wild places and staying in luxurious hotels in Paris and Italy. She could have adventures just like she used to have, money for whatever she wanted, now that I would be out of the way.

Brown Suitcase was opened one more time, after years of waiting, unpacking, and repacking whispering from its worn threads and corners. It snapped open and welcomed my treasures into its belly. All my suits and sweaters from Saks Fifth Avenue and my jewelry and diary were carefully tucked inside. I took nothing of Penelope's, not even one book. In the leaps through clouds between Duxbury and Squaw Valley, I dreamed of the moment I would see Gardiner. The plane landed in Reno, and I was dressed in my best Saks Fifth Avenue suit of armor. I held my head high, and when I saw him, the warrior took over without my even asking, and the faceplate slammed down. There was no access to the vault; the queen in her shining armor greeted all visitors with her sword and shield, guarding me against all intruders and inquisitors. It was she who greeted my father with a formal hug and a regal greeting.

45
STARTING A NEW LIFE
IV

I DID NOT RUN TO HIM; I strode. I did not lean into the embrace; I hugged without touching. I did not cry. "Hi, Dad," I said, smiling through Elizabeth Arden lipstick.

"Well, hullo, Kacey," he said and looked at me. "You're all grown up!"

"Yes," I said. "I am."

Within the first ten minutes of our reunion, he said, "Well, I suppose you'll be needing some birth control pills." He was chuckling. I couldn't come up with an answer and looked at him between the slits of faceplate.

We drove west on Interstate 80 toward Truckee—the same road we'd driven exactly four years before when I had asked him about his affair with Sammie. It was January, and the stubble of forest-fire-ravaged trees along the foothills of the Sierra Nevada were blanketed with deep snow. I loved to look to the west and see the first glimpse of the High Sierra toward Donner Pass; it was still there and still beautiful against a cerulean winter sky.

As we drove into Squaw Valley, my heart leapt at the shape of the familiar mountains encircling the valley floor like arms, embracing its meadow now covered by a serene blanket of snow. "We're going to have dinner at the Klaussen's house," Gardiner told me. I was excited to see the Klaussens again, having spent so many nights at their house as a worried child when Penelope was in hospitals most of the time. They knew why I was coming home to Gardiner, and I wanted to show them that I was a serene, sophisticated woman, not a messed-up kid whose mother couldn't take care of her. In my mind, I thought I would be playful and bubbly when my father walked into their house without knocking, as he always had, announcing his presence. But playfulness and bubbliness were not what came out when I went inside. The warrior appeared, ensuring my safety, securing the armor, making sure that I showed only dignity and maturity. I became Penelope.

"How *are* you?" I asked, standing some distance from myself and them, safe inside my armor, emphasizing the middle word of my sentence as Penelope did.

"Well, *we* are fine, but how are *you*, my dear?" asked Mrs. Klaussen, behaving as if she knew me.

"I am *fine* . . . just *fine*." I said, believing it was true. And then she asked, "How is your mother, dear?"

Penelope took over, operating controls inside my jaws, and I stepped away from myself, saying in a voice like Penelope's, "Oh, she's doing *quite* well. She . . . no . . . *we* decided . . . together, that is, that she needed time to renew her career, and she is going to spend some time traveling around Europe with Fish . . . I mean Helene. So, you know, she'll do that, and she'll be better off without me there."

And then I smiled and said, "So tell me about how everyone is here?" I would put a hasty stop on any further questions about my life with Penelope. Any inquisitors would buy my story and then leave it alone. I would raise the drawbridge, shutting out intruders, and I would smile.

When we went home to what was once my house, I discovered other people living in the rooms, including my old bedroom. "What's *this*? What have you done to my room?" I asked Gardiner. I'd expected everything to be the same as it was—my drawings on the wall, my books in the shelves, and my bed undisturbed. But I'd been removed.

"I have renters in here, since Sammie and I just live in the upstairs," he said sheepishly.

When he took me back, Sammie packed up her shit and left for

Columbine Creek, a budding ski resort in the Rocky Mountains, where they'd bought a piece of land. They'd planned to live there permanently until I complicated things by coming back. He didn't want to be here; he wanted to be with her. That was obvious to me. He seemed parked in the house as if he were just going to run in for a minute, leaving the car running and the emergency flashers on. He had a few things hanging in the closet, but his dresser was cleared of everything; his drawers were mostly empty, and most of the books on the shelves were packed in boxes. I turned and went downstairs to my old room. "Where am I sleeping?" I asked, looking around and seeing that it was full of someone else's stuff. I could still see the faint remnants of all the drawings I'd done in crayon all over the walls and the horse I'd drawn in orange crayon on my closet door.

"We'll sleep upstairs. In the room your mother and I . . ." he trailed off.

"There is only *one* bed in there," I said, feeling ready to argue.

"Yes," he said flatly.

"I don't want to sleep with *you*," I said, channeling Penelope. "Can I just go to a motel then?" That's what Penelope would have done, I thought.

"Look," he said wearily, "I don't like it any more than you do, but it's all I can do for now. And no, you can't go to a motel, for Christ's sake."

There were strangers upstairs in the kitchen and in the living room. I felt sick and tired as I realized that my fantasy of what it would be like to come home wasn't even close to the reality. The front door opened, and people were laughing and talking as they came upstairs. They greeted Gardiner and stared at me smiling, as if I were a stranger he'd picked up hitchhiking. Gardiner introduced me to the three people who were living in my house now. Two of them were dressed in Squaw Valley ski school uniforms, and the other guy had a ski patrol jacket on. Al and Diane, a young couple, were living in my old room, and the ski patrolman, Ed, lived in our old guestroom with his dog and a very nice stereo system.

It was late Saturday afternoon, and Gardiner went to the hospital to make rounds. I stayed home to unpack. I looked in Penelope's closet to see if one of her sweaters might be in there. I would bury my nose in the cashmere and perhaps catch the faintest whisper of her perfume. But it was empty, and it smelled like Sammie's drugstore perfume. It was getting late and I realized I was hungry. I wandered to the kitchen where Diane was preparing a meal using Penelope's cookware. I looked in the refrigerator for food and began to fix something to eat. Diane said, "I don't know what we're going to do about the food situation."

"What *food* situation?" I asked, wondering what the fuck she was talking about.

"Well, we like . . . all buy our own food here and . . . like, well, this is *our* food," she said, pointing to the bread and peanut butter I had in my hands. Feeling the orphan inside me arise, I just put the food down and left the room. When Gardiner came home, he said that we would go buy food and take turns cooking.

"I don't want them here. Can't you tell them to leave?"

"I *have* told them, but it's going to be another couple of weeks before they move," he said.

And then there was the school issue. Brown Suitcase was hardly unpacked before Gardiner took me to Truckee to register me at the high school, a prison-like brick fortress, menacing and devoid of any features suggesting it might be fun to be there. I was okay with it because I actually thought it would be fun to be normal, but then again I didn't really know how. I looked at what everyone was wearing and realized I had no clothes for winter weather, nor did I have anything that looked like normal Squaw Valley teenager clothes. I had all my Saks clothes and maybe a couple of pairs of casual pants, but that was it.

"I need clothes. Can we go buy me some corduroy Levi's or something, so I don't look like a freak?"

"I can't afford to buy a lot of crap," Gardiner said. "But I guess we can go get a few things." He seemed irritated and impatient with all my questions. I hadn't thought that my arrival back in his life was any big deal, but it was. I tried not to be that much trouble and to be less of a problem by offering to cook and clean. He said my stew had too much oregano and that my omelets were tough.

I still had not been to McDonald's, nor had I tried pizza, which all the kids I'd known seemed to love. I'd gone to one eighth-grade school dance and vowed never to go again. I didn't have any school pictures or yearbooks from Duxbury or from any period of time since I'd left Squaw Valley. And I'd never had a boyfriend or a date. The closest I'd come was when I kissed the Thai waiter in New York when I was fourteen, or kissing boys during games of Pass the Butt in eighth grade.

46

GOODBYE PENELOPE

I REMEMBERED THE LAST WORDS I'D EVER heard from Penelope on that January day at the "Bent Peter" Hospital: "I would be the best mother in the world! I would change everything!" She must have thought she wasn't the best mother, but she had never told me she'd felt that way. In fact, she'd always told me how lucky I was that she'd survived at all considering the brutality with which Gardiner had treated her on top of her having a life-threatening disease. She had always been successful in shaming me out of any feelings of resentment I'd had toward her, or the really evil thoughts I'd had about wishing she were dead. Or that I was.

I do not remember any phone conversations with Penelope after she was released from the hospital and went home to Duxbury in March of 1974. I needed to believe she was glad to be rid of me. I'd cut off the old life and started the new one, just as Penelope had shown me we could do so many times. I looked deeply into the shelves of another closet, where Penelope used to keep her best shoes, all nicely tucked into a shoe bag that hung on the door, and her cameras, guns, and other precious things that reminded her of her old life before Gardiner and me. I reached way back in the shelves of her closet and touched the stacks of her scrapbooks and photo albums. A pile of glossy black-and-white photos of her had been stuffed in between the pages of her big leather scrapbook, in a way that suggested she shouldn't be visible anywhere in the house in which she used to belong. It was the big leather scrapbook Penelope and I used to look through when I was a little girl. I took them out and carefully tacked them up on my bedroom wall. Then I took them down again, feeling I was lying to myself. I couldn't celebrate having abandoned her. I tucked them back inside the scrapbook and retold myself the story that she would be better off without me now. She could go to Davos and live with Fishballs without being hassled about it.

Ann was at our Duxbury house with the dogs while Penelope finished her stay at Peter Bent. Gardiner refused to let me bring them to Squaw Valley with me, but he told me Ann had moved into our house to take care of them until Penelope was released. At least Penelope wasn't alone, but Ann's gallon of vodka a day made for collusion in addiction, not practical nursing. They probably sang songs and staggered around the house dancing with the dogs. They probably ate when the drugs wore off and made grand plans at the heights of their highs and never did anything about them.

It was probably one of those New England afternoons in March, when the wind blows and the sun tries to warm the new blossoms, but it's cold enough to need a jacket even though one is reluctant to put it on. Penelope must have emerged from her bedroom and called down the steep stairs to Ann, who was probably in the living room watching television, "Annie twinkle, be a duck and run to the A&P and fetch me some cigarettes, will you? Get me two packs of Benson & Hedges 100s. Regulars, not that horrible menthol."

And Ann probably climbed into Grandpa's beat-up, old, green Dodge and went to the A&P. She'd only just run inside for the cigarettes and maybe just one more bottle. One should never risk a dry hour. And perhaps just a little snort on the way home at the bar. She was gone an hour. Or maybe two. She didn't wear a watch.

I wasn't there to steer Penelope back to bed and insist on bringing her soup upstairs to her on a tray, or to make sure there was an ashtray on her bedside table. Maybe it was on purpose that she staggered down the stairs and went to the kitchen, turned on the gas without lighting the stove, and forgot what she was doing. Maybe she got distracted in her narcotic fog and forgot. She'd always said I was her reason for living and now I was gone. But then, she also said I was her reason for wanting to die.

Maybe she leaned down to light her cigarette from the gas flame, but there was none. Maybe she perched her lit cigarette on the stove and turned on the gas, thinking she might make some soup as she'd done many times in a narcotic stupor. Or maybe she decided to die that afternoon instead and knelt down to breathe in the gas from the open oven door. The cigarette burned and the gas met its little orange embers like a woman meeting her lover.

The flames roared to life and quickly consumed her red-plaid, cashmere, Brooks Brothers bathrobe, so quick to burn. They slapped her face and then ate her hair and slapped and slapped until they had consumed almost every inch of her delicate flesh. And curling down to the floor, Penelope had to give in.

Smoke filled the kitchen, and when Ann returned home, she couldn't see inside. Strangely, the kitchen door had been locked. Had she locked it? She couldn't have. She ran around to the front door, and it too was locked. Where were the dogs? She called, and they came running from the woods. Penelope must have let them out. Ann screamed and banged on the window. But there was no response.

Ann drove the mile or so to the Duxbury police station, managing only to cry and scream about her baby sister Penelope on the floor. The police knew the house well, having been called many times by the school to drop by and threaten me with juvenile detention.

On March 23, 1974, when it was getting dark outside, Penelope Converse Pier was pronounced dead. The coroner's report, written in barely legible handwriting, read, "Victim was found lying by the kitchen stove where the fire originated. Victim's red plaid wrapper caught fire. Victim had third-degree burns to face, chest, and arms. Cause of death: cardiac arrest."

But I knew it wasn't cardiac arrest. He'd just had to say something other than suicide. I'd had a dream that week, just after I turned sixteen, as I slept in the same bed she'd used to sleep in, in our house in Squaw Valley. I slept on her side of the bed and thought I could even smell the sweetness of her skin on my pillow. I dreamed she'd died and had come to say goodbye to me. But that was before I knew that dreams were the language of the soul.

When Gardiner called me, I had just woken up, having stayed the night at a friend's house—I'd reunited with Heidi Chisholm, whom I had always thought of as Redheaded Heidi, and we were just being teenagers, having a good time, staying up most of the night smoking and gossiping. I knew he was going to tell me Penelope was dead before he even told me. He asked me to come down to his office right away, but I didn't ask what he wanted. I just said I would walk there, without asking what he wanted. Redheaded Heidi walked with me. We were planning to cut school, and she worried our plans would be foiled.

"Don't worry," I said. "It's probably nothing. I'm probably in trouble for not cleaning the house or some shit."

After Gardiner told me, "Your mother is gone," he began to cry, and I comforted him. I felt myself leaning toward the door where Redheaded Heidi was waiting for me.

We skipped school and skied all day. As we walked home, I thought that didn't want to go to my house. I wanted to stay at her house. Mrs. Chisholm greeted us at the door, her eyes filled with tears. "Oh Kimmy," she began.

I felt myself withdraw into the armor. "It's okay," I said. "I'm fine, but can I just stay here tonight?"

"Of course, my darling," she said. "You can stay as long as you want."

I thought of how comfortable I would be living in Redheaded Heidi's room and forgetting the last four years of my life, as if they had just been a horrible dream.

I wanted to go with Gardiner to her funeral, but he told me he couldn't afford to take me. I asked him to bring the dogs back with him, but he refused, saying it would be too expensive. I asked him to ship all our furniture and belongings so I could go through all of it, but he sold it all instead. All those uncomfortable antiques of Penelope's were sold to pay off her bills, mostly at the Duxbury pharmacies. He brought back a few of her things—a red Eddie Bauer jacket that she'd worn all the time in winter; a gold bracelet that had been a gift from Fishballs; a couple of her sweaters; her odd pieces of jewelry, like a necklace made of old spurs and a ring shaped like a Western saddle; her fur hat; and her Chanel airplane suits. A couple of years later, the gold bracelet was stolen by one of the stray men I took in to rent a room in our house. I wore the sweaters until they were full of holes. The hat was eaten by moths, but I held onto the Eddie Bauer jacket and wore it until it was threadbare.

In the months following her death, after Al and Diane moved out of my room, I gathered all of Penelope's belongings from around our house and put them way back in my closet, hiding them underneath my clothes where they would be safe from Gardiner and Sammie. I found two more of Penelope's scrapbooks inside an old trunk in the garage, which had been pushed under his tool bench, out of sight, as if Gardiner were trying to deny her existence but couldn't quite bring himself to throw her completely away. I pulled the huge books out and opened the big black one I remembered from long ago. Inside were all the clippings and articles about mountain lion hunts and skiing and mountain climbing in Switzerland. "Tell me about the lion hunt again, Mummy," I would beg, and she'd pull the scrapbook out and lay it on her bed, and we'd spend hours looking at them as she told stories of her adventures before I was born. There was a series of photos and an article about an avalanche rescue, where she had modeled as the victim. In the picture, a dog was digging her out of the snow, and she looked dead. Then there was a photo of men putting her on a sled and putting an oxygen hose in her mouth. Now I looked at the yellowed article and thought of how many times I'd seen her on other kinds of emergency transporters with oxygen masks and tubes. I turned the page.

I saw the lion hunt photos from Kanab, Utah, her first trip west, with Fishballs as her guide to the wild canyons and mountains; I saw the photos of the climb on the Matterhorn and the photo of her that made the cover of *Glamour* magazine in 1950. And at the back of the book were all the black-and-white photos of her that she'd used for her modeling portfolio. I took them out and carefully tacked them to my bedroom wall until it was almost completely covered.

Then I took out the big, blue leather photo album from way back in the closet. It was dusty and a little warped as if it had been left out in the garage. The blue album was where she'd kept all the pictures she'd taken of me. There was a picture of me taken four hours after I was born, and then there were hundreds of pictures of me up until I was about eight. And then everything ended. All the remaining pages were blank starting with 1966, marking the point in time when sickness had taken us all away from Christmas and playing with dogs and singing to Penelope's accordion and Gardiner's harmonica while the dogs howled in delight. Gardiner had built her a darkroom downstairs so she could develop her own pictures. And there were hundreds of them on proof sheets inside the album. Some were circled in red pencil—the ones she'd meant to develop one day. The proof sheets were tattered and cracked now, having been stuffed inside the album in haste as if she would have time later.

I put the trunk back under the tool bench and took the big, black scrapbook up the long path to our house. I wrapped the scrapbook in towels and shoved it under my bed, where Gardiner wouldn't know I had it, and where it was safe from Sammie. I stuffed the blue album in my dresser drawer and covered it with sweaters.

I didn't know how to be in the world without Penelope. There was so much space, and I wasn't anyone's reason to live anymore. I didn't know how to be my own reason to live. It seemed I was only in Gardiner's way, and I wanted to make it easy for him to leave. At least I could be astonishingly easy. And I made being astonishingly easy my specialty, a craft, like acting.

47

CAPTURING LOVE

I COULD ACT AS IF I DIDN'T really need anything; it felt better to be an endless supply of abundance, to be the giver of long back rubs, the one who always made the cookies to bring to school to share, the one to offer up a cigarette or give up my lunch money to a boy, secretly hoping to become his forever girl. I lingered where the boys gathered along the heat register at school, hoping to be chosen, as if I had a reason to be where they were. I pretended to read or search my purse with intense focus, as if finding the right pen were all I really wanted. Penelope had told me not to have sex until I was married. That would have been easy, but in order to get love, it seemed I would have to have sex.

I asked my friend Jeri how to capture the boy I liked—a boy who had just had a loud fight with his girlfriend out in the hallway after French class. Barely fifteen, Jeri had breasts that were big and beautiful, perfectly shaped honeydews, much more than handfuls unless the boys had very large hands. But she had a boyfriend who was equally as beautiful, like one of those surfer boys I'd lusted after when I'd lived in Laguna Beach. Blond, narrow-hipped, well-muscled, and tan, he and Jeri were the perfect pair. They'd been going out together for two years, and Jeri said they had sex all the time, sometimes standing up or in the car or in the shower. She'd put a lot of miles on her vagina already and knew exactly what to do. My vagina was like a foreign land I only visited occasionally, stopping by for a moment only to clean its cage or feed it a tampon as if it were a lonesome parakeet.

"Just take off your pants and lie on your back," she said. "It might hurt, but whatever you do, don't cry or make a big deal out of it. He'll think you're a dork. And moan a lot or breathe hard so he knows you like it." I could attain such rapture by myself, safe in the world of fantasy, but Jeri made it sound like sex was really fun and easy once you got the hang of it. Like making it all the way to tensies playing jacks.

And so I lured him, wearing a sweater that showed my breasts pretty well, including the nipples if I got cold enough. He made it a point to hold my hand when his ex-girlfriend was around, and we kissed goodbye after each class. After three whole days, he asked me to meet him at Jeri's house after school. I was practically hysterical with excitement and sought counsel from Jeri one more time about how to have sex.

He began to kiss me and caress me, and I felt warm and willing, as long as my clothes were on. But once he put his hand on my crotch, I left my body and closed down, fear gripping me about losing my virginity, something Penelope had told me I should hang onto and protect, as if it were some kind of treasure men would want and attempt to steal, like a red Corvette. I was about to hand over my red Corvette without a wedding or even the promise of a return phone call, yet I felt I could not say no. I could never say no to anything, the word having been absent from my vocabulary for quite some time.

My underpants made it to my ankles, and then I kicked one foot out as he pried my legs apart with his knees. They dangled from one foot as he pushed his pants down just far enough. His shoes were still on. I bit my lip and hoped I wouldn't bleed too much. It was over before I could begin the moaning and panting performance. I lay on my back, stunned and worried. Was I supposed to feel something? And then he said he had to get going, but I thought we would get married. I leaned on him the next day at school, having marked him as my territory. He shrugged me off like an itchy sweater. He went back to his girlfriend, and I ate two boxes of Ritz Crackers and half a jar of Skippy chunky peanut butter.

48

MY BODY —
WINTER 1974

IN THE HOT, MUGGY SUMMERS IN Duxbury and New York City with
Penelope, I had missed Squaw Valley so much that it ached in my chest.
I'd wanted to wear a bikini, but each one I'd tried on in the privacy of dressing
rooms had been a reminder that my body still looked like Scooter's, not
Barbie's. At fourteen, I had worried that I looked ridiculous with no hips
or breasts. But now, at sixteen, I stood in front of the mirror and saw a girl
I didn't know or recognize. I had breasts, but I wasn't lean, not even close
to Barbie, with my thickish thighs and doughy belly. I stood there hoping
I would turn into Penelope, whose warnings about having a huge ass and
thighs like tree trunks echoed in my head. The mirror confirmed that I did
not look like Barbie, and I didn't look like Penelope either.

Gardiner came up behind me. "Dad, do you think I'm fat?" He grabbed
the fleshy handles sitting above my hips. I froze and held my breath, reflex-
ively holding my stomach in as hard as I could. I'd never been fat, not even
close, until now. Penelope had seen to that, with her daily warnings about

looking like Gardiner's mother, Grannie Pier, whom I'd always thought had a comfortable grandmother's butt and soft, squishy breasts.

"You'd better do some sit-ups and get some regular exercise right quick," he said and left me standing there, hating the girl in the mirror even more, the imprints of his fingers still on my fat-rippled flesh.

The hope of ever winning his approval or love dropped over the horizon. I learned to hide, as best I could, my longing that he would just be my daddy again. I still had my armor and could slip into it when I needed to pretend it didn't hurt. His criticism of me served to strengthen his case for leaving me behind. He found more reasons to assign me to the category of juvenile delinquent because I smoked and failed to be a ski racer or a good student.

The boys could feel the grasping and clutching even before my fingers had a chance to brush the locks of hair away from their eyes or touch the skin along their muscled thighs, and then, soon enough, they would find reasons to leave and never call. I learned to be so deeply ashamed of my body that I couldn't stand myself and hid underneath big t-shirts and loose pants, hoping that my ugliness wouldn't show. I wanted to starve myself but could only last a day or two before emptiness overcame me and I ate so much so quickly that I hated myself even more.

49

THE DAY TOM KELLY CHANGED MY LIFE — WINTER 1974

I CHAIN-SMOKED VIRGINIA SLIMS MENTHOLS BEHIND TRUCKEE High School, cutting algebra until there was no hope of passing. Then I cut school entirely and went skiing instead, which made it easier for Gardiner to conclude that Sammie was right, and I *was* a juvenile delinquent. He kept insisting that I return to the ski-racing scene, like all the other kids from a long time ago in another life, thinking it was what I needed to acquire the self-discipline he thought I lacked. Ski racing in Squaw was a whole new scene now. No more playtime and lemon drops during dry-land training, like when I was eight. And the slalom courses weren't on Gold Coast, where there was always the option to ski off into the trees to avoid embarrassment; now they were on the steep runs out in the open where everyone could watch. Nobody else seemed intimidated by having an audience.

"Just go for it. This is not so tough," said my Austrian coach with disdain. Believing in myself was so foreign that when I was told to believe in myself, I felt like I needed a set of instructions for assembly of a self and then a switch so I could turn it on. What was a self, and what did it mean to believe in it? All I could feel was fear—fear of sleeping in the dark, fear of being left behind, fear of not being loved . . . and, mostly, fear that I didn't belong anywhere anymore. My existence had been occupied, colonized, evaporated, and absorbed by Penelope. Now I had no palpable reason to exist, and I just groped around for something to hang onto—a pastrami sandwich, a cigarette, a boy. Standing at the top of a racecourse, the only voice I heard in my head was Gardiner's telling me to get on with it and quit being such a sissy. He wanted me to have goals, make him the proud father of a U.S. Ski Team member, and if I couldn't, it would be easy for him to give up on me.

Tom Kelly was among the coaches for one of the Squaw Valley ski teams, now with a few more wrinkles than he'd had when I was a kid. All the wrinkles were the result of years of smiling and laughing. I wasn't with Tom's elite group; I was with the coach for those of us who couldn't put a fast race together, the slow ones whose pants didn't fit and who would have preferred to get stoned if not for demanding parents. I fell or skied out of the course on each race, knowing Gardiner would be angry. The rides home with him were silent except for his expressions of disappointment and frustration that I couldn't get my shit together.

Occasionally, there were races where we losers got to race with the elite racers. One day, when the light was flat in Squaw, the giant slalom was set on Red Dog, exposed and steep, at least for me, and I would have an opportunity to fall flat on my butt in front of the entire valley. The other kids were laughing and joking around, warming up, riding on the lift together. I waited for my green chair just for luck. Maybe I would feel better, more like a ski racer instead of an imposter, a mule in a corral full of racehorses.

Standing at the top of the course, I felt like I was sacrificing myself to a dark sea full of hungry sharks. I would fall to my death and be devoured in the dark sea of my own shame. I shook and quaked at the top of the course, swallowing vomit and holding my pee. It was almost my turn, and the ruts were deep. Tom was at the top of the course to give pep talks and course instructions with Warren Gibson, the coach for a few of the nation's elite young male ski racers, for all of whom I longed.

Tom and Warren saw me shaking so hard that my poles rattled; tears welled up in my eyes and steamed up the lenses of my goggles. Then I saw Gardiner walking over to the bottom of the racecourse from his office, and my heart sank. His presence was almost a guarantee of my failure to complete the run. Any remotely loving thoughts I had about myself flailed and struggled against the fierce tug of self-hatred to which I succumbed, sinking lower and lower until I disappeared into Gardiner's assessment of who I was. With only a few minutes until the countdown, when I would project myself out of the starting gate and try just to get through my ordeal, I felt a presence move up next to me.

Tom was laughing, and, of course, the smile took up most of his face. "Vell?" he said, breaking into robust Irish laughter. The Austrian accent was our little joke. I imitated Hans, whose frustration with me had come out one day when we were running slalom gates. I had done what I usually did at practices, falling and skiing with my ass stuck out and my skis so far apart that a cat fight could have taken place between my legs and I wouldn't even have known it. "Vell?" Hans had demanded, his arms spread as if to indicate hopelessness, perhaps an end to schnapps and strudel forever. "I don't know . . . you ski like my sick grandmother." He shook his his head and waved me off for yet another run. I imitated Hans whenever I saw Tom, and he would burst into laughter and exclaim, "Vell?!"

"Yahvole!" I would exclaim. "I ski like his sick grandmother!"

Now as I readied myself for the run, I managed a nauseated laugh as Tom grabbed me with one arm, lifting me up off the snow at the top of the racecourse. "Kimmy, Kimmy!" he laughed, teasing me with my childhood nickname.

He set me down right in front of him. What he said in the next moment changed my life. "Hey, now listen," he said softly. "Ski racing is supposed to be fun! This is for *you*. Just you. It's not for your dad or me or anybody else. This is for you to have fun and just let it all go. It's not life and death; it's just a race! So just laugh and have a good time! Forget about your dad. And . . . I want you to smile the whole way down, okay? Yahvole! Hahahaaa!" And he held me close.

Then Warren sidestepped down beside me and gave me another piece of wisdom that I never forgot: "And remember, your primary need is oxygen. Breathe."

I went to the starting gate, doubting the whole smiling idea. But the countdown began, and I pushed myself free. I flew down the course and, somehow, I remembered to smile. Everything just slowed down, and I could hear my breath mingling with the sounds of my edges carving through each gate, years of shame and sorrow falling from my body like dross from a burning star. *For me*, I thought. *This is for me.* The weight of performing to fulfill someone else's idea for me lifted, and for the first time in my life, I felt the lightness of joy, the playfulness available in doing something out of sheer love. I won the race that day and did not acknowledge Gardiner as I skied past him at the bottom and got on the lift to ski for fun and revel in my newfound identity as a winner.

Sometimes, it only takes one person in one moment to change everything. It had never occurred to me that I deserved to have fun and that I could do something just for myself rather than making everything I did an effort to please someone else.

50
BILLY – SPRING 1974

Jeri's boyfriend, Dane, lived in the Klaussen's old house. It had many rooms, all of which I remembered from the many nights I had spent there when Penelope had been sick and Gardiner on emergency calls. My favorite room had built-in bunk beds, great for playing hide and seek, but bedtime had meant darkness and worrying about whether Penelope was going to die in the night.

Dane's mother had taken in a ski racer, and when I saw him I decided he would be mine forever. I loved ski racers; they were so muscular and boyish, always smelling vaguely of dirty socks and sweaty long underwear, but this one actually showered regularly. They wore tight pants and never combed their hair, seeming not to care what the girls thought. Billy's hair was reckless, black and curly. And his jeans rode his hipbones like raspberry jam on warm bread. I'd already lost my virginity for nothing. I figured it didn't matter anymore, and Penelope was dead, so what good was virginity now, anyway? Maybe he wouldn't notice I was used. I'd felt nothing when I'd had sex and wondered why it was such a big deal. I worried that my vagina didn't work, that maybe I'd been given a faulty vagina. I knew everything worked fine when I found my clitoris, but I thought something magical was supposed to happen when a penis arrived on the scene, as if I would no longer need my clitoris. But it turned out that my clitoris was the key to everything wonderful in my entire sexual range. I was all about the clitoris, and I thought something was terribly amiss with that. But that could be my secret, just like killing Penelope. I could just live with the fact that I was the only girl on the planet whose vagina was defective, and that my only source of sexual satisfaction would be my clitoris and my finger. I would certainly never tell Billy that he should just forget about my vagina and pay attention to my clitoris. So I just left my body and tried to make all the right noises so that he might think I was phenomenal and choose me to be his one and only forever.

I laid seductively on Billy's bed after he got out of the shower and watched him in the mirror as he combed his beautiful dark curls and then shaved off the five or six hairs on his chin. I knew I had him pretty well hooked when his erection poked through his blue terrycloth bathrobe like a salute to the Third Reich, and I hadn't really been doing anything much other than changing positions a lot on his bed trying to make sure my breasts were showing a little. I strained to keep from giggling when I saw his weasel; he didn't seem to know it was out. I did not immediately address it, deciding to demurely turn away and look out the window as if fascinated by the view of the back porch.

I was his first, and I wanted it to be special, so we decided we would make love in front of the fireplace on Dane's mother's fake bearskin rug. "Do you have a condom?" I asked breathlessly when the situation reached a point of no return.

"No!" he said with an expression of sheer panic on his face. I thought quickly and arose from my supine position and dashed into the kitchen. "Where are you *going?*!" he asked in a tone suggesting imminent cardiac arrest. I rifled through the kitchen drawers until I found a box of Glad sandwich bags. "Here," I said, racing back to my position on the bearskin rug. "We can use this."

"How will we use a sandwich bag?" he exclaimed, attempting to wrap his purple, swollen penis with shaking hands. "Like this," I said snatching the bag off of it and stuffing it into my vagina. "It will be like a shield. Nothing can get past it, don't worry," I said reassuringly. "Now get in!" And so he did, and it was over in seconds. We lay there on the rug, my fingers running through his hair, loving each curl. He went to sleep for a while in my arms, but I felt I might never sleep again.

"I think I love you," he said when he woke up. Those magical, blissful words I longed to hear.

I was lost in him, completely absorbed in fixing his meals, doing his laundry, and following him everywhere. His mother brought him a large box full of small kitchen appliances—one designed to cook bacon perfectly, another for making waffles, and another for making grilled cheese sandwiches. Penelope had been dead a whole month, long enough for Gardiner to finish packing all his books and clothes and begin his move to Columbine Creek. He made sure he only took a few tools, and then a few shirts at a time, so it seemed like he was still a little bit here, not quite in Columbine Creek forever. Billy and I would have Gardiner's house mostly to ourselves. Only one housemate remained in one of the rooms downstairs, but by spring he had gone on a trip to Argentina. I was grateful he'd left his dog to keep me company.

"He likes da sandviches," Billy's mother Yana said in her Czech accent. "He likes about three or four for lunch vid a lodda cheese." She unloaded several loaves of bread and several pounds of cheese. "And he like crêpes." She pulled out a crêpe pan. "You know how to make?"

"No," I admitted.

And then she removed a blender from the box. "Come, I show you," she said brusquely, wrapping her kerchief around her head. And so I learned the care and maintenance of Billy from his mother, who left only after she had run through the meal plan several times and instructed me on the feeding schedule.

We had sex almost all the time, and I tried to feel something, begging my vagina to please be normal, but I was frozen inside, so closed up that I couldn't stay and had to leave my body every time. I rose to the ceiling, watching myself perform and wondering what could be wrong with me. I could never tell him; he would leave me for sure if he knew I was broken, so I pretended to be the queen of orgasms, my screams echoing off the granite around Squaw Valley for all the neighbors to hear.

I wasn't expecting to feel such despair whenever he left for more than a day. When he left for training or races away from Squaw Valley, I went into mourning, as though he'd died. I could barely move under its weight, the tears welling without prompting, and Gardiner telling me I was being ridiculous, which made me wish I could be different or better somehow.

When my Billy left with the team for training down near Mammoth, California, I was frantic that I couldn't even talk to him on the phone. Our reunions were like the return of Orpheus to Eurydice. I waited on our front porch, pacing back and forth on the day I knew he would come home, and when the team van dropped him off, he ran as fast as he could, up the sixty-four concrete steps Gardiner had built, sometimes leaping three at a time, and caught me, swinging me off my feet and around and around, finally stopping, breathless and panting. Our eyes locked, and he kissed me as if I were an ice cream sundae. His eyes were big and blue, fringed with dark lashes, and he wasn't afraid to look directly into mine. I wasn't afraid to go to sleep with him. I could hardly ever sleep by myself, but I could sleep with Billy.

He moved into our house for part of the summer while Gardiner went back and forth between Squaw and Columbine Creek in a frenzied attempt to appease Sammie and also not completely abandon me, but unlike me, Sammie had the power to keep him scared of losing her, or at least losing access to her vagina.

Billy's mother wanted him to go home to Berkeley over the summer, so he could work and earn some money for all his expensive ski racing equipment. She invited me to come, too, knowing how attached Billy and I were and not wanting me to be rattling around alone in my house in Squaw.

I felt like a caged animal in the rush and din of this new city without a way to go anywhere, too uncertain to figure out how I could venture out all day while he and his mother worked. I was all alone with food, all day. In the past, food had never really been anything but a sort of innocuous presence in the refrigerator or the cupboard.

In my life with Penelope, we'd sometimes had food and sometimes not. When we'd run out, she would send me to the store with a check, which was likely to bounce, and I would be given a note that I had permission to buy wine and cigarettes. I bought what I knew Penelope would eat: Sara Lee frozen blueberry cheesecakes; packaged Carl Buddig turkey or beef for sandwiches, along with Hellman's mayonnaise, yellow mustard, bread, and various soups; Triscuits; and Pepperidge Farm chocolate chip cookies. She'd liked Campbell's tomato soup; I liked Campbell's Bean with Bacon. I'd bought vegetable soup and chicken noodle soup, too, just for a change now and then, and a few Swanson TV dinners, usually fried chicken or turkey, or any dinner with mashed potatoes and a decent dessert. And we had always needed dog food. We'd never eaten fresh fruits or vegetables. Vegetables required thought and preparation, whereas the soups had the vegetables already in them. I'd rarely even bothered to cook the bean with bacon soup, preferring to eat spoonfuls directly from the can and then put the unused portion back in the fridge, tin lid pressed down over the pasty soup to keep it from drying out. We'd never bothered with tin foil or Saran Wrap. Soup had been stored in the pot with the lid on.

Now, having discovered that there was a whole world of food beyond Swanson and Campbell's Soup, and that I wasn't responsible for buying it and explaining to the store manager later why the check had bounced and should be sent through a second time, food was suddenly available. I began to gain weight, a problem I had been mostly unfamiliar with except when Penelope had looked at my blossoming hips and breasts and warned me that if I continued to eat french fries, I would end up looking like Gardiner's mother. "Grannie has an ass as big as the side of a barn, and her legs look like tree stumps. It's a sign of her poor breeding, so at least you don't have *that* problem, but you better watch it. You could end up having a body from your *father's* side of the family," she would say disdainfully, putting breathy emphasis on the word "father," and then remarking on how her tiny hips and broad shoulders were a mark of exquisite breeding.

Since I'd come back to live with Gardiner, I couldn't help myself. The food tasted so delicious, especially the school lunches. At school, I would go to the line and pick exactly what I wanted and eat it outside or in the gym with Redheaded Heidi and a few other kids I'd known since we were all in kindergarten. I'd never had pizza fresh from the oven, dripping with cheese and pepperoni floating in little ponds of its own fat; I'd never eaten a pastrami sandwich with mustard and cheese, warmed in the oven, or had hamburgers on buns with cheese and bacon. I began chasing my school lunches with ice cream sandwiches, and after a month or so, I noticed I couldn't zip my pants anymore. I hadn't paid much attention; Penelope was dead and she couldn't see that I was beginning to look like my Grannie. But Gardiner noticed. And from the moment he'd grabbed the handfuls of tender teenage flesh around my waist, I'd felt deeply and irreversibly ashamed and vowed never to eat pastrami again. I tried to skip lunches and dinners, but I hated being hungry and always gave in after a day or so of starving myself.

Food became my torturer, a predator waiting for me to ruin my nice streak of starvation and eat in a frenzy of anxiety and shame. But now that I was in Berkeley for a few weeks and alone all day, I began a pattern of eating as if there would be no other opportunity ever again, and then I felt sick for several days afterward. The feeling of unbearable fullness was followed by a longing for the feeling of emptiness. The fearsome cavern inside was never far away, and neither was the emptiness.

Billy didn't seem to notice. He had a focus; I had none other than him. I wished I had something that called me other than an insatiable need for his attention. He was disciplined in his training regimen, spending hours out running or doing ski-racing drills, flexing in front of the mirror, asking me to watch him flex different sets of muscles every two minutes. "See, look at these," he said, flexing and posing. "These are my pecs. And these are my delts . . . see? Watch. I can flex them independently of all other muscles."

I tried to sound admiring over the stifling voice of my insecurity about my own body, which was getting fatter despite my efforts to starve. I could manage a diet of carrots and celery for a couple of days, putting saccharine tablets in my coffee instead of sugar, smoking more cigarettes, reading diet books, and counting calories. Food had become the lurking predator that attacked when I was alone. When nobody was around, I didn't know what to do with myself, and soon a nibble of something turned into a blind fury of eating everything I could get my hands on, until I was so full it hurt to move. The speed and intensity with which food gripped my attention was terrifying, and even worse was the aftermath of guilt and fear as I worried about how I would ever work off all that I had eaten. The fear of throwing up superseded all, so my only option was a strict regimen of starvation and furious exercise as repentance for my sins. The emptiness always felt so good on day two or three of not eating. I felt safe in the space of deprivation.

I didn't know what to do with myself while he was at work or working out or playing with his slot cars. I often waited hours for him to wake up on his days off, anticipating spending many hours together, but teenage boys can sleep longer than sloths. They can also eat twenty times their own weight. He was always hungry, and I was always trying to restrain myself from eating. The reality that my happiness depended upon whether he was paying attention to me felt like trying to capture water in my hands.

51

LEFT BEHIND —
SUMMER 1974

WHEN GARDINER WOULD RETURN TO SQUAW to pack up more of his things, he would come and get me in Berkeley so that we could have some time together to go for hikes or play tennis. Those were the tiny windows of time when I hoped Gardiner would see how much better it could be to live with me instead of Sammie. But on one particular occasion, Sammie came along, and I didn't know about it until we got home, when I saw her taking a box of her belongings down to the garage.

"Why is *she* here?" I demanded. "I thought we were going to have time together without her."

Gardiner looked annoyed. "She's going to pack the last of her things and then go visit her mother in Reno. She won't be here long, so you'll just have to be polite and deal with it." I had no intention of being polite and went to stay at the Chisholm's house until she left.

She had taken over the house right after Penelope and I had departed for Laguna Beach in the spring of 1970. I don't think the exhaust had cleared from the tailpipe of Penelope's Porsche before Sammie moved her children and her collection of Coty frosted lipsticks into the house I'd once believed nobody could ever live in except Penelope, Gardiner, me, and our dogs. She shoved all evidence of Penelope into the darkest reaches of the cellar and the closets. She must have refused to sleep on Penelope's side of the bed and slept on Gardiner's side instead. I knew which side Gardiner had slept on because I'd discovered a device for maintaining an erection, a penis-enlarging device, and porn magazines on Penelope's bedside table drawer when I'd returned home and had to sleep in the king-sized bed Penelope and Gardiner had once slept in.

Sammie was crafty, sinister, like a fatter, trashier version of Cruella De Vil, planning ways to show Gardiner that I wasn't worth keeping. Once, I had discovered maggots in one of the cupboards and asked Gardiner what they were. Sammie stood with her arms folded, a smoldering Winston dangling from the corner of her coral-frosted lips. "I saw her put groceries away and she put the meat in there I bet, Gardy. Look way back in the cupboard." She was yanking out maggot-covered cans and packages of spaghetti and throwing them at my feet. "I asked her to put the groceries away, and she put the meat in there, *see?*" and she pulled out the white package of rotting hamburger crawling with maggots. "*This* is what I'm talking about," she hissed. "She's irresponsible and sneaky, and I will not live with this!" She stormed out screaming, "It's either *her* or *me*, Gardy! You fucking decide!"

A few months back, I'd overheard Sammie tell him that I should be sent to juvenile detention and could not be trusted alone in the house. His watch had disappeared, and she claimed to have torn the house apart and found his expensive watch in my underwear drawer. She stole money from his wallet and hid it in my pants pockets and told him he ought to go through all my clothing, that she was certain he would find it. He had been planning to move to Columbine Creek anyway, but now that I was on his hands, I was in the way. In the summer of my sixteenth year, she was throwing her stuff in boxes while Gardiner tried to plead with her to calm down. He was following her around waving away the clouds of cigarette smoke from her Winston. She stopped in front of Penelope's dresser and began to shove drawers in and yank them out, grabbing her stuff and throwing it in boxes. "You need to make a decision, Gardy. But I'm not living with that little bitch of a daughter of yours," she shouted, blowing the smoke through her frosted lips and tapping her pink sneakers on the floor, arms folded, squeezing her tits up out of her sleeveless pink shirt.

I was watching from the door of Penelope's bedroom, where she had infected Penelope's closet with her poor taste in clothing but was now packing the last of it. I hoped she would leave and that Gardiner would go with her. Then I could live by myself in my own house. Just me and Penelope's ghost. There was no invitation for me to move with them to Columbine Creek, and I never asked. They would move away and bring only Darryl, Sammie's son, who was about to enter high school; the two girls were old enough to be on their own. Tammy Jo was living with various men and participating in every wet t-shirt contest held at the Bear Pen on Friday nights. She'd become Gardiner's daughter over the past several years and occupied the same place in his life that I once had, including being his shadow at his office.

Sammie was in Columbine Creek fixing up their new house, while he stayed here to finish up seeing patients he'd treated over the past fifteen years of being in Squaw Valley. Gardiner was more like his old self now, and it occurred to me that maybe Gardiner had taken me back because he had known there would be money in it for him, or maybe Sammie had encouraged him to take me back so that the money would be available to her. At least while he was in Squaw, he didn't have to worry about Sammie rebuking him for spending time with me. We went for long hikes around the mountains in Squaw, we played tennis, we went for swims in Lake Tahoe, and we had long talks. Those were the times when I thought, just for a little while, that he would love me the best and choose me instead. If I could be stoic and understanding, he would see that I was worth keeping. So we talked about all his troubles with Sammie, and I was always a good listener.

I still had my old guitar, and I sang to him. He loved the John Denver songs I'd learned to play, and he especially loved "Angel from Montgomery," by John Prine, or any song about Colorado. Gardiner had grown weary of Squaw Valley and felt he'd found a new frontier in Columbine Creek, a place where he could start a brand new life. And there were no vestiges of Penelope there, no reminders of the conversations they'd once had about retiring at sea, like the Owl and the Pussycat who sailed away in a beautiful pea-green boat.

52

BELONGING

WHEN I CAME HOME FROM BERKELEY after being there for several weeks, Gardiner had moved almost all of his belongings to Columbine Creek. It was now midsummer, and Billy was coming up to stay with me so that he could participate in dry-land ski training with the rest of the boys on the elite boys' race team. I felt comfortable being in my own house. The summer was soft and warm, the purple lupines in full bloom on the hillside in back of the house, and the meadow was green and full of wildflowers; the mountains were bare of snow, and the creeks ran full.

Dry land ski racing training had been a part of my summer as a child. The same Squaw Valley kids I'd done push-ups and sit-ups with as a child were still doing the same calisthenics now. Back then, on weekends in the late summer and throughout the fall, we had been wrested from Saturday morning sleep and herded down to the base of the mountain where we would run up the mountain a ways, and then turn around to run down, pretending that we were skiing through a slalom race course. We would groan and collapse on our stomachs at the top, feigning death from exhaustion, but we would soon be laughing as we ran down. We would then gather on the big lawn in back of the Squaw Valley Lodge and do the calisthenics followed by a soccer game. We were not allowed to be late to practice and never missed a day. Our coaches were fathers of the kids on the team—all were tanned, athletic, handsome, and strong. They herded us up and down the mountains of Squaw Valley like little goats. When one of us lagged behind on the hikes, Tom would pull a bag of lemon drops from his pocket to boost our plummeting blood sugar, encouraging us with threats of pushups. The two Austrian weren't the lemon-drop types, expecting us to show fidelity to the Austrian tradition—a reverence for ski racing, no whining or complaining about being tired. wheezing and wishing I could turn around and go home without being noticed. I loved the hikes and the calisthenics; it was choosing up sides for soccer games afterward that I dreaded. We all had to play soccer because it built strength and agility for ski racing. But there were always arguments over who would get stuck with me. I believed that nobody was as trustworthy as I with a soccer ball, therefore I had volunteered to play all positions. I was willing to give up the ball only when under threat of serious injury. Why couldn't they see how capable and worthy I was of being a member of the team? I'd tried harder, unyielding in my grasp of that ball, determined to show that I was worth choosing.

Now, as a sixteen-year-old, I lagged behind when we ran up the mountains, my lungs straining against the tar and nicotine of the Virginia Slims menthols that I smoked when I was away from all the kids who were so good and pure and who had Olympic dreams. In the soccer games, I avoided the ball, timidly clutching my hands to my chest, trying to be invisible on the field while the world whirled around me. Only a few months had passed after Penelope's death, and Gardiner's expectation of me was to join the Squaw Valley race team scene, as if no time had passed, and nothing significant had occurred to disrupt my childhood. It seemed Gardiner wanted a seamless transition, from being a carefree seven year-old before Penelope got sick, to a a well-adjusted, well-behaved sixteen year-old who wouldn't cause him any trouble. He wanted me to be an athlete, an honor student, an all-around good kid who stayed out of trouble. But I smoked, I didn't want to ski race, and the pastrami sandwiches at school were so delicious, especially with cheese, and so were those ice cream sandwiches for dessert. I was not particularly athletic looking, which he had noticed and commented on.

I had kept my inner world private during my life with Penelope. It was like a train wreck in my head, and trying to explain how I felt seemed tiresome and pointless. Gardiner just wanted me to do my homework and get good grades, and I tried. I really did, but my brain wouldn't let me pay attention. Having missed so much school, I was lost and had to pretend I knew what was going on, too ashamed to ask for help. I thought maybe if I sat in class, I would just understand it, but none of it made any sense. Fruit flies, Gregor Mendel, binomial equations . . . I couldn't make sense of any of it and wandered through my days at school hoping I could just get by. I sat before my biology book, intent upon doing the homework, wanting so badly to be in Gardiner's good graces. He kept telling me I was lazy, lacking the self-discipline I needed. I swallowed his criticism, too worn out to fight it. He wasn't happy that I was back in his life, and I knew it.

He traveled between Squaw Valley and Columbine Creek, moving a few more of his items with each trip, and his absences grew longer. He let me stay in our house, which I was grateful for, even if I had to share it with the renters who weren't around much. I didn't have to pretend to love ski racing or to be a good student in my own house. I could smoke Virginia Slims, read, listen to Elton John, and be terrified of life without anyone telling me I should just try harder. The Franklin stove was still there, and some of the same kitchen tools were in still in the drawer, the ones I had loved to play with the most while Penelope cooked—the egg beater, the potato masher, and the big spoon with holes in it. Gardiner had built shelves in the broom closet for Penelope's opera collection, but now that was gone. There were a few operas that remained gathering dust, the ones she hadn't liked very much, and the soundtracks from the Broadway musicals she and Gardiner used to love—*Camelot, My Fair Lady* with Rex Harrison and Julie Andrews, *Show Boat*, and *The Most Happy Fella*—were shoved way back in the corner. The new people had put their own records where Penelope's had been—Crosby, Stills & Nash, Janis Joplin, and Jimi Hendrix. I put them downstairs in the renter's rooms. They could keep their fucking records there, play them on their own fucking record players, and not infect Penelope's opera closet or play them on her beloved stereo system.

After I cleaned all of Penelope's drawers with Pine-Sol, trying to get rid of the Sammie residue, I moved my clothes into the built-in bureau, exactly the same as Gardiner's on the opposite side of their bedroom, and I inhaled the smell of the wood. I looked in all the drawers, including Gardiner's, to see if I could find anything left of her, maybe a forgotten scarf or a piece of jewelry, but the drawers were empty. Some of her things still hung in her closet, and I could still smell her if I closed my eyes.

53

ORPHANED AGAIN —
FALL 1974

PENELOPE HAD TOLD ME NEVER TO be an easy lay. "Why buy a cow when one can get milk through the fence?" was her reasoning for resisting the temptation to flaunt my udders and raise my tail for easy entry by the throngs of bulls who would line up on the other side of the fence. But the bulls hadn't lined up. They must have sensed that I was the cow with a complex and stayed far away in other pastures where the psychologically balanced cows were.

Billy left for Austria for a ski-racing camp in September of 1974 just as the meadow grass began to turn gold and things began to die before we were ready. He would be gone for a month, and I awoke each morning after restless sleep feeling the heaviness of despair. Gardiner was gone most of the time now. I always told him I was fine, and he liked that about me, that I made it easy for him to leave. I knew Sammie had warned him about choosing me instead. I was too afraid to sleep alone in our big house, feeling Penelope's ghost wandering and restless in the rooms at night, as if trying to retrieve her stolen life.

When Billy left, I cried as if he had died, but I told him I would wait for him, imagining that I could. But once he was gone for a week or two, I left my lonely, pitiful self behind, so sick of her helplessness and suffering, and another girl emerged from her skin, a bad, flirtatious girl who lingered by the heater at school near the boys. Billy had probably forgotten me anyway, I reasoned; I was easy to leave. I was so brave about it, Gardiner told me when he was packing his things, and so understanding and mature about it. So despite being a disappointment to him in so many other ways, my one redeeming quality was making it easy for him to leave. I felt good inside knowing he thought I was so brave and mature. I made it my mission to seem aloof and without any need at all for attention, but the harder I tried, the hungrier I felt.

I tried to do what Penelope had taught me about getting the boys to like me—be aloof, act as if you don't care, and, whatever you do, don't let them have their cake and eat it, too. But I cared so much that I might as well have been wearing a thick coat of chocolate frosting with yellow lettering on my butt that said, "Please take all the frosting you want and don't bother with the cake."

I didn't know exactly when Billy was coming home; he had said he'd call. But I must not have been home. He was frantic to see me, racked with guilt over having had sex with his old girlfriend somewhere between Oakland and Austria. He paced the living room while his mother unpacked his suitcase, pulling out dirty laundry. Sighing heavily, she finally said, "Vy you don't just take my car and go to Squaw." She held out her keys, and Billy snatched them, threw some stuff into his bag, and started his mother's red Datsun 510 station wagon, which had made far too many trips over Donner Pass and was beginning to resist, topping out at forty miles per hour as it groaned toward the summit and then, finally, over the top and down the other side toward Squaw.

I was preparing dinner for one of the boys from Warren's collection. I'd managed to lure him to my house with a promise of a back rub and chocolate cake for dessert when I heard the familiar sound of the Datsun. Its muffler needed repair, and it couldn't park without a few burps and loud farts. Billy was racing toward the front door, which I'd hastily locked when I'd heard the car. I wanted to pretend I wasn't home, but he knocked and knocked, and

I finally relented and went to the door, leaving my guest at the dinner table confused but nonetheless absorbed in his spaghetti. Billy's face was beaming with excitement when I opened the door. "You can't come in," I said coldly.

Billy's face fell. "Why?" he asked, his beautiful black curls peeking out from under his wool hat.

"Because I just don't want you here, that's all," I said, feeling a pang of shame for not waiting as I'd sworn I would.

"Are you breaking up with me?" he asked, tears welling in his eyes.

"I . . . I don't know. I'll talk to you about it tomorrow. Now, please, just go."

Billy managed to find a place to stay with his coach that night, and I carried on as if nothing had happened, returning to my new boy. I fed him dessert and then offered to rub his back, hoping he would want to kiss me and have sex with me and stay overnight, and possibly marry me. But he left after the back rub and never called me again.

54
BOYS

I COULDN'T EVEN FAKE BEING HARD TO get, and I devised ways to get more boys. I offered to cook for everyone on Warren's ski team—all beautiful, strong boys, the fifteen-year-olds still smooth and hairless, the eighteen-year-olds with Dionysian temperaments and bodies that grew out of the forests of Gilgamesh. Yes, I would be their Ereshkigal and tame their wildness with my undercooked, gluey spaghetti and sauce with too much oregano, or my warm willingness to massage their backs, my hope for their attention oozing from my every hair follicle. These young, playful gods with rivers of testosterone, wild and sweaty hair, and eager penises would be mine as long as I was willing to do whatever they asked me to do, and if they didn't ask, I would offer until they gave in and accepted. One of the boys showed me how to cook the spaghetti so it didn't stick together. He reached around my waist from behind me and poured a little olive oil into the roiling pot of noodles, took my hand, and stirred gently, whispering in my ear, "The oil keeps it nice and slippery."

I learned quickly to embody my work, fingering each succulent ingredient and tenderly adding each to the pots and sauté pans. I wore long skirts without underpants, allowing my nakedness to taste the fabric, my t-shirts showing my long-desired, peach-like breasts, just newly ripe. I tasted, allowing my fingers to linger on my tongue. The moves between the food and my body were indistinguishable.

I worked on my back-rubbing technique, adding soft laps and strokes that barely caressed frontal hip bones and the beauty of the forest below, and they would often fall asleep in my lap. But, more often, I knew my fingers could invite and beckon them into my body, and I wouldn't have to ask them to stay with me. We just drifted into my bed. I was hopeful that my boys would be captivated by my well-practiced ability to writhe and moan at precisely the right moments, that they would marvel at my apparently overflowing and easy eroticism so much that they would follow me like lemmings to the sea.

I could have painful, unsatisfying sex with the boys every day, if there was any hope of winning their eternal love. I'd heard them call me "Gibson's whore" a few times, but I pretended it didn't hurt, in the same way I pretended to have cataclysmic orgasms with each boy. My acting had to be timed with precision; they were usually done quicker than a rodeo cowboy on a bull ride.

But the boys spread the word among themselves, and each wanted his turn with me, but none wanted more than one turn. I overheard them one night as I stirred their soup on the stove, referring to me in whispers. They stifled smiles when I looked over at them. Somewhere inside, I knew it was not love they felt, and I tried harder to pretend it was not love I needed. One boy asked me what I really wanted, and I dared to tell him. "I just want you to stay with me and sleep next to me." And he did. He held me close all night, and I allowed myself to sleep. When he left the next morning, I felt sick and shook all over. I wanted Billy back. I wanted the safety of sleeping right up against his back, where I could feel his heart beat and match my breath with his. I went to where he lived, and he was sitting on the front porch. He looked at me and put his face down, looking at his hands. "What do you want?" he asked quietly.

I swallowed and sat down next to him. "Well . . . it's just that I've been thinking I might have made a mistake, and I was wondering if . . . could we maybe try again?" I asked.

He shook his head. He knew what I'd been doing. "I don't think so," he said, still looking down at his hands. There was nothing to do but walk home. I curled up in a ball and stayed that way all night, sweating, shaking, and being afraid of throwing up.

55

THE BLUE PHOTO

ALBUM

I HAD DROPPED OUT OF SCHOOL IN November of 1974, two months into my junior year. I didn't need school, I thought; I would just take correspondence courses like all the other ski racers, even though I sucked at ski racing. Gardiner was gone, and Billy wouldn't come back to me. I decided it was time to get rid of everything that reminded me of the old life. The house was for sale, and there was so much stuff. Might as well just throw it all away, I thought. It would feel good. Like starting a new life. I just wanted to be rid of everything that reminded me of a time when life had seemed as steady and familiar as the mountains around Squaw that had held me and nurtured my little family so faithfully. So I took the big, blue leather photo album of pictures Penelope had taken of me as a child and leafed through it one last time.

There was the story in photos Penelope had taken of me with Rufus, the little fawn Gardiner had rescued in 1965. That night, he was driving home from Tahoe Forest Hospital in his light-blue VW Beetle one afternoon as the light was growing dim. He rounded a corner and noticed a doe lying on the shoulder of the road and her fawn standing right next to her. He pulled over and got out his stethoscope to see if the doe was still alive. But first, he approached the little fawn by getting down on his knees and speaking softly so it wouldn't be frightened and run out into the middle of Highway 89. Animals loved Gardiner, especially dogs—except maybe Felix, who had routinely ruined Gardiner's mornings by crapping on our rug.

Gardiner lifted the little fawn in his arms and put him in the back seat of the VW Beetle and roared home to Squaw Valley. He carried the fawn up the driveway and up the sixty-four concrete steps to the front door and walked in with the fawn in his arms. The dogs went nuts, including Felix, who had never been much impressed with Gardiner anyway, being the only other boy in the household. Penelope immediately set about making a bed for Rufus in the bathroom, where it was nice and cozy and where he would be safe from the inquisitive Vizslas. Eventually, the dogs calmed down and crawled into the bed Penelope had made out of Gardiner's old military wool overcoat and some nice wool blankets. Rufus drank from a bottle, although I'm not sure the cow's milk was the best thing for him, but he drank hungrily, nearly pulling the bottle out of my hand every time. After a few weeks, we left the sliding door open so Rufus could wander in and out as he pleased. But he always came home in time for supper. Those were the days when one could wander about Squaw Valley without fear of trespassing. If you were a dog, anyone's garbage pail was fair game, and you could pee and crap to your heart's content because people didn't have lawns and the weeds didn't seem to mind. When summer was at its end, Rufus's spots began to fade, and he spent more time out in the woods, where he must have known he belonged. And one day, Rufus just didn't come home at all. Fortunately, Gardiner and Penelope had prepared me for that day by telling me that it would be a day of rejoicing, not grieving. And, so, crying a few little-girl tears, I threw his bottle away and went outside to play.

There were photos of me on my red tricycle on our front porch; there were pictures of Penelope and me horseback riding in the meadow on J. P., and of all our Christmases and birthday parties and playing outside in the wildflowers. I took that album and threw it in the garbage can in front of the garage of our house on Sandy Way.

On November 24, —Penelope would have turned fifty. I had kept her scrapbooks, with all her stories and pictures in magazines of her adventures with Fishballs to Utah, to Alaska, and all over Europe. I had kept her favorite jacket. I wore her hiking boots everywhere, and I wore her leather shirts with the leather fringes. I wore as much of her as I could.

The angels must have whispered into Joan Klaussen's ear on that November day, telling her she ought to take a different route to the post office, and she drove past my house in her red convertible. Seeing the blue photo album beckoning from the garbage can, she stopped and plucked it out and took it home with her.

56

MARCH 1975 –
A YEAR AFTER I HAD
KILLED PENELOPE

I EMANCIPATED LEGALLY WHEN I TURNED SEVENTEEN on March 11.
I'd recently received a letter addressed to Gardiner and me from the
Merchants Bank of Boston, the bank Penelope's Uncle Frank had started
back in 1925. The letter said Gardiner was the trustee for Penelope's estate
and that I was to receive the funds according to his discretion. But Gardiner
had not told me he was keeping all the checks he'd received so far. It wasn't
much, maybe a few hundred dollars a month, but it was enough to make the
car payments on Sammie's new Audi.

When I emancipated, Gardiner could no longer receive the money from
Penelope's family's estate; it would go to me. And I did not spend it on my
college education or badly needed dental work. I was living on my own, and I
could do what I wanted. As soon as I turned seventeen, I got a job as a cook
and spent most of the money on a new red Porsche, just like Penelope's old one.

The boys began to seem too young, and I turned my eyes to the young men who ran in packs, their boisterous laughter deep with manliness, carefree as it echoed through the trees. They were just a short leap from the breathlessness of adolescence, young but shaving every day, old enough to drink and have jobs but young enough to prioritize play over work. Their parties went on all night, and the playing went on all day with the aid of elixirs and herbs to keep their libidos crested to overflowing. I found Timothy in a camper parked at the ski area. Blond, blue eyed, broad-shouldered, and aloof, he drew me in with the challenge of dissolving his resistance.

I wasn't sure what I wanted from Timothy, who actually lived in his camper all the time and eschewed any trappings of conventional culture, like bathrooms and kitchens, which at first seemed wild and free. In fact, the word "freedom" showed up frequently in all his conversations, which made me all the more determined to capture him. I made all the right sex noises, bucking like a belly dancer, so that he did not notice that I disappeared, leaving my body and the bed once the act commenced. I was the mad painter, creating all the scenery necessary to offer an illusion of devotion and belonging. I rubbed his back, I cooked the food, I cleaned the camper, and, eventually, when he gave in to a more civilized way of life, I kept house. I barely kept up with him as we ran up the steep mountain trails. The effort brought forth rage, unharnessed and mysterious, and it traveled like a missile from my heart into my throat, where it cut off my breath. When I stopped, the tears let loose and I cried unabashedly, in the same way I had when I had been seven and crashed on my blue Schwinn, screaming, howling, and then down to my knees whimpering. Timothy walked up the mountain a ways to give me time to get my shit back together.

I crumpled like an orphan left on the coldest night of winter when he parted from me for a job far from home. "I'm not leaving you." He was impatient with my childish weeping, but believing he was leaving me somehow felt safer than hoping he would come back. I could find no peace in separateness, but he seemed to be able to do so easily. I mourned and wept daily, wandering the earth as the abandoned one, spending inordinate amounts of time writing him long letters that I could not send. He was without any permanence in his camper, often just in a parking place by a river where there were no phones or post offices. When he was gone, the relationship was gone, and there was nothing but empty space. Other women seemed to be just fine when their boyfriends left on ski trips or for work elsewhere; they even seemed to enjoy it. They laughed lightheartedly at my suffering and told me to buck up. I sighed and turned to trail running for relief, but every step felt like I had cement boots on, and tears choked in my throat.

Gardiner only came back to Squaw from time to time to make sure I hadn't destroyed our house, which he'd put up for sale. I swallowed the truth that I was not welcome in his life, and I did so without emotion, too numb to cry and too exhausted from the life I'd led so far to fight. It must have been late summer or early fall when he started yelling at me for something. I remembered the moment when I had made it easy for him to leave and move to Columbine Creek with Sammie. We had been in front of the garage, and he'd told me I'd ruined his life by coming back. I had told him he'd ruined his own life, and that he should move to fucking Columbine Creek, that I'd be fine on my own.

I had thought I *would* be fine on my own, but I hadn't been prepared to be afraid of the dark, afraid of all the empty space, afraid to be alone for more than a few hours.

Now, I had to entice my camper man into marrying me, but I had to invest some time into seeming as if I were like other Tahoe girls, comfortable with myself and wanting my freedom, but freedom seemed terrifying to me. I wanted to belong to someone—a very uncool way to be for a Tahoe girl.

I would show him how I could outdo any girlfriend he'd ever had, pretending not to be needy, and he would be out of his camper and into my house in no time. He kept talking about freedom, and I kept trying to show him how fantastic being my prisoner of love could be. But it seemed that no matter how many back rubs I gave on demand, no matter the time of day or night, the sumptuous meals prepared and served according to his wishes and pot-driven cravings, the loaves of banana bread I baked, or sexual acrobatics I performed, I couldn't be enough. He could leave at any moment if I ever became too much. If I cried or whined, he could simply tell me that if I didn't like what he offered, he could easily climb into his camper, take his dog, and park in someone else's driveway.

I was grocery shopping one day, carefully filling my cart only with my favorite snack foods—barbecue-flavored Corn Nuts, Diet Pepsi, a few Slim

Jims, and a six-pack of Diet Pepsi, when a man I barely knew looked me up and down in the aisle.

He looked like an old, fat rhinoceros, but he scrutinized me right there in the soft-drink aisle in Lucky Supermarket as if he were a judge at the Miss America Pageant. "Hey, you know you'd be pretty cute if your boobs stuck out farther than your stomach," he said, laughing boisterously at his own repartee. That was the magic trigger that made it possible for me to resist food and welcome the hunger as I watched the needle on the scale move farther and farther to the left. Starvation was familiar, like reconnecting with a part of myself I'd lost when I had been a skinny fourteen-year-old who wore Saks Fifth Avenue suits and never went to school.

I had tried being a normal teenager who ate pizza without worrying about how many calories each bite had, and who went to school regularly, but I missed the hungry, skinny self who could make a little of anything go a long way, whether it was Penelope's approval, my father's attention, or a bag of M&M's. Even now, I buy a cookie or a muffin, take one bite of it, and put the rest away for later. A cookie often lasts me for a week as I savor each bite and wrap the rest up to eat when I'm really hungry again. Hunger and emptiness feel normal. Fullness feels uncomfortable, as if I want to leave my body.

57
RUNNING

AFTER THAT FAT RHINOCEROS GUY COMMENTED on my body, I became a master at counting calories and resisting food, even when the hunger was so intense that I felt like one big, empty stomach. For dinner, I only ate salad and canned mini shrimp with soy sauce for dressing because it only had nine calories per tablespoon. I ate massive amounts of carrots. I drank only Diet Pepsi, and had popcorn with no butter and massive amounts of Lawry's seasoning salt for dessert. I ate a half a cantaloupe for breakfast and an apple for lunch. I dropped from a hundred and twenty-five pounds to a hundred and one within several weeks, and I loved the feeling of my bones. I started to run up the mountain trails and enjoyed the lightness and the pain of hunger. Being hungry matched how I felt most of the time, like an orphan from a Charles Dickens tale—bereft, unwelcome, easily left in a doorway with her empty food bowl.

Running made me feel like I could love myself a little. My heart pounded and my lungs strained against the tar and nicotine from my Virginia Slims habit. There was no other sound until I stopped and all was quiet inside. I never wanted to go back down into the world; I wanted only to stay and sleep on the huge granite rocks that flanked the creeks. The water smelled like snowmelt and tasted like I was part of its purity—cold, sweet, and clear.

Just a tiny bit of self-esteem had begun to grow as I discovered I could run faster and harder. It felt so good that I decided to cut back on smoking. Timothy had introduced me to cocaine, and I loved it, but the binges left me feeling regretful after the all-nighters. I didn't want to end up a cocaine-addicted, pot-smoking burnout with rotting teeth, capable only of being a house cleaner. I clearly needed to find a new path so I wouldn't lose all my teeth from cocaine and malnourishment and die living in a house with ten other fucked-up people, which was common in Tahoe. I'd begun to regret dropping out of high school.

So when I turned eighteen, I decided to apply to Sierra College in Rocklin, California, thinking I would not be accepted but hoping for a miracle. I managed to pass an entrance exam, but with the provision that I would take remedial math. I barely knew fractions and was completely in the dark about algebra and geometry, having developed a pathological fear of both in the brief time I had been in high school. I was mostly worried about where I would run in a place like Rocklin, sixty miles away from Squaw Valley in the flatlands. I approached the cross-country team coach and asked if I could run with the group, just to get to know the trails, and he suggested I join the women's cross-country team. I had never considered competing, and the thought terrified me.

"I can't do that!" I exclaimed. "I'm not good enough!"

"It's our very first year of having a women's cross-country team and we need participants. C'mon! It'll be fun!" he said. It was indeed the dawn of women's running, but I didn't know until a few years later that I was a part of a revolution. He finally convinced me to join, but I was so anxious the night before the first practice that I must have gone through an entire pack of Virginia Slims Menthols. I could never sleep the night before races and made myself so miserable with anxiety that I cried and begged Timothy to tell the coach I was sick and couldn't participate. He told me I'd be fine once the gun went off. I shook so hard on the starting line that I was sure I would collapse, and when I heard the pop of the starting gun, I ran as hard as I could for the entire three miles, not understanding how to pace myself, which was how I was with everything. I won every race by running scared, in oxygen debt, and collapsing at the finish line. Once I'd won, I felt I needed to win every race. My first loss crushed me, and I spent several days eating barbecue-flavored Corn Nuts and Slim Jims washed down with Diet Pepsi, wallowing in self-degradation.

I ran every practice afterward knotted up in fear, fists clenched, face contorted with agony, barely making it through the workouts. It seemed the harder I pushed, the slower I went. And then I remembered what Tom Kelly had taught me about relaxing, smiling, and having fun, rather than making practices and races such an unpleasant, high-pressure ordeal. It was like a miracle, telling myself to imagine being graceful, light, and relaxed. I learned to flow and breathe, to smile and enjoy myself for the most part. I still had my moments of being frantic that I wouldn't win, but losing was no longer so debilitating that I would vow to quit, do a lot of cocaine, smoke a lot of cigarettes, and starve myself. I'd actually quit smoking, realizing that no matter how much I lied to myself about how I could be a great runner *and* have my Virginia Slims Menthols, I still felt ashamed about not behaving like a devoted athlete. I ended my first year having won the regional championships and placing second in the Northern California Championships. I was fifth at the state championships, which was surprising to me—not because I doubted myself, but actually because I didn't think that there were four other women who were better than I was. One or two was acceptable, but not four. I decided to train harder over the following summer, which I did, until I got pregnant.

58

THE ABORTION

I LIED ABOUT IT FOR MANY YEARS, murdering my unborn child. I added it to the lie I told about killing Penelope, about leaving her so she could go back to her old life with Fishballs. Barely eighteen, I was now responsible for two deaths: hers and that of my accidental baby. And I could not see myself as anything but a despicable human being. Penelope had gotten pregnant with me by accident, and she'd kept me, reluctantly at first, but she'd kept me despite Gardiner's insistence that she abort me. As a zygote, I must have heard her shouting from the deck of her houseboat as she threw his shaving equipment into the San Francisco Bay, "Fuck you, Gardy! I'm going to have this child, and you will not have anything to do with it, so why don't you just go home to your wife and leave me the hell alone!"

A sudden, sharp cramp while I was running up in the mountains above Squaw Valley signaled something was wrong. It was a cramp that doubled me over and made me feel pressure on the floor of my pelvis, as if my vagina were going to open up and puke out a boulder. I was ragged, uneducated, and wild. My menses had always been erratic, like my life, and I'd surfed the waves, never prepared, always out of Tampax, always surprised when I had seen blood at all. I took passing notice that my breasts were sore and swollen, that I had suddenly developed an aversion to cherry tomatoes and

Wrigley's spearmint gum, but I figured it was just one of those weird things. I felt fat and swollen but thought I wasn't exercising enough and put myself on a more demanding training schedule while I was home from college for the summer. Despite my fear of getting fat, my obsession with being thin, and my desire to be an athlete, my body still insisted on being female. And it did what it could to maintain its female functioning.

Gardiner had been in Columbine Creek for over a year now, but his old office was within a few minutes of where I was doubled over, up on the Red Dog run on the dirt road. It was so weird to walk in and see everyone I knew there but him. The first person I saw was Bunny, and I was relieved she was working that day. I told her my stomach had started hurting really bad all of a sudden. She put me on the exam table and asked me when my last period had been. I didn't have a clue.

When Dr. Charlie, Gardiner's best friend and partner, came into the exam room, he performed the dreaded vaginal exam and then looked at me from behind his wire-rimmed glasses and full beard. "Well . . . your stomach hurts because you're pregnant," he said without any hint of judgment in his voice. Then he measured the light brown stripe from my pubic bone to the top of my navel that I had not even noticed. "I'd say between seventeen and twenty weeks," he said.

I began to hyperventilate. There was no way I could be pregnant. Shit like that just didn't happen to me. "I can't *have* a baby!" I cried, tears streaming down my cheeks onto the crisp, virgin-white exam table paper.

That was when I called Gardiner in Columbine Creek. Timothy had always said he was sterile, that his mother had had German measles when she had been pregnant. So this probably meant the baby was from a bass player I'd been having unsatisfying sex with. Another tryst with a man who'd had way too much energy to spend on himself.

I always shook with fear when I called Gardiner, praying that Sammie wouldn't answer, but she did. I handed the phone to Bunny, unable to speak through my tears. Sammie didn't mess with Bunny; she only messed with people she could bully. When Gardiner came to the phone, Bunny said, "Hi Gardy. We have your daughter here, and she needs to talk to you." I expected exactly what he gave me, but I leaned into the velocity of his anger and squeezed my eyes closed. I needed his help and took whatever he had to say. I was instructed to get rid of the damn thing and do it quickly. And he told me to hand the phone to Charlie. I curled up in a ball, crying in my paper dress, trying to cover my awfulness with it. Bunny brought me a blanket.

"There, there, sweetie, it's all going to be okay," she said. I loved Bunny. She was so progressive. There was a hospital in Oakland that did late-term abortions. I didn't have the four hundred dollars. I worked full time, but all my money went to rent and the payment on the Porsche I'd had no business buying. I begged Gardiner to loan me the money, which he did, but only after I promised to give him Penelope's precious Rolleiflex cameras as collateral.

I had to make up a lie about why I was killing my unborn child. The cramping and pelvic pressure were not particularly dangerous, Charlie said, just a sign that I needed to take it easy. But I told people that I would have lost the baby anyway, that the cramping meant I was in labor and that I would miscarry unless I stayed in bed for the remainder of the pregnancy. There was no bleeding, but I had to make it sound bad, so I added bleeding to the story. I really had no choice but to have an abortion, I would tell people. Timothy dropped me off at the hospital in Oakland and then left to go to his mother's. "It isn't mine," he said with a shrug.

Ten years later, he and his wife had two kids.

I was led to a room with three other women. Or girls, I should say. Girls who were willing to have unsatisfying and often painful sex with men they hardly knew in hopes of being chosen. We swapped man stories in between screams of pain. I spread my legs on the bed in the Oakland inner city hospital and felt the stab of seaweed sticks tearing through the tiny opening of my cervix. The nurse said nothing and then prepared a syringe with a long needle. She did not tell me what she was going to do with the needle, but quick as an eagle snatching a salmon from a river, she plunged it into my abdomen and down into the delicate flesh of my uterus. I screamed and moaned as she drew out the amniotic fluid. I was overcome by nausea and cold sweats as my fluttering, pounding heart warned me that a terrible invasion had occurred. When the nausea and shakes subsided, I heaved for breath, gripping the sheets with my hands. The other girls were looking at me from their beds. "It will feel better soon," the one in the bed next to me said. "I've been through this before."

The nurse put an IV needle in my forearm and taped it down. A bottle of Pitocin dangled above my narrow bed. "This will start the contractions. They'll be pretty strong, so you'll need to breathe through them," she said and left the room.

Nobody could have prepared me for what I would experience through the night. The sheets turned scarlet as I bled rivers and rivers, screaming with every savage contraction. My toes dug into the metal bedstead, my body writhing and tensing, bracing against the pain. There was water in a pitcher, but I could not bring myself to put anything in my mouth. My lips were dry and cracking. The girl next to me got up and put an ice cube to my mouth. "Here," she said, "This will help your mouth from getting so dry, but you must drink."

Surely I must stop bleeding soon, I thought, but I believed I deserved to bleed and suffer this way. Maybe I would die and the score would be even. The other three women in the room rocked and screamed, curled up, sweating, crying, begging for mercy. We were the worst of the worst. The scourge and scum because we had waited so long. Our babies were formed with arms and legs. We should feel every stab. We should be made to lie in our own blood and shit and vomit. A commode had been placed by each of our beds where we were instructed to expel the contents of our ragged uteruses. I didn't know when the parts of the baby I carried would come out, or what they would look like, and I was too horrified and ashamed to look. Through the night, I writhed in pain, sweating, gagging, sobbing, regretting, hoping I would be forgiven, but feeling I didn't deserve it.

When the dawn came, and I had bled all I could bleed and felt pain beyond comprehension, my grief and shame still were not quiet. My legs, stuck together with blood, shaking and weak, were forced abruptly apart by a man, as they'd been so many times without my resistance. The doctor shoved two latex-gloved fingers up inside my tender, ravaged vagina. "Get ready for a D and C," he told the nurse and snapped the glove off. She leaned down and whispered close into my ear, "I'm trying to *have* a baby." Her narrowed eyes glistened with contempt.

When the steel instrument was inserted without anesthesia, I screamed up into the bright surgical light, which became an eye and then a black moon, and I joined my dead baby at the altar, laid open to hell and fury and then blessed purple darkness. Perhaps death would be kind enough to take me.

Within days, my breasts swelled to feed the baby they thought I'd birthed. They dripped and ached, becoming rock hard and engorged. I went to Bunny, arms held out away from my body to avoid touching my breasts. "What do I do?" I sobbed. She gave me an ice pack and told me to lie down while she got some Ace bandages. Then she held me and wrapped my breasts tightly in the bandages. "I'm so bad," I whimpered into her white nurse's uniform.

"No, sweetie, you're not bad. You're young, and it's all gonna be okay."

I began to bleed brown, putrid chunks and had to lie down on the floor at work curled up, barely able to manage the pain in my abdomen, a fever burning hot inside my belly, making me dizzy and sick. I looked at the pieces of infected tissue, evidence that I had killed, and was once again invited to eat my shame. Bunny rocked me again when I slumped on the exam room table and sobbed. The depression enveloped me. I sold my belongings, everything, wanting to punish myself. I couldn't see my way out of the darkness, the shame too great to give room for the loss I wasn't allowed to feel. I punished and punished myself, but no amount of remorse was enough to cleanse me.

PART III

BECOMING KIMBALL –
NOT BEING PENELOPE
1975 AND BEYOND

59
REDEMPTION — 1979

I WAS CERTAIN GOD WOULD EVEN THE score by making me barren. But God, or whatever was in charge of deciding my destiny, had a different plan. It was the fall of 1979, and I was twenty-one, old enough to buy Kahlua at Safeway, which I would occasionally mix with half and half or ice cream if I didn't feel fat that day. It was a nice day in September out on the treeless plains of Gunnison, Colorado, and the barbed wire caught on my hair as I tried to crawl beneath it. The other boys kept running, but Oscar remained behind to help me untangled my hair. It was expected that the boys wouldn't wait; I was the lone female on Western State College's cross-country running team, and I would never ask the boys to wait. A few of the boys wished I would go play volleyball or badminton, but I would show them I could run with them and hold my own. They kept their tobacco tucked behind their bottom lips and spat as we ran, spraying my shoes with the shit-brown juice.

I had thought Gunnison would be a mountain town, not like the flatlands of Palo Alto, where I'd been offered a running scholarship at Stanford after my second year of successful competition at Sierra College. I'd returned to training as soon as I'd recovered from the abortion and the subsequent depression and shame.

I had turned down the offer, certain I would fail at a place like Stanford. Besides, I didn't like to run on pavement, and there weren't any mountain trails or pine trees or lakes in Palo Alto. A small college in the mountains closer to Columbine Creek where Gardiner lived seemed more realistic and appealing. I loved Columbine Creek, and although I was never welcome at Gardiner's house, I had spent the summer there house-sitting for one of his patients. But when I arrived in Gunnison after the long drive from California, all I saw were brown, brush-covered, but otherwise treeless hills, and cows, a *lot* of cows. Bored and brindle brown, like the dirt, they lumbered along the brown landscape, shit-caked tails swishing at the flies, looking for something green to eat.

The sign read, "Welcome to Gunnison, Home of Western State College— Elevation 7,700 feet, Population 3,403." The Take-Away Gas Station and Convenience Store advertised cigarettes for a buck fifty and six-packs of Coors beer for a buck ninety-nine. Downtown Gunnison reminded me of Truckee with its rows of old brick buildings—a variety store, a drugstore, a bank, a few clothing stores, and restaurants where the ranchers gathered and the college kids got hangover breakfasts of two eggs with a choice of sausages, bacon, or ham with hash browns and toast, all for just two-fifty, and all the coffee you could drink.

I went to the cross-country team coach and told him I was ready to run. He seemed surprised, looking at me up and down. "You mean the cross-coun-try *ski* team, don't you?"

"No, I said cross-country when I wrote you about joining," I said, begin-ning to worry.

"We don't have a women's running team," he said, moving the tobacco to his other cheek.

"I'll just run with the men," I told him, ready to hear him say that I couldn't, but surprisingly he agreed.

"Long as you know not to expect your own room on road trips, and you'll be running with the men in the races," the coach warned me. "No special treatment."

Happy just to be included, I settled in a double-wide trailer he owned at the Shady Acres RV Park, with another girl who was on the cross-country ski team. It was so cold at night that I awoke with a coating of frost on my blankets.

Gunnison winters are cold, bleak, and lonely; the leafless trees are paralyzed with ice, and the plains covered with snow carved into striated sculptures by the cruel winds that scoured one's flesh discouraged joy, bullying one's patience until even the staunchest atheist might consider salvation.

I joined a Fundamentalist Christian church in hopes that God would see that I was truly making an effort to be good. And I was looking to Jesus to help me out. All the pictures of him I'd seen suggested he was open-minded and willing to hang out with heathens like me. I'd gone back to my sinful ways over the summer in California, mixing hard training and work with days of doing coke and smoking and having unprotected sex with men who didn't care about me.

I thought I'd gotten saved once in a church in Grand Junction. I had been house-sitting for Gardiner's patient and had begun running with a guy from Columbine Creek who'd said he was a saved Christian. He was a special education teacher who always wore a suit, not to mention the coach of the wrestling team, a school bus driver, and an all-around popular guy, the kind of Christian who told people he would pray for them when they were having a bad day. He went to Bible study and rented a room in an old woman's house.

"She needs the help, 'specially in the winter," he said, furrowing his black eyebrows.

I wondered if he wanted to experience sinning; he was a really cute guy for a goody two-shoes, with legs that showed every muscle; abdominal muscles rippling beneath smooth, unblemished skin; and sinewy, strong arms. His teeth gleamed white and perfect, unlike mine, which were crooked and rotting from too much Wrigley's Doublemint gum and not enough dental care. I had always chosen to buy Porsches or cocaine with any spare money. I had decided to stay in Columbine Creek for a few more months and rented a room in a house where a widow lived with her two young boys. She was a saved Christian, too, so I was surrounded.

He could run like a deer, and the sweat beaded on his brow and dripped down onto his long, black eyelashes that shaded eyes as blue as morning on the lakes. His disposition oozed such sweetness that it made my teeth ache, as if I'd eaten an entire box of sugar doughnuts. The kids loved him. He played games with them and spent time with each of them, patiently going over the lessons until they earned a sticker or a little toy from the treasure chest he kept in his desk drawer. He went to one of those churches where people spoke in tongues and everyone had a slight Southern accent, even if they weren't from the South.

I wanted to marry this guy, but he told me I had to accept Jesus as my personal savior first. So we went to a big church in Grand Junction, where the pastor looked at me with eyes like warm amber lanterns, and I felt I was ready to ask Jesus into my life, to be my personal savior, and hoped he wouldn't turn me down. And I did feel something along the lines of rapture I thought. It was a feeling of surrender, which was so overwhelming that I cried. And I was a good Christian for a few weeks or so, but I kept sinning, and I had to keep asking Jesus to help me stop having sex with the schoolteacher out of wedlock, or write bad checks. I was pretty sure Jesus was disgusted with me, but I kept praying anyway.

The teacher turned out to be a psychopath. He had borrowed a washing machine part from my housemate. I explained to him that with two small boys who wet their beds, her laundry was piling up, and she needed it back. I expected that he would graciously oblige, like he usually did whenever anyone asked him for anything. But like a sudden darkening of the sky before a tornado, his eyes changed—his pupils dilated, turning his eyes from blue to black, and suddenly I was against the wall shielding my face and body as he threw punch after punch until I crumpled to the floor screaming. My housemate heard me a block away and came to take me home.

Of course, nobody believed he'd beaten me, because he was a saved Christian and I was the heathen who'd seduced him into my heathen bed. It took several beatings for me to understand that no amount of understanding or forgiveness whispered into his dark, wavy hair when he was on his knees telling me he was sorry after he'd bloodied my nose and called me a stupid, uneducated cunt was going to change him.

Now, I saw the sandwich board sign along Gunnison's dusty main road: "Jesus Loves You! Join us on Sunday at 9:00 and let Jesus into your heart!" I felt drawn to the idea that Jesus might still accept me into His family, even if Gardiner wouldn't, and I would feel welcome, like an orphan finding her way home again. And I thought, perhaps, if I surrendered, sitting in the lap of Jesus, that He would forgive me, and I would magically stop hating myself for sleeping with men I wasn't married to, for having an abortion, for buying cocaine when I should have paid rent, and for writing checks when I had no idea whether I had money. I wrote checks as though someone at the bank would make sure I had enough money to cover them. Penelope's way of handling the banks when her checks bounced had been to send me in to explain with the story about Gardiner leaving us without a pot to pee in or a window to throw it out. Or she would haughtily remind bank employees that she was an exception to the rules because she was a Converse.

Gunnison didn't have a bowling alley or an indoor recreation center, and the outdoor ice rink was tiny. I could go running if I bundled up with several layers, a face mask, and goggles to keep my eyes from freezing shut, but otherwise, the only other thing to do was go to church, and then go to the potlucks afterward, where all the women gathered in the church kitchen wearing skirts and warm tights (Jesus didn't like women to wear pants, even when it was forty below zero), and sweaters with little flowers or jewels on them, and their hair long and ponytailed, with ribbons to match their sweaters. They made tuna casseroles, chili, salads with iceberg lettuce and a few cherry tomatoes, and Jell-O molds with pieces of fruit suspended in red and green gelatin castles with Cool Whip moats. The heathen college kids found their entertainment on dollar beer night at the Dos Rios, where the Western State students drank until they ended up dancing naked on the tables or puking out the windows of the dorm rooms. The kids who belonged to the Campus Crusade for Christ went to Bible study and made out in their cars afterward.

Oscar was easy to be best friends with, and we did almost everything together. By November, he told me he thought he was falling in love with me.

Since Billy, I had seemed to love men who made me worry about whether I was good enough to stay with, the most recent being the schoolteacher, who had moved to Gunnison from Columbine Creek when I had. He had a perfect right to be there. He had sneered at me when I'd told him to stay away from me; he'd gone to the college before I had, and he would do whatever he wanted. He had inserted himself into the cross-country team just to run with the boys, he said. We had been on a training run one day, and he had lagged behind close to me and begun to shove me. I had made the mistake of turning back toward to school, thinking I could outrun him. After he'd held my head over a drainage ditch full of angry, brown water mixed with cow shit and threatened to kill me, I went to the police and showed them the bruises on my throat and ribs. They said they were sorry but nothing could be done unless they'd actually *seen* him beat me. After that, I was afraid to go anywhere alone and would sleep with the lights on. Oscar came over every night and slept on the sofa to protect me.

Oscar was easy and kind, and he followed me everywhere, waiting for me after our classes, walking me to my next one, as if his sole reason for living were to take care of me. I was unaccustomed to feeling safe with a man. Love had always been coupled with fear, and, frankly, it was a little boring not to worry all the time about when he would leave or when he might hit me or sleep with another woman. I told him he would probably get over it. He was my protector, a watchdog ensuring that the psychotic special education teacher could never get close enough to hurt me again. Oscar waited for me on the long runs through the cow pastures and mountains, never losing sight of me, always holding up the barbed wire fence so I could get through safely. He was the one I trusted to share a bed with me when we went to cross-country meets; he honored my privacy by sleeping with all his clothes on, and he guarded the bathroom when I needed privacy.

It was during the Thanksgiving break that I felt the familiar dread of being alone. I had always felt like an orphan, abandoned and unwelcome anywhere. I was never invited to Gardiner and Sammie's home, even though I was now only two hours away from Columbine Creek, and Oscar was spending Thanksgiving at the dorm cafeteria with other students for whom the journey home was too long and expensive. I spent it with my roommate and her family in Durango, but the loneliness I felt was so painful and filling that I could feel the rushes of grief explode in my chest and run like ice water down my arms and legs. So I called Oscar and told him I was in love with him and no longer wanted to be an orphan.

But orphans can never feel safe for long. Soon, the familiar feeling of fear returned, and I felt an overwhelming need to ensure we could seal the deal. So I hinted around about rings and marriage and practically proposed for him. He was passive enough that when I asked him to repeat after me, "Kimball, will you marry me?" he actually did it. We got married a month later during Christmas break in Kona, Hawaii, where his parents lived. His mother, Eleanor, thought it would be a good idea to get it done when the whole family was there anyway. It would be economical and sensible, with a minimal amount of planning. Gardiner, now sixty-seven, had been slaving away in towns like Temecula and Tehachapi in the dried-out plains of California, working twenty-four-hour shifts in emergency rooms to support Sammie. Coincidentally, she'd browbeaten him into buying her a house in Kona so she could sit on her ass in the sun. She had told Gardiner that she might grow orchids and sell them to contribute financially, but she never did. Gardiner happened to be in Kona at the same time we were, so I asked him if he would give me away, but Sammie threatened to leave him if he even so much as drove by the church on our wedding day. So Eleanor, intimidating, intrusive, and even terrifying as she shouted instructions, who demanded action without excuse, however substantive, was comforting and reassuring. She enlisted a neighbor who agreed to stand in for Gardiner and give me away. She shook her head about Gardiner's flaccidity, but she did not know Sammie's rage as I did.

Oscar seemed to be in a daze as the whirlwind of planning a wedding in a two-week time period went on around him. He couldn't escape; we were on an island, and he'd never successfully stood up to Eleanor, so he succumbed and smiled on our wedding day, as wedding guests and family patted him on the back and said, "Good choice, Oscar! Well done!" He became violently ill on our wedding night, which we spent at the Kona Village Family Resort before returning to the cold, gray winter of Gunnison the following day.

I felt Oscar's fear and reticence over the next several months. He refused to have sex, saying he was tired from training; he was unable to eat and threw up everything I tried to feed him. I asked him if he regretted getting married, and he was almost too emphatic in his insistence that he was very happy to have married me, that it was all just stress around school, and could I please stop asking him questions about how he was feeling. We had been married just over a year when I became pregnant.

We'd moved to Anchorage, Alaska, at Eleanor's insistence, so that Oscar could participate in the family construction business. I was excited, having opened Penelope's old scrapbooks to revisit the photos of her in Alaska back in the 1950s, hunting Dall sheep with Fishballs and taking pictures of grizzly bears from the pontoons of a float plane. She had camped out in the wild with her guns and her fishing pole, surrounded by rough men and horses, with Fishballs to pay for everything and protect Penelope from having sex with anyone but her. Seeing the Chugach Range encircling Anchorage, all I wanted to do was run as fast as I could into their majesty and beauty, but Eleanor quickly shut down any opportunity for such silliness. "You're going to be a mother soon. You can't run anymore, especially here. You'll get eaten by a bear or raped by a drunken Eskimo." Eleanor called all Native Alaskans "Eskimos," just as she called all African-American people "niggers," all Jewish people "kikes," and all Japanese people "slitty-eyed yellow bastards." Penelope at least had used words like "negro" when speaking of black people; Jewish people had been "those *Jews*," and all people of Asian descent had been "Orientals." So I had learned to otherize at a very young age, but Penelope had been more discreet about being a racist; Oscar's parents were out and proud about it.

Oscar and I lived in his parents' Winnebago in the Klondike Trails RV Park across the street from a shopping mall. I wanted to kill myself, it was so ugly. I wondered where I could run, seeing no access to the mountain trails Oscar had told me about, only broken-down bike trails that seemed to lead nowhere and dusty streets lined with smelly bars. I got a job at Alma's, a German delicatessen across from the RV park, where I fought waves of pregnancy nausea from the smell of knackwurst and cabbage.

There was no escape from Alaska. I was thousands of miles from the softer, more civilized "lower forty-eight," as Alaskans called the rest of the United States. I came across a flyer posted on a telephone pole that read, "In crisis? We're here to help!" I tucked the flyer in my purse and called from the phone booth in the RV park, needing only a listening ear. "I'm in the wrong life," I began, sobbing. "I shouldn't be here. I am trapped in this Godforsaken shithole, and I have no friends, and I'm pregnant. My husband is never around, and I hate my mother-in-law!" This place was nothing like the photos in Penelope's photo album, although she had written this in her journal about Anchorage back in the 1950s:

Anchorage was deposited along a road one mile in length and had been given the legendary name, "Main Street." At each end of Main Street, the tar surface abruptly ended in mud that almost swallowed me whole. The buildings lining the street were lopsided tar-paper-and-plywood shacks, unpainted, as if their destiny was to supply only temporary shelter. There were fifty-two saloons, two hotels, a brothel, and a drugstore showcasing items most needed for the Alaskan frontier: trusses, supports, heavy work boots, fishing supplies, liniment, beer, cigarettes, and aspirin. I felt the unrest and heard the snippets of conversation as I walked past the doors of the saloons, where the men talked in groups about floatplanes, weather, tents and supplies, and, of course, gold, a fever that had not yet remitted in the frontier. Beyond the end of the road, I could smell the putrid earthiness of the tundra emerging from the hard freeze of winter.

Penelope hadn't been in Anchorage for long. Her mission had been to fly into the wilderness around Mt. McKinley with Fishballs and photograph bears and Dall sheep for hunting magazines. She'd camped in the wild, eaten the fish caught in the rivers, and drunk whiskey around the campfire in the evenings with Fishballs, the guides, and the floatplane pilot.

At Alma's Delicatessen, I spent my days making quiches and grating carrots and cabbage. As my belly grew, I felt better, less nauseated, and I was given the blessed job of managing another Alma's Delicatessen in Girdwood, south of Anchorage, a little village a lot like the photos of Davos and the Alps in Penelope's scrapbooks. I spent two nights a week in the little deli, which had been converted from an A-frame ski cabin. It had a loft that looked out onto the green mountainside, and I lay in the soft, warm bed feeling my baby move around inside me. I loved to go out in the morning and walk up the trails into the sharp, gray mountains with all the wildflowers in full blossom.

I constantly checked to see if she would move when I pushed on my belly. I could not believe I had been granted a reprieve and held onto her with all my muscles and all of my heart. So fearful she would be taken away from me somehow, I checked for blood in my underpants several times each day, noticing every little drop of anything, becoming frantic with each little cramp and ache, and I cried daily, trying to rinse away the anxiety that I would lose her because I deserved it. I had held on so tightly to her from the moment I discovered I was pregnant that my pelvic floor muscles could have held an entire ocean. When I began to feel the rhythmic contractions, and I felt the release of the mucous plug, it was as if I had cemented her in place with worry that I would lose her. I delighted in the sensations of contracting, but she wasn't moving, and I was failing to move her. I went to the hospital, and they sent me home saying it was too early.

"You're only two centimeters," said the nurse, snapping her glove off. 'You can go home and come back when the contractions get closer together." She shook her head ever so slightly as she walked away and went to the women who were in real labor, not just fake labor. I left the hospital in shame, vowing not to bother anyone until the baby was hanging halfway out and I had to hold her in with my hands.

I went home and waited, trying to will myself to open up. I couldn't sleep, nor could I feel legitimately in labor. It had been two days, and I hadn't slept because the intensity had been just enough to make me awaken and pant, but not enough to push my baby down to where she needed to be to get through. But when I returned to the hospital, the nurses rolled their eyes, shaming me for taking up space, for not being real or legitimate, for being a faker in the maternity ward, an uninvited intruder. I did not belong; I was just an unwelcome imposter taking up space. The doctor, an old woman with Matterhorn tits that reminded me of Fishballs, was furious with me for being such a pain in everyone's ass.

"You want me to section you?" she demanded angrily. "That'll teach you to harass the nurses." She ordered an x-ray to see if I might be telling the truth or to affirm that I was indeed being dramatic and making trouble, just like I had when I had feigned injury so long ago to get Wes Schimmelpfenig's attention. She returned to my bedside and told me my baby was stuck between my ischial spines and that I would need a C-section.

And so I was vindicated. My little girl was surgically removed from my uterus, but unlike the time in the hospital for sinners, where we had to feel the full physical import of our choice to abort, I was given the sweet milk of numbness from the chest down. And I watched as she was brought into this world by the gentle hands of a giant black man, a pediatrician and former college football star, whose eyes shone like moons and whose voice was like velvet. His hands were warm and welcoming as he held her tiny body and placed her at my breast. She was numinous, surreal in her beauty, and I could hardly believe she had come from my scarred and troubled uterus, a vessel that, despite my lack of love and respect, had remained strong and viable, and I thanked it each day of my pregnancy for embracing and nourishing my baby into being.

Several months after Jessie was born, I received a large, heavy package in the mail from Mrs. Chisholm filled with baby clothes, baby toys, and baby blankets, in addition to her weekly phone calls to check up on me. And I received a smaller, heavy package from Mrs. Klaussen. When I unwrapped it, I was astonished to find the big, blue leather photo album, with all the proof sheets tucked inside, undisturbed, and every photo still pasted on each page. Inside the front cover was a note that read:

Dear Kimmy:
This is a "found object," and I hope you will accept these beautiful pictures into your life at this time. Someday, they will be treasures for your children and your grandchildren. I'm getting very sentimental as the wrinkles deepen and the head goes white. There is great meaning in continuity.
Love & Joy, Joan K.

60

NOT BEING PENELOPE

FIVE YEARS LATER, IN 1987, OSCAR, Jessie, and I moved to Seattle after the oil market boom in Alaska bottomed out and the construction business ground to a halt. I was five months pregnant with our second child, and we had just enough money to make it to Seattle and rent an apartment. We packed up my little red VW Golf, which had a big dent in the fender from sliding on the icy roads into a moose, who lumbered off into the woods completely unharmed. Oscar found work as a Volkswagen salesman, and I got a job in a clothing store in a mall. But in my seventh month, with all the time I was spending on my feet at work, I went into early labor. Again, the fear of losing my baby overwhelmed me, and I was willing to do anything to hang onto him. I even surrendered to bedrest until it was safe for me to not to I asked Oscar to listen to my belly several times a day and breathed a sigh a relief when he could hear the baby's heartbeat loud and strong.

On September 25, 1987, I went into labor, and this time, it was real labor with pains unlike anything I'd ever experienced with Jessie—powerful, like big hands kneading and squeezing down on my uterus, moving the baby down. I felt like a member of a sacred circle as I felt my first pang of active labor. I wanted the deep, dull ache of each pain as they sharpened and peaked in intervals. I was anxious that they would stop and that I would end up not being able to give birth without a Caesarian section. I worried that I would go to the hospital and that they'd tell me to go home, that the labor was all in my mind, that I was a fake and did not deserve to be a member of the sacred circle, but they welcomed me into the maternity department four centimeters dilated and progressing nicely, a bona fide woman in labor. I spent hours and hours in labor, far into the night, pacing, stopping, squatting, and groaning as I became something else: a primal being, a root, then a flower opening to sunlight, a cry, a howl, a fish, a roar, and a breath, all in the rise and fall of each contraction.

I would give birth to a son, this time without surgical intervention. A second pregnancy would move me beyond Penelope, who, upon my delivery into the world, had made sure she would never give birth again. And a second birth would make me a part of the world of motherhood to which I had wanted to belong. I would be able to say I had two children now, and my life would have the weight and substance of a real family that I could say was really mine. I would welcome the chaos and coordination of Girl Scout meetings, soccer practices, and games, and I now felt I *really* needed a membership at Costco.

It was two o'clock a.m., and, after ten hours of labor, the contractions felt less powerful and painful. I grasped at each one, wanting it to get worse, a sign that I was closer. The nurse encouraged me to walk more and get into the warm pool to encourage my body on. I cried in disappointment that I wasn't progressing beyond eight centimeters and that my water had not yet broken. Why couldn't I just be normal? Why did this have to end up being another complicated birth full of drama? I was exhausted but so ready to do whatever I needed to do to get to ten centimeters and start pushing. "Why can't you just poke a hole in the fluid sac?" I shouted at the nurse. She checked my blood pressure and then told me she was going to insert an internal monitor. "You cannot be fucking serious!" I cried. "Please don't put anything in there that makes it hard for anything to get out!"

She chuckled. "That baby will come out just fine, don't you worry!" An IV pumped much-needed fluid into my dehydrated body, which seemed to help, but the pain was getting to the point where I couldn't manage it.

I had to surrender. "Can I please have an epidural now?" I had decided that if they said no, I would rise up, grab my IV bottle, pole and all, and scream at the nurses until I got the drugs. If they denied me drugs, I don't know . . . maybe I would just break things or run down the hallway and out the door into the street. Then they'd have to knock me out.

"Okay, all right, honey, just take it easy. I'll get the doctor. 'Bout time you asked for an epidural. You've been very brave!" Those words vindicated me, and I could stop hearing the voice of Gardiner in my mind telling me I was just being a goddamn sissy.

The numbness was delicious, and suddenly I felt friendly again. The nurse checked the dilation, and she beamed when her head bobbed up from under the sheet. "Well, honey . . . you can start pushing!"

And so, full of vigor and renewed energy, I followed the voice of the doctor to push and then pant and wait. Ever the driven athlete, I had expected to have my baby born after several pushes, but it seemed he was stuck. I pushed until my strength was gone and the pain was once again overwhelming. "I can't," I panted, tears rolling down my cheeks. Oscar paced and worried next to the bed, trying his best to cheer me on as if it were one of so many races he'd seen me win. The doctor ordered another epidural, but my blood pressure was dropping, and so was the baby's. They flipped me over on my left side and propped me up. "Come on now, you can do this!" the doctor said. "Let's have a couple of big pushes, and he'll be out!" And with all I had left inside, I pushed so hard that I felt like I would split wide open from the top of my chest to the edges of my pelvis, as if I could push all my insides out onto the sheets. And then . . . I felt release as his shoulders were born, and then his little body was out, all seven pounds of him, crying softly as his lungs gasped in his first breaths. It had taken two and a half hours of pushing and a vacuum extractor to pull my baby boy from my bony pelvis into the dawn of his life. They let me hold him to my heaving chest for a moment before whisking him away. He was exhausted from his ordeal, too, but we were reunited a short time later, and I held him to my breast. I had two babies now, a daughter and a son, created on purpose, loved beyond what I had thought possible.

I was really not Penelope now. I was a mother with a 1978 Volkswagen bus and a Costco membership. I was going to bake cookies for classroom parties and be a Brownie troop leader; I would read *Good Housekeeping* and never do cocaine again; I would never tell them I was going to kill myself because they made my life miserable, and they would call me "Mommy," and I would always answer.

I often shared with my children how grossly inadequate I felt sometimes trying to mother them, especially when they asked me to play with them, something I had forgotten how to do when I was about eleven, never having felt playful much after that. I have had to ask for their forgiveness many times for my clumsiness or self-centeredness.

I regret all the times I said, "Not now, Mommy is busy," when I wasn't that busy. I treasure all the times I spent in bed with my children reading them *Little House on the Prairie* books, and I am thankful I took the memories of Gardiner reading me stories and planted them in my life as a mother. I feel heartache when I remember the times I was caught up in feeling fat and spiraling into despair, or in having a slow race and then blaming it on being too fat and spending the entire day being cranky. Or the times when I was just lazy and couldn't be bothered to pay attention when they wanted me to watch them on the swings or participate in building a castle out of toilet paper. All the times when I forgot that it was my day to bring snacks to a soccer game or when I was late to pick them up from daycare made me feel I'd failed to meet my expectations of being everything Penelope wasn't. Penelope would never have shown up at a soccer game or been a counselor at a Girl Scouts' campout. I stood out in the rain at the grocery store with my daughter selling Girl Scout cookies, wishing I could be elsewhere, but I never regretted the time spent. I went to every soccer game and talent show and helped with homework to the extent I could, having dropped out of high school. I didn't want to miss a single drop of being a mother. However, the scars from life with Penelope and longing for Gardiner's attention were there, just under the surface.

The times of being impulsive and stupid and making decisions that affected my children's well-being, or raging at them in the grocery store in front of other horrified mothers, or just being an asshole all still make me cry and wish for a do-over. At least, I tell myself, I never told them I wished they'd never been born, though, as Penelope's mother had told her so many times. And I never made them choose between their father and me when I ended our marriage. And despite depression that sat on my shoulders like a damp stole of wet moss, I never attempted suicide. I thought about it . . . a lot ... but I developed a relationship with the thoughts, interrogating myself about how valid they really were, and I always concluded that I did have an obligation to live. This state of mind dissipates like morning fog most of the time and gives way to a viewpoint that this place of being in the vale is simply part of my neurochemistry. It's usually a good time to write.

Despite memories that left an indelible imprint in my bones and muscles and psyche, I have no wish that things could have been different in my life with Penelope. Maybe she was so exhausting to live with that I'd had enough of her, and I never allowed myself just to be okay with that. I treasure the sweet and delicious time with Penelope that seeded all the memories I keep untarnished, unspoiled by the sieges with her when I longed for escape and fought not to be swallowed up in her wake.

And maybe she'd just had enough of life, worn out just from being Penelope. Maybe it was just fine to choose death, like retiring when your audience still wants more.

On the morning of March 24, 1974, when the phone call from Gardiner came, I was getting ready to skip school and go skiing with Redheaded Heidi instead. The sun was out, and we had money for cigarettes and lunch. We were still the kids that never made the race team and wore hats without stripes, which marked us as losers, but we didn't care anymore. We wore jeans skiing and smoked on the chairlift. Bunny tapped on his door with the brass sign saying, "Gardiner Pier, M.D."

"Come on in, Kacey," he said. It was quiet except for the sound of the phone ringing, as it always did first thing in the morning. He put all the lines on hold so that only the lights would flash.

It took him a while to stop crying after he told me she was dead. I'd left her. I hadn't been there to snatch away the cigarette burning a hole in the blanket or to tell her to go back to bed. I hadn't been there to hide the pills, fix the soup, or be her only reason for living.

"What are you going to do today, Kacey?" he asked with swollen eyes. "Are you all right?"

"Sure, Dad, I'm fine," I said. "I'm going skiing with Heidi."

"Great," he said. "I'll talk to you later on."

"Are *you* going to be okay, Dad?"

"Sure," he said with his usual smile. "I'll be fine."

And I went outside to meet Redheaded Heidi. "My mom died," I told her.

"Oh, wow! So . . . are you okay?" she asked. "Do you want to go home?"

"Nah. Let's just go. KT looks good today. I just wanna go skiing." And we poled over to the chairlift. "I'm going to wait for the green chair," I said when Heidi zoomed into the loading zone.

"Okay. Meet you up there," she said.

And I rode up into the sky in my exceptional, one-of-a-kind green chair.

EPILOGUE

GARDINER AND ME

RECONCILIATION

Over the years, Gardiner and I had talked by phone whenever he was not with Sammie. He'd started an urgent care practice on Maui when they'd settled permanently in Kona, so for her to interfere would have required an airplane trip—not as easy as what she usually had done, which was to pick up the extension and scream at him to get off the phone, or barge into the room and demand that he hang up or just start packing.

He lived in a separate room in the same building as the urgent care practice. He had enough room for a bed, a small kitchenette, and a table for his television set. We would talk for hours when he was settling in for the night and my children had gone to bed. Such sweet conversations, remembering the early years in Squaw Valley and his love for Penelope, which had not died after all. We also talked at length about our relationship problems—my marriage to Oscar, which had not matched my fantasies of deep conversations, parenting Jessie and James together, and enjoying time outdoors as we once had. He was absent even when he was home, and the marriage died of malnourishment. We divorced in 1991, after twelve years together. Plus, I'd gotten myself involved with a married Catholic guy with three kids and a foster daughter, which is a whole other book. Oscar knew about this affair that I'd told myself was love, and he behaved as if it didn't matter to him as long as his routine didn't change. He could get up, go to work for twelve hours (even when he didn't have to be there), come home to a nice supper, and watch television. He would ask how my day was and whether I'd seen "Bruce the Married Catholic Guy," which he'd sing to the tune of "Puff, the Magic Dragon." I couldn't stand myself.

I was earning enough money as a professional runner and a house cleaner to support our children and myself, but just barely. The conversations I had with Gardiner were my lifeline. He was always comforting, never critical or judgmental, even when I confessed the worst of my behavior. He'd tell me that anything that I had done, he'd done the same and probably worse.

Sammie never changed. Gardiner had become more and more afraid of upsetting her, which didn't take much. She found things to criticize and blame him for; she had successfully alienated him from his friends and family, and he had become like a mangy little mouse with post-traumatic stress disorder. Despite her unceasing attempts to isolate him, people were drawn to him wherever he happened to be working, and the friendships he made lasted until he died at the age of ninety-one. All I wanted to do was love him and cherish what I could redeem from our past, which had healed like a huge, untended wound, the scars tough and jagged, like a fissure in an ancient landscape. We talked so easily that it seemed as if the past had never happened, until he forgot my birthday, and I had to remind him.

"Oh *damn*," he said with a sigh. "I'm such a shitty father." And, of course, I was quick to refute his assessment, which worked every time to revive his conscience. Or, if a week went by and I didn't need him to help me through yet another relationship crisis, he'd call and tell me he had been so worried about me because I hadn't called. I refrained from reminding him that he could have called me if he was worried. Something about him claiming to be worried about me got stuck in my throat like a tiny piece of a popcorn kernel, vaguely annoying and difficult to dislodge.

After so many conversations when he'd tell me about Sammie's most recent reason to berate him, her raging and abuse wearing him down to defeat and exhaustion, I campaigned for him to leave her and come live near me. "Dad, you need to retire. You're too old to be staying up all night taking care of drunken tourists and screaming babies with ear infections."

"I suppose you're right," he said. "I worry that I'm going to leave a piece of gauze or my tweezers in someone's wound one of these days."

"Your grandchildren would love to get to know you, too," I told him, hoping to entice him with visions of family reunions, which would include his three other children and nine other grandchildren, none of whom he had been allowed to visit. Sammie had made it nearly impossible for him to stay connected with any of his family or old friends, especially from the Penelope days.

In 1992, when he was nearly eighty, he finally surrendered, realizing that he was truly too old and in too much pain to function very well working so hard. When Gardiner arrived in Seattle, he carried his few belongings in Brown Suitcase, now as wrinkled and beat up as he was, reinforced by a rope in case its clasps failed. In his other hand, he carried his black medical bag, the same one he had carried so many years ago when he had made house calls in Squaw Valley.

I had found an apartment for Gardiner, and we had bought him furniture at Sears after we'd discovered he had a Sears credit card.

"Huh," he said, pulling the battered card from his battered wallet. "Wonder if this thing still works." Fortunately, it did, and its credit limit had allowed us to furnish the entire one-bedroom apartment. He was especially fond of the reclining chair and the new television, in front of which he planned to spend time cheering for the 49ers, his favorite football team.

In the early months of his arrival, it was like a new romance, where everything seems so incredibly perfect. But I had failed to consider how massive this life change might be, especially for Gardiner. He had been a physician for fifty-five years and was now uncertain as to what to call himself or what to be. He had always introduced himself to patients by saying, "Hi, my name is Dr. Pier, and I will be removing the marble from your child's nose," or "I will be sewing up your head today," and offering reassurance that all would be well. Suddenly, there was nothing but his television and too much empty space to occupy his time, and he seemed like a man who had been shoved out of an airplane with no parachute. He was lonely. I had thought his grandchildren and I would be enough, but Gardiner had always had a woman; Sammie was at least someone he could say was his wife, despite her litany of pathological personality disorders.

He'd announced he was going to begin writing his memoir on yellow legal pads, but the half-hearted sentences trailed off, left behind like orphans by the side of a lonely dirt road. He made friends in his apartment complex, but they weren't his people. They read *People* magazine or *National Enquirer*, consuming Cheetos and Pepsi as they sat and read on their little porches. They loved Gardiner, who also loved Cheetos, but he read books by Hemingway and anything written about sailing, and he watched old World War II movies and reruns of *M.A.S.H.* on television, not *The Simpsons* or *Buffy the Vampire Slayer*. He tended to their ailments, black medical bag ready and stocked, but they weren't sick often enough to keep him busy.

"I'm going to see if they need a doctor over at the University of Washington Medical Center," he said. "A Harvard classmate of mine was a pretty well-known doctor there once, so maybe if I drop his name, they'll give me a job." I was irritated with him for not being able to relax and enjoy sitting around watching television and reading. He was broken down physically from having had polio during his first year of residency, and then suffering a bout of post-polio syndrome in his early seventies. The polio had affected his left side, and he had always walked with a slight limp, but now it was more pronounced, and his back hurt almost all the time.

Gardiner was a master at fishing for attention from women, but he did it in ways that were charming and genuine, like asking Mrs. Klaussen to cut his hair, or soliciting the nurses' opinions on his choice of neckties. Now he sought attention from me and from Jessie, who just wanted a grandfather she could love. She was angry with Oscar for abdicating his role as her father. He had moved to Berkeley and remarried, fortunately to a woman who didn't allow him to forget he had children. Jessie despised her other grandfather, who had invaded her privacy by pulling her pants down when she was five. I had taught her to be vigilant about her boundaries and intolerant of anyone who attempted to breach them, and it only took one offense to get on Jessie's shit list. Oscar's father rocketed to the top and stayed there.

Jessie had hopes that Gardiner would quench her thirst for healthy male attention, but he was yet another disappointment for her. He wanted her to take care of him, cook for him, trim his eyebrows, and clean his apartment. James, being a boy, got the grandfatherly treatment. Gardiner taught him how to draw and carve a canoe out of a piece of wood, and how to shoot a bow and arrow. Jessie added Gardiner to her shit list when she knocked on his door one afternoon and he answered it stark naked. She ran home sobbing and told me what had happened.

Suddenly, all the reweaving of my tattered relationship with Gardiner unraveled like a spool of steel cable snapped from its anchor. Memories long since suppressed forced their way into my consciousness—all those little games we'd played when I had been a child, when he lain down on his back and I had stepped on his hands for him to lift me up, or when he had wanted me to stand on my head wearing only my nightie. I had always worn a nightie with no underpants on, innocently thinking it was perfectly natural and safe. I remembered all the backpacking trips we'd taken when he had insisted that I be naked when we swam in the lakes, and his fondness for being naked in front of me in our house, sometimes partially erect. I had thought it was funny when he'd emerged from his bedroom in the morning wearing nothing but his huge leather sheepskin-lined moccasins and his glasses. He'd put on his bathrobe after he had put the water on for morning coffee, but it seemed he liked being naked around me whenever possible. It was with a wave of horror that I wondered if he'd gotten into bed with me when I'd been sick so that he could be naked with me there, too.

The rage over those memories, and the way he'd left Penelope and me with such finality, came roaring back, and I felt as though I'd collided with a speeding Kenworth. I went over to his apartment and unleashed, my breath shallow, my heart racing, and my mouth dry. I felt the rage, white hot, so powerful I could not contain it, and screamed at him with vengeance I had not felt since I'd been fourteen, on an occasion when I'd burned Penelope's toast. She had thrown the toast at me and told me that I was selfish and useless, that I'd deliberately burned her toast and that I ought to go back to Gardiner because we were so alike. I had hated her in that moment for comparing me to Gardiner, and I'd wanted to kill her. This rage at Gardiner felt that powerful.

I could not speak to him for many months. He wrote me a letter telling me he was going to the Philippines to meet a woman some close friends of his thought he might like. He was so lonely, he wrote, and needed companionship, especially since I wasn't speaking to him. He married her while he was in Manila and brought her back to Seattle. He was enraptured over this tiny little angel of a woman he had found, and he begged me to meet her, but I refused, thinking it was just another one of his stupid, impulsive decisions. It wasn't until she called me herself and asked if she could meet me that I softened.

Lita turned out to be the medicine that healed some of the losses in Gardiner's life. Innocent, unabashedly openhearted, and devoted to her values around family and kinship, she made it her mission to reconnect him with his children and grandchildren, and his old friends in Squaw Valley. Gardiner couldn't get over how capable Lita was at doing just about everything. Having come from the small island of Negros, Lita knew how to get by with very little in the way of modern conveniences. She had grown up without running water or electricity, in a little house built above the ground so that the livestock could be kept underneath it. She was one of ten children, all of whom had been expected to work on the family farm. Lita had gone to school until she'd passed the eighth grade, at which point she was told she had to go to work, which she did.

Now, her world revolved around taking care of Gardiner, and I was relieved of any guilt over not wanting to do so myself. If not for Lita's persistent invitations to "bring the childrens to see dere grandfadder," I might never have spoken to Gardiner in person again. Instead, I wrote him long letters detailing every act of cruelty and abandonment he'd ever committed. I wanted to hold his feet to the fire until . . . until what? I wasn't sure. I thought continuing to feed my rage would make me feel better, but it seemed that all it did was bring more rage. Gardiner heard it all and did not defend himself. He only asked if I could forgive him, and I couldn't. I seemed to be locked up in that old armor I had worn whenever I'd needed to keep vulnerability in check. I was disappointed in myself for not being able to maintain the euphoria over finally having my daddy all to myself, and I was astonished at the intensity of my rage. It had been twenty years of not having a relationship in the safety of fiber optic phone lines or sending letters back and forth. Now here he was, and my fantasies had imploded. He was broken down and needy, unlike the daddy I remembered from the days in Squaw Valley when he would catch me as I hurtled down the hill on my blue Schwinn, certain that the brakes wouldn't work.

Over the next nine years, I visited Gardiner and Lita more, but I argued with myself about whether to call in sick or just go over and eat

Lita's dried-out pot roast, redeemed only by her *lumpia*, which James loved. Gardiner was a good conversationalist, and I enjoyed our visits, but I was so anxious to leave that I sat on the edge of the sofa as if preparing for a fire drill.

I have a cherished memory of a series of interviews I did with Gardiner in 1996 for a graduate school project, for which we had been instructed to identify all the family members from whom we had cut ourselves off. Unearthing some of Gardiner's history and our history as father and daughter was less painful when I could set up the video camera and ask specific questions as if I were Oprah Winfrey interviewing Tom Cruise. I think Gardiner liked being videotaped; he was at ease telling stories about himself and answering my very blunt questions. For example, when I asked him why on earth he'd stayed with that shrew Sammie for twenty years, he said, "I don't know really . . . I guess I felt so guilty about leaving your mother that I felt I ought to stay with Sammie. I'd made my bed, so to speak."

I asked him questions about how he could reconcile staying with Penelope, even though she'd continued an intimate relationship with Fishballs.

"Well," he said, furrowing his long white eyebrows and removing his glasses, "I loved your mother, and part of loving her was accepting the fact that Fishballs was not going to disappear."

And so we grew another relationship, more as friends, I suppose. I couldn't be the doting daughter he expected me to be, and I'm sure he was disappointed. He behaved like an alcoholic who, after thirty years of being drunk and unavailable, expect his family to forget all the heartache and trauma inflicted and instantly rebound, celebrating his return with rapture equal to an evangelical revival.

I told him in no uncertain terms that I did not feel like a part of his family, and that I never had. When Joan or Susie, his other daughters, had come came to visit him and Lita, I had avoided invitations to join in and behave as a part of the family. I just couldn't do it. I thought I *should* rejoice in the idea of reconnecting with my half-siblings and felt ashamed that I just couldn't, but all I really wanted to do was keep my distance. They had not made any attempts in the past to include me, and yet, suddenly, because Gardiner had decided it was time to be a family, I was expected to join in, like a caboose that had been left behind by the rest of its train for thirty years.

In 1995, I married Bruce. In 1992, he had left a marriage that nobody in his family or his circle of friends thought would ever end. The divorce took three years cost him enough money to buy a nice house in Aspen, and he was bitter about everything. Our marriage ended after eight exhausting and mostly painful years. It turned out that trying to create an instant family by stealing someone else's husband and children had brought me into full contact with what had happened between Sammie and Gardiner, and I was horrified at myself for doing the exact thing I had said I would never do.

So, after seventeen years of city life, I felt it was time to go home to Lake Tahoe, and on a fine summer morning, I merged onto I-5 and headed south.

Gardiner was ninety-one when I left, and he was losing his memory. Lita had taken a job at a nursing home in Seattle as a housekeeper in order to help support them, but he was getting more forgetful and had begun to sleep all day while she was at work. He would forget when he'd taken his last dose of Oxycodone and then take more, and then he would forget where she was and go into a panic and call me sobbing, "Lita has left me and gone back to Manila!"

"Dad, she's just gone to work," I would reassure him. "She'll be back." And then he would forget I'd told him and call me again. I had taught him how to use a cell phone, but he would always forget.

"Goddamn this thing," he would mutter. "I want a *real* telephone with a receiver and a dial."

It had been a year since I'd convinced him he couldn't drive anymore. The final straw for his ability to live at home was when he drove to downtown Seattle and couldn't remember how to get home. Still, he clung tenaciously to his last bit of freedom.

"Goddammit, Kacey! I am not a child for, Christ's sake!" he would say, standing up as tall as his disintegrating spine would allow. He surrendered only when I reminded him that he'd run into another car backing out of his carport and hadn't even noticed the frantic woman waving him down as she stood next to her blue Buick with a newly smashed passenger door.

My plan was to get settled in Reno since Squaw Valley, now occupied mostly by huge homes for second-home owners, was out of my price range, and then move Gardiner and Lita down to live next door to me. Dr. Charlie, who was still doctoring at Gardiner's old Squaw Valley office, said he'd never survive at higher altitudes, so I made up my mind that Reno would be close enough. My reunion with Lake Tahoe was resonant and right, and my faith in establishing a new life was unwavering, for the most part, with only a few small episodes of terror and self-doubt. I returned to Seattle once I'd secured an apartment a couple of buildings up from mine.

"I was afraid you weren't going to come back for us," said Gardiner.

James drove Gardiner's Ford Contour, and being seventeen, he relished the opportunity to drive anything, even a dorky Ford Contour. I would drive the U-Haul filled with furniture and box upon box full of Lita's knick-knacks. Lita loved to shop at the dollar stores and thrift stores. They appealed to the Filipina part of her that loved bustling, crowded marketplaces where everyone talked at the same time, picking through the goods and loading their multicolored plastic shopping bags. I put Gardiner and Lita on a flight to Reno, knowing that Gardiner's back would not tolerate a two-day car trip. They would stay with an old doctor friend of his until James and I arrived with the U-Haul. It felt good to be completely out of Seattle and to have Gardiner and Lita close to me.

I had gotten a job as an intern therapist, having spent the 1990s completing my undergraduate and graduate degrees in Seattle, and now I was ready to practice. The job was an hour's drive from Reno, so an eight-hour day always lasted at least ten hours. I'd brought my two miniature dachshunds, Gertie and Rosie, back from Seattle, and they were overjoyed to be with Gardiner and Lita while I was at work. Everything was working beautifully until one morning in early November when Gardiner called me at seven o'clock.

"I think I'm having a mild heart attack, and I'm going to drive myself to the emergency room now," he announced without any hint of alarm. I told him he would do no such thing, and that he was to stay put while I called 911. As the paramedics loaded him onto the stretcher, he said, "My name is Pier. I used to be a doctor."

The paramedics instantly addressed him as "Dr. Pier" and told him they were going to see to it that he was safely transported to the emergency room in the same hospital in Reno where he had told Penelope he didn't love her anymore and that he was in love with Sammie.

Gardiner was correct; he was having a mild heart attack. The doctors expected that he would recover without any complications and that they would be releasing him the next day. I was out for a run, expecting to pick him up after I was finished, but when I got to the car, there was a message from the hospital on my cell phone.

"Your father has had a stroke and is in a coma. We need you to come to the hospital right away." My heart leaped and the adrenaline rushed through my bloodstream, giving me the energy and focus I needed to make decisions, as I'd done so many times with Penelope. Lita was falling apart—the doctor had told her that he had little chance of living, and that he had signed a "Do Not Resuscitate" agreement upon being admitted. She could not bear the idea of letting Gardiner die and, clutching her rosary, begged God to do something to keep him alive. Lita was Catholic and believed that only God should make such decisions. I was annoyed with her for being so attached to keeping him alive no matter what.

"If he doesn't come out of the coma," I said to the attending physician, "please take him off the ventilator. He would not want extraordinary measures." But then, after eight hours in a coma, Gardiner woke up. He was alert and seemingly cognizant of what was going on around him until the doctor asked him what year it was.

"It's 1944," said Gardiner with certainty. "And I have to get to the hospital for rounds." He then proceeded to leave his bed, IV tubes straining against their bandages on his wrists.

"Get these goddamned things off of me, for Christ's sake," he barked. "I have work to do."

I restrained my urge to laugh and eased him back into his bed. He'd had a stroke and was not able to speak coherently or use his right side. Within one day's time, he developed pneumonia in his right lung and was put on the strongest antibiotics available to fight the raging infection. His cognitive ability returned at least to the extent that he knew what had happened and where he was. He was not responding to the antibiotics and began to show signs of congestive heart failure and kidney failure.

"Dad, you're going into multiple organ system failure. Do you want the doctors to keep you going? If you choose not to have the ventilator or a feeding tube, you'd better speak up now."

"Hell, no," he said. "I've been around long enough. How old am I, anyway?" he asked, a question I had answered several times daily over the past year or so.

"You're ninety-one, Dad."

"Jesus, I should be *dead*, for Christ's sake!"

"So do you want me to sign the DNR? I have power of attorney. Lita won't sign it."

"Yes, please do," he said. And with that, Gardiner began the process of leaving his body. The view from his hospital room was of the mountains he'd loved when he had first come to Lake Tahoe in the early 1940s, but his bed faced the wall. "Could you turn my bed so I can look out the window?" he asked me.

Gardiner slipped in and out of sleep, but when he was awake, he looked out the window, his gaze seeming to be on something we could not see.

Lita continued to try to get him to eat, thinking if he ate, that meant he wasn't dying. Joan and Susie arrived and Gardiner cried when he saw them, as he did now so often when he remembered something. The day before we brought him home, so that he could spend his last days surrounded by familiar books and his pictures on the walls, he asked to be taken outside.

"I want to breathe the mountain air one last time," he said. Gardiner had been put on oxygen twenty-four hours a day to help him breathe, but the nurse took the nasal cannula out of his nose.

"Just for a little while, Dr. Pier," she said patting his hand. We bundled his tiny little body up in blankets and put on his favorite blue knit hat. When he took his first breath, he cried out, "I think I'm going to *puke!*" and he began to pant. Gardiner had been suffering panic attacks in recent months, and he would often say he was about to puke, but he responded to reassurance that he was just feeling fear and that it was going to be okay as long as he didn't pant.

"It's all okay, Dad," I told him softly, looking into his eyes. 'You're just breathing the November air, and it's hard on your lungs. Just breathe easy if you can."

In the brief times he was awake, we had conversations where he would tell me his about his dreams.

"I keep having the same dream over and over again," he said tearfully. "Your mother and I were on our boat . . . the one we were going to have built when I retired. We were way out at sea and it was perfectly calm. I was holding her in my arms and she kept saying, 'Save me, Gardy. Don't let me die.' And I told her I couldn't save her.

"You always asked me why you were crying all the time," I reminded him.

"And you always told me it was because I had a lot to mourn." Gardiner remembered the days when I was alone with Penelope in New York. He sobbed freely and deeply as he recalled my frantic phone calls to him, pleading with him to help me, and how he would often hang up, especially when I asked him for money. "How could I have *been* so cruel and heartless," he sobbed. "You were only a child, and I left you to manage Penelope all alone!" I just listened, not knowing what to say, intuition telling me not to reassure him or minimize what he was saying, because all of it was true. It seemed he simply needed me to witness him allowing all the memories to surface.

When we brought him home, he had stopped sipping even the tiniest amounts of water, and he slept almost all the time, the hum of the oxygen concentrator humming away in the living room. Joan, Susie, and I had never been together in the same room. Now, they were in their early sixties and I was forty-six. Susie read, Joan knitted, and I wrote what Gardiner and I had said to each other so that I would never forget it. Lita continued to try to get him to take water in the brief moments he was awake.

Dr. Charlie, Joan Klaussen, and so many other old friends had come to say goodbye, and it seemed there was no reason for him to be alive any longer, but he hung on for almost a week after being brought home, his heart rate at a hundred and thirty beats per minute, which was really high for a ninety-one-year-old man close to death. He had always been very fit, but it seemed he was in a race of some sort as he slept, perhaps running from death's inevitable, final decision.

Thanksgiving was late in November that year, and Lita made the full meal with turkey and stuffing, pie, and mashed potatoes, enough to feed the entire apartment complex. She thought perhaps Gardiner would miraculously recover and prepared a full plate for him.

"Honey, please eat food," she said softly, stroking his hair. "It will be good for you." Of course, he didn't stir, and Lita sighed and wrapped his plate in foil. "Maybe he eat later."

James, who had never been fond of Thanksgiving, came over to see his grandpa, who was drifting in and out of sleep as we ate and talked. When James put his hand on Gardiner's arm, he awoke, looked at James, and smiled,

"How's my grandson?" he exclaimed, patting James's hand.

"Fine, Grandpa," James said. "How are *you* doing?"

"Great," said Gardiner. "Just dandy."

And those were the last words Gardiner ever spoke. Joan and Susie and I assured him that he could let go, talking to him as we sat at his bedside later than evening, knowing that the sense of hearing is the last sense to shut down.

"He's just refusing to die because he loves the attention," said Joan, whose feelings for Gardiner were a mix of contempt and love, if that was possible. "He's always loved being the center of attention."

Susie went home, her own life and family calling for her attention. She left Joan and me feeling torn, tearful, and frustrated that Gardiner had not taken advantage of all three of his daughters being present to finally pass away. Perhaps Gardiner had made a bargain with Death to pass in privacy, taking his last breath in the darkest hours of the night. I got the phone call from Lita at around two a.m. on December 1, 2004. She'd called me a couple of times over the past few nights thinking he had died, but each time, she had been dreaming. Each of those times, I'd given her one of Gardiner's Ativan tablets and put her back to bed.

I roused Joan, who had been staying with me, and threw on our clothes to go see if, this time, it was true. All was silent when we went inside, the oxygen concentrator off and Gardiner lying still, finally at rest, free of his demons and ghosts. We huddled together in the bedroom as the coroner zipped his body up in a black bag, an unbearable sight to witness. I had asked Gardiner whether he'd wanted to be buried or cremated.

"I'm not going to be in a coffin in the ground, where I wouldn't do any good at all, for Christ's sake! Just throw me in the incinerator and spread my ashes around Squaw Valley."

Over the next two weeks, I was caught up in a flurry of attending to cremation details, taking care of Lita (who was in pieces), and organizing a memorial service at the little church in Squaw Valley where I had once gone to Sunday school. The church was filled to capacity, and many stories were told of the days when Gardiner had made house calls on snowshoes, birthed babies, sewn up people's cuts, and casted broken legs at the Squaw Valley office, which was still staffed by Dr. Charlie and many of the nurses Gardiner had hired on when he'd first started the practice in 1959.

On December 25, I took his ashes in a Ziploc bag to Squaw Valley to spread them along the mountain ridges as he had requested. It had snowed at least a couple of feet, but it had warmed up and the snow was soft. The sun was brilliant and the sky so blue that it looked like a painted ceiling. I had my snowshoes and a backpack containing warm clothing in case the weather changed, and I set out to climb. Gardiner and I had a lovely conversation as we climbed along the mountainsides we had explored together when I had been a child.

I carried him all the way around the ridgeline, and then we sat down on one of our favorite granite rock outcroppings.

"I have one last handful to spread. The rest is for your daughter, Joanie. I promised her I would save her some of you."

Gardiner chuckled. "Are you sure she even wants me? She doesn't have much good to say about me."

I took a handful of ashes and brought my hand back to give them a good toss over the granite cliffs.

"Bye, Daddy," I said.

"Bye, Kacey." I heard a clinking sound on the granite under my feet and saw that it was one of his gold crowns, which had survived the grinding machine. He laughed.

"That's disgusting, Dad," I giggled and tossed the crown over the cliff.

I removed my snowshoes and put them into my backpack when I began to traverse a rocky face with patches of snow in the cracks and crevices. I stepped onto what I thought was a secure snow bridge and ended up standing waist-deep in snow with my feet in the creek underneath. My backpack flopped open, scattering the contents, which I hastened to pick up before they got wet in the creek. I did not discover until I arrived at the parking lot far below that I hadn't quite retrieved everything.

I searched for the Ziploc bag containing the rest of Gardiner, but he wasn't there. I had left him somewhere around the place I'd fallen, in the creek along with one of my fleece mittens and a nice pullover. It was Christmas Day and I had a turkey to roast and I panicked. I had no time to go back and search for the remaining ashes meant for Joan. I wondered if perhaps he didn't want to go with Joan, preferring to remain in the canyon where the ashes of so many other friends had been spread, including those of Mrs. Chisholm, who had died of cancer in 1987.

I called Joan and told her what had happened, and we planned to make a pilgrimage up the trail when the snow melted to see if we could find him, but the winter of 2005 was long and heavy, and the snow didn't begin to melt off that mountainside until late May. On May 30, which would have been his ninety-second birthday, I drove into Squaw Valley and looked up toward the mountainside where I thought Gardiner might be. Memorial Day weekend was coming and I didn't want to take a chance that his Ziploc might be presumed to be litter by an environmentally conscious hiker. So on this beautiful, warm afternoon, I began to run up the mountain trail, picking my way over snow patches and crossing the swollen creeks.

When I got close to the place I'd fallen, I called to him. "Dad? Where are you? I need a hint." I heard him tell me to walk just a little farther. The trail was partially covered with snow, and the bare trail was a stream.

"Look down," he said. I looked down and spotted one of my fleece mittens in the water, which I picked up and wrung out.

"A few more steps," he said. "Here I am." And there he was, half submerged in the water inside his Ziploc bag, next to my favorite pullover.

"Dad!" I said out loud and recognized the voice as the one I'd had about forty years ago.

"Hi, Kace," he said. "Where have you been? I've been waiting for you."

"You knew I'd find you, didn't you?" I said and carried him over to a dry, sunny spot on the rocks. I tenderly emptied out the water inside the Ziploc bag surrounding the plastic bag with his ashes inside.

"You always knew exactly where I was." *Yes, I really did.* "I'm glad we're home, Kace."

"Me too, Dad."

Photo by Chris Werner

ABOUT THE AUTHOR

KIMBALL CONVERSE PIER, PH.D., IS A depth psychologist and psycho-therapist who lives and practices in Truckee, California. She lives with her husband, Jon L. Weedn, and their two miniature Dachshunds, Penny and Ruthie. She has two grown children, a daughter who is a social worker and a son who loves anything to do with a board (snow, surf, or skate).

Made in the USA
Las Vegas, NV
25 January 2021

16543082R00187